Introducing Biblical Theology

Introducing Biblical Theology

Sigurd Grindheim

BLOOMSBURY
LONDON • NEW DELHI • NEW YORK • SYDNEY

Bloomsbury T&T Clark
An imprint of Bloomsbury Publishing Plc

50 Bedford Square
London
WC1B 3DP
UK

175 Fifth Avenue
New York
NY 10010
USA

www.bloomsbury.com

First published 2013

© Sigurd Grindheim, 2013

All rights reserved. No part of this publication may be reproduced or transmitted in any form or by any means, electronic or mechanical, including photocopying, recording, or any information storage or retrieval system, without prior permission in writing from the publishers.

Sigurd Grindheim has asserted his right under the Copyright, Designs and Patents Act, 1988, to be identified as Author of this work.

No responsibility for loss caused to any individual or organization acting on or refraining from action as a result of the material in this publication can be accepted by Bloomsbury Academic or the author.

British Library Cataloguing-in-Publication Data
A catalogue record for this book is available from the British Library.

ISBN: HB: 978-0-567-45815-5
PB: 978-0-567-45687-8

Library of Congress Cataloging-in-Publication Data
A catalog record for this book is available from the Library of Congress.

Typeset by Newgen Imaging Systems Pvt Ltd, Chennai, India
Printed and bound in India

Contents

List of Abbreviations — vii

Introduction — 1

1 The God Who Interacts — 4

2 Obedient and Rebellious Subjects: Angels and Demons — 17

3 Made for Fellowship: Human Beings as Created — 27

4 Breaking the Relationship: Human Sin — 33

5 God Makes It Personal: God's Interaction with His People in the Old Testament — 47

6 Mending the Relationship with God: Restitution for Sin in the Old Testament — 67

7 A New Ruler and a New Order: The Old Testament Messianic Hope — 74

8 God Came to Us: The New Testament Picture of Jesus — 89

9 What Human Beings Could Not Do: The Work of God in Christ — 123

10 Enjoying Favor with God: Salvation in the New Testament — 138

11 The Most Intimate Fellowship: The Gift of the Holy Spirit — 157

12 A Life Transformed: The New Life of the Believer — 167

13 God's New Community: The Church — 179

14 The Covenant Rituals of the New Community:
Baptism and the Lord's Supper ... 203

15 Perfect Union: The Last Things ... 215

Scripture Index ... 229

Index of Ancient Writings ... 261

Subject Index ... 263

Abbreviations

CEB	Common English Bible
CEV	Contemporary English Version
1 Chron.	1 Chronicles
2 Chron.	2 Chronicles
Col.	Colossians
1 Cor.	1 Corinthians
2 Cor.	2 Corinthians
Dan.	Daniel
Deut.	Deuteronomy
ed.	edition
ed.	editor
eds	editors
e.g.	*exempli gratia* (for example)
Eph.	Ephesians
ESV	English Standard Version
et al	*et alii* (and others)
etc.	*et cetera* (and other things)
Exod.	Exodus
Ezek.	Ezekiel
Gal.	Galatians
Gen.	Genesis
GNB	Good News Bible
Hab.	Habakkuk
HCSB	Holman Christian Standard Bible
Heb.	Hebrews
Hebr.	Hebrew
Hos.	Hosea
Isa.	Isaiah
ISV	International Standard Version
Jas	James
Jer.	Jeremiah
Jn	John
1 Jn	1 John

Abbreviations

Jon.	Jonah
Josh.	Joshua
Judg.	Judges
1 Kgdms	1 Kingdoms
1 Kgs	1 Kings
2 Kgs	2 Kings
KJV	King James' Version
Lam.	Lamentations
Lev.	Leviticus
Lk.	Luke
2 Macc.	2 Maccabees
Mal.	Malachi
Mk	Mark
Mt.	Matthew
Mic.	Micah
NAB	New American Bible
Nah.	Nahum
Neh.	Nehemiah
NIrV	New International Reader's Version
NIV	New International Version (1984)
NJB	New Jerusalem Bible
NKJV	New King James' Version
NRSV	New Revised Standard Version
Num.	Numbers
Obad.	Obadiah
par.	and parallels
1 Pet.	1 Peter
2 Pet.	2 Peter
Phil.	Philippians
Phlm.	Philemon
Prov.	Proverbs
Ps.	Psalm
Pss	Psalms
Repr.	Reprint
Rev.	Revelation
Rom.	Romans
1 Sam.	1 Samuel
2 Sam.	2 Samuel

1 Thess.	1 Thessalonians
2 Thess.	2 Thessalonians
1 Tim.	1 Timothy
2 Tim.	2 Timothy
TNIV	Today's New International Version
Tit.	Titus
Zech.	Zechariah
Zeph.	Zephaniah

Unless otherwise noted, all Scripture references are from Today's New International Version.

Introduction

On the way to Emmaus, Jesus gave two of his disciples a unique Bible study. "Beginning with Moses and all the Prophets, he explained to them what was said in all the Scriptures concerning himself" (Lk. 24.27). Jesus understood all the books of the Old Testament to have one theme. That theme was himself.

Jesus taught his disciples to read the Old Testament in the same way he did. The authors of the New Testament were therefore convinced that the Old Testament prophets pointed forward to the fulfillment in Jesus Christ (2 Cor. 1.20). According to 1 Peter 1.12, the Old Testament prophets "were not serving themselves but you, when they spoke of the things that have now been told you by those who have preached the gospel to you by the Holy Spirit sent from heaven." The church father Augustine (354–430 CE) said it like this: "The New Testament lies hidden in the Old and the Old Testament is unveiled in the New."

Christians therefore believe that the canonical books of the Old and the New Testaments belong together as one book. This book is held together by a unifying theme: the good news of Jesus Christ.

There is a story that runs through all of the biblical books: the story of God's salvation in Jesus Christ. This is the story of the Triune God, the God who interacts. As the crown of his creation, he makes human beings who enjoy a harmonious relationship with him. This relationship is broken because of human sin, but God continues to reach out to human beings through covenants and through the election of Israel as his people. However, human beings constantly fail to be faithful to him, and this failure shows that God needs to intervene in a more direct way. In his Son Jesus Christ, he comes to earth as a human being. Jesus dies in the place of sinners, but is resurrected from the dead. In Jesus Christ, God brings reconciliation between himself and the world. In Christ, God brings a new creation where there is harmony between God and human beings and where the power of death has been broken. Through faith in Jesus Christ, human beings may enjoy God's favor.

God sends them his Holy Spirit, transforms human beings from the inside, and brings them together in a new community, a community that once again enjoys intimacy with God. This new community reaches its completion in the new heaven and the new earth.

In this book, we will learn from Jesus and the apostles how to read the Bible, and we will see how the good news about Jesus Christ emerges as the central theme.

We will not forget that the 66 books of the Bible were written by many different authors over the course of many hundreds of years. The individual books originated in many different historical circumstances, they were written with many different purposes, and they reflect the individual characteristics of their human authors. But with all their differences, all the books are witnesses of the one God and his master plan: salvation in Jesus Christ.

We may liken the many books of the Bible to the different building blocks that are used to build a house. Each of these building blocks may have a fascinating history of their own. Some of them may even contain materials that originally were used for completely different purposes. But when the house is built, each of the blocks becomes a part of the building. So also with the books of the Bible. Each book has its own history, but in the end they all become a part of the final product, the Bible.

Books about the Bible may also be compared to books about a house. It would be possible to write about the background and characteristics of each one of the building blocks. Such a book could be written even if the house had never been completed. But it would also be possible to write a book that explains how all the building blocks function in the design of the house, how some blocks support others, and how all of them together form a beautiful building. There are many books that describe the background and characteristics of the individual books of the Bible. These books are very useful to read. But the book you are now reading is of a different kind. It is a book about how all the books fit together. This approach is often called a canonical reading or interpretation of Scripture.

Further Reading

Barr, James. *The Concept of Biblical Theology: An Old Testament Perspective.* Minneapolis: Fortress, 1999.

Introduction

Hafemann, Scott J., ed. *Biblical Theology: Retrospect and Prospect*. Downers Grove: IVP, 2002.

Mead, James K. *Biblical Theology: Issues, Methods, and Themes*. Louisville: Westminster John Knox, 2007.

Review Questions

What is unique about the discipline of biblical theology?

What is canonical interpretation?

1
The God Who Interacts

Chapter Outline
God's Name	5
A Holy God	7
To See God	8
God's Presence	9
Only God	9
Father	10
God as Male	11
God as the Triune God	11
God and Evil	13
God's Knowledge	14
Summary	15

The God of the Bible is the God who makes himself known to us. We do not meet him by searching within ourselves. He is a God who acts, and he is known through his actions. The first book of the Bible introduces him with the words: "In the beginning God created the heavens and the earth" (Gen. 1.1). The Bible presupposes that God is there. There is no need to argue that he exists.

The Bible does not use philosophical ideas to describe him. God is not a power, not an idea; he is a person. He interacts with the world, and we learn about who he is through his works and through the way he interacts.

God's Name

God is a person who has a name. He revealed this name to Moses when he spoke to him from a burning bush. "God said to Moses, 'I AM WHO I AM. This is what you are to say to the Israelites: "I AM has sent me to you."' God also said to Moses: "Say to the Israelites, '[Yahweh], the God of your fathers—the God of Abraham, the God of Isaac and the God of Jacob—has sent me to you.' This is my name forever, the name you shall call me from generation to generation" (Exod. 3.14-15).

The Hebrew name Yahweh is translated "Lord" (in most English translations usually with capital letters: LORD). This translation is based on the way the name was read out loud in the Jewish tradition. When the Jews read the Bible in the synagogue and they came to the name Yahweh, they said "*Adonai*." They did not want to pronounce God's name because they considered it to be too holy to be pronounced. The Hebrew word "*Adonai*" means "Lord."

Sometimes the name Yahweh is rendered Jehovah. When the Old Testament was first written down and copied, the writers only wrote with consonants (as they also do in modern Hebrew). They did not use vowels. When they added the vowels later, the scribes did not include the vowels for Yahweh. Instead, they wrote the vowels for the word *Adonai*, which was what they read out loud. Out of respect for the written text, they preserved the consonants for God's name, YHWH, but the vowels were those from *Adonai*. Those who were unfamiliar with the Jewish practice would read the consonants of YHWH together with the vowels for *Adonai*, and it became Jehovah. This is the result of a misunderstanding. We know that the correct pronunciation of the name must have been Yahweh because there are many names in the Bible that are formed with God's name. Two of these names are Jeremiah (Yahweh exalts) and Isaiah (Yahweh is salvation). These names end in *-yah*, and show us that God's name should be pronounced Yahweh.

The name Yahweh is probably related to the Hebrew word for "I am" (*ehyeh*), and the phrase "I AM WHO I AM" is an explanation of God's name Yahweh.

This name is puzzling; it both conceals and reveals. It conceals because God does not explain who he is. He is who he is. In itself, this name does not reveal anything, but it refers Moses and the Israelites to the works God will do. The works that he is about to do will reveal who he is.

6 Introducing Biblical Theology

God reveals his name to Moses right before he is about to show his might in Egypt. He will defeat Pharaoh and the Egyptian gods and set Israel free. In this way, he shows that he is God, not only over Israel but also over all the world. He is supreme over all other powers, both in the physical world and in the spiritual world. And he uses his power to save his people.

At the same time, the name "I AM" shows that God does not depend on anyone or anything else for his existence or for what he does. He is the only true God. This is how the prophet Isaiah explains God's name: "I am [Yahweh], and there is no other; apart from me there is no God" (Isa. 45.5).

God is the one who always is. As Isaiah continues to explain, this means that he is eternal: "Who has done this and carried it through, calling forth the generations from the beginning? I, [Yahweh]—with the first of them and with the last—I am he" (Isa. 41.4). The book of Revelation develops the name "I AM" even further. God is "the Alpha and the Omega . . . who is, and who was, and who is to come, the Almighty" (Rev. 1.8). He always was and he always will be. He always is.

But that God is "I AM" does not mean that he is a God in isolation. Yahweh is a name that emphasizes God's relationship with his people. It is the name of the God who enters into covenant with his people. That God's name is Yahweh means that he is a God who is reaching out to the people he created and establishes a relationship with them. It also means that he will go to great lengths to preserve and restore this relationship.

Table 1.1 Elaborations on the name Yahweh

The one who is I AM	God said to Moses: "I AM WHO I AM. This is what you are to say to the Israelites: 'I AM has sent me to you.'" God also said to Moses: "Say to the Israelites, '[Yahweh], the God of your fathers—the God of Abraham, the God of Isaac and the God of Jacob—has sent me to you'" (Exod. 3.14-15).
Only God	I am [Yahweh], and there is no other; apart from me there is no God (Isa. 45.5).
Eternal	I, [Yahweh]—with the first of them and with the last—I am he (Isa. 41.4). "I am the Alpha and the Omega," says the Lord God, "who is, and who was, and who is to come, the Almighty" (Rev. 1.8).
Redeemer	I will take you as my own people, and I will be your God. Then you will know that I am [Yahweh] your God, who brought you out from under the yoke of the Egyptians (Exod. 6.7).
The Covenant God	[Yahweh, Yahweh], the compassionate and gracious God, slow to anger, abounding in love and faithfulness, maintaining love to thousands, and forgiving wickedness, rebellion and sin. Yet he does not leave the guilty unpunished; he punishes the children and their children for the sin of the parents to the third and fourth generation (Exod. 34.5-7).

When God prepared Moses for what he was going to do in Egypt, he told him: "I am [Yahweh]. I appeared to Abraham, to Isaac and to Jacob as God Almighty, but by my name [Yahweh] I did not make myself known to them" (Exod. 6.2-3). This statement is surprising to us because we find the name Yahweh (Lord) frequently in the Bible, even before the account in Exodus 6 (Gen. 2.4 etc.).

To understand what God means, we must consider the full significance of the verb "to make known." That God made himself known by the name Yahweh did not simply mean that he taught Israel how to say a new word. In biblical language, the word "to know" often means to know by experience. When God makes himself known, it means that he lets the people experience who he is. He will let Israel know through experience that he is Yahweh.

The experience that God will give to Israel is that he liberates them from oppression and slavery in Egypt. To know God as Yahweh is to know him as deliverer, as savior and redeemer. It is to experience what he does when he uses his might to save his people (Exod. 6.6). The reason why God will do this is that he remembers his covenant (Exod. 6.4, 8). To know God as Yahweh is to know God as the one who enters into a relationship with his creatures and who spares no expense to preserve and restore that relationship. It is to know God as the one who proclaims: "I will take you as my own people, and I will be your God. Then you will know that I am [Yahweh] your God, who brought you out from under the yoke of the Egyptians" (Exod. 6.7).

Yahweh is the savior God of the covenant. It is his nature to show mercy to his people. He renewed his covenant with Israel even after the people had committed idolatry with the golden calf. "Then [Yahweh] came down in the cloud and stood there with him and proclaimed his name, [Yahweh]. And he passed in front of Moses, proclaiming, '[Yahweh, Yahweh], the compassionate and gracious God, slow to anger, abounding in love and faithfulness, maintaining love to thousands, and forgiving wickedness, rebellion and sin. Yet he does not leave the guilty unpunished; he punishes the children and their children for the sin of the parents to the third and fourth generation'" (Exod. 34.5-7).

A Holy God

The prophet Isaiah's favorite name for God is "the holy one of Israel" (Isa. 1.4 etc.). Isaiah had learned about God's holiness when God called him to go to Israel as a prophet. He had seen "the Lord seated on a throne, high and exalted, and the train of his robe filled the temple. Above him were seraphs, each with six wings: With two wings they covered their faces, with two they covered their feet, and with two they were flying. And they were calling to one another: 'Holy, holy, holy is the Lord Almighty; the whole earth is full of his glory'" (Isa. 6.1-3).

Isaiah had seen God in his majesty, as the one exalted above all of creation and above all other powers. That God is holy means that he is separate from everything and everyone else. The heavenly beings, the seraphs, praised him as the one who is three times holy, a Hebrew way of saying that he is the most holy of all. Because God is holy, he fills the world with his glory, splendor, and abundance.

It is natural that God's holiness and majesty inspires fear. When someone who is not holy enters into the presence of the holy one, it has terrible consequences. God explained to Moses that if anyone entered the Most Holy Place, they would die. Only the high priest could enter, once a year, with the right sacrifices that would make him acceptable in the Lord's presence (Lev. 16.2). When Isaiah met God in his holiness, he was convinced that he was doomed (Isa. 6.5), but he was saved by the atoning sacrifice from the altar (6.6-7). Ezekiel also "fell facedown," when he saw a vision "of the likeness of the glory of the Lord" (Ezek. 1.28).

To See God

Even though Isaiah saw the Lord, he did not give any description of what he looked like. He could only describe the things that surrounded God: the throne, the robe, the seraphs, and the smoke (Isa. 6.1-4). Isaiah saw the majesty of the Lord, but was unable to describe his appearance. In his vision "of the likeness of the glory of the Lord" (Ezek. 1.28), Ezekiel saw "a figure like that of a man" (1.26). But Ezekiel could not describe the features of this figure. The light was so overwhelming that all Ezekiel had to say was that "he looked like glowing metal, as if full of fire" (1.27). When he revealed himself to Moses, God explained why: "you cannot see my face, for no one may see me and live" (Exod. 33.20). Moses was therefore only allowed to see God's back (Exod. 33.23). Ever since then, the saints longed to see God's face (Pss 11.7; 42.2).

This changed when Jesus came. In him, "all the fullness of the Deity lives in bodily form" (Col. 2.9). In him, it is therefore possible to see God. "No one has ever seen God; the only God, who is at the Father's side, he has made him known" (Jn 1.18 ESV; 1 Jn 3.2). In Jesus, we can see God as he truly is, for Jesus has been given God's name, "the name that is above every name" (Phil. 2.9), Yahweh (ch. 8).

God's Presence

The Bible refers to God as living in heaven (1 Kgs 8.49; Eccl. 5.2), but we must remember that this heaven is not a physical place. It must be understood spiritually. The biblical authors knew very well that God was too great to fit into the physical heaven (1 Kgs 8.27; 2 Chron. 6.18). When the Bible says that God dwells in heaven, the point is that he is much greater than those who live on earth (Isa. 57.15).

God is present everywhere (Jer. 23.24), and it is impossible to escape from his presence (Ps. 139.7-12). But the Bible distinguishes between different kinds of God's presence. He was graciously present with the ark of the covenant in the tabernacle and the temple. Israel could worship him and pray to him, and he blessed and protected them (Exod. 20.24; 1 Kgs 8.37-40). This presence is a special privilege that should not be taken for granted (1 Sam. 4.3-11; Jer. 7.4). God can take it away (Ezek. 10.4, 18-19).

In the New Testament, God's presence is in Jesus Christ, who is Immanuel, "God with us" (Mt. 1.23). The Gospel of Matthew focuses on Jesus' own personal presence. He promises to be present with his disciples always and everywhere (Mt. 18.20; 28.20). In the Gospel of John, Jesus explains that both he and his Father will be present and make their home in Jesus' disciples (Jn 14.23). Jesus' disciples will also be in him (15.4-5). This presence takes place through the Holy Spirit, the Advocate (14.17).

Only God

The Bible teaches us that God is the only God. There may be other beings that are called "gods," but they are powerless compared to God. In the book of Isaiah, God calls on the idols to "tell us what the future holds, so we may know that you are gods. Do something, whether good or bad, so that we will be dismayed and filled with fear. But you are less than nothing and you can do nothing; those who choose you are detestable" (Isa. 41.23-24). At the time of the Old Testament, many people believed that there was one god for every nation or every country. But God makes it clear that he is not only God in Israel; he is God everywhere. He controls everything that happens anywhere in the world. He can raise up Cyrus as the king of Persia and use him for his own purpose: to bring his people back from exile (Isa. 44.28). The king of Babylon had to realize that he had no power of his own; he depended on God for his very existence (Dan. 5.23; 6.27-28).

God is the only creator. Other gods cannot cause anything to exist, but God "spoke, and it came to be; he commanded, and it stood firm" (Ps. 33.9). He is therefore the universal king, not only in Israel, but everywhere (1 Chron. 29.11-12), in the heavens above and on the earth below (Ps. 103.19).

This means that other "gods" are not really gods. "I am the Lord, and there is no other; apart from me there is no God" (Isa. 45.5; 1 Cor. 8.4-6). Moses' words in Deuteronomy 6.4 are Israel's confession of faith: "Hear, O Israel: The Lord our God, the Lord is one." Because God is the only God, he is the only one we should worship (Deut. 6.13; 10.20). Other gods are no threat to God, but his concern is for his relationship with his creatures. It is important to him that we do not treat anything or anyone else as God. God does not share his honor with anyone. "The Lord, whose name is Jealous, is a jealous God" (Exod. 34.14). His people are his bride, and he does not tolerate that his bride gives her devotion to anyone else (Hos. 1.2; 2 Cor. 11.2).

Father

That God is the bridegroom (Isa. 54.5; 62.5) shows us the love he has for his people. God is also a loving father, who cares for his children (Ps. 103.13; Jer. 3.4). Jesus shows us that our relationship to God is first and foremost a relationship of children to a father. He taught us to pray "Our Father in heaven" (Mt. 6.9). This was very unusual for Jews in the first century. Even though they knew that God was a father, it was not common for people to pray to God as "my Father" or "our Father." When he taught us to pray in this way, Jesus showed us that we can have a very intimate relationship with God. We can talk to him as "our Father."

The apostle Paul explains that the Christians believers have received the Spirit that "brought about [their] adoption to sonship" (Rom. 8.15). It is therefore characteristic of Christians that they "cry, 'Abba, Father'" (Rom. 8.15; Gal. 4.6), just like Jesus did (Mk 14.36).

Abba is the word for "father" in Aramaic, the language Jesus spoke. Even though the New Testament was written in Greek, the word *Abba* occurs a few times. Jesus' use of this word must have been so characteristic of him that the New Testament authors felt they had to keep it just like he said it.

God as Male

When God is a husband and a father, it is natural to think of him as male. But the Bible also describes God's care for us with female metaphors. He carries his people in his arms, "as a nurse carries an infant" (Num. 11.12); he gave birth to his people (Deut. 32.18); he is like a mother who cannot "forget the baby at her breast [or] have no compassion on the child she has borne" (Isa. 49.15); and he comforts them "as a mother comforts her child" (Isa. 66.13).

The many different images that the Bible uses for God show us that God is greater than our understanding (Pss 40.5; 139.6). But this must not lead us to think that the way he has revealed himself is not fully trustworthy. God has motherly characteristics, but he has taught us to call him "Father." Jesus, who has made him known (Jn 1.18), came to earth as a man. God's own revelation therefore requires of us that we understand God as male, rather than female.

This does not mean that we should think about God as a man in the biological sense of the word or in the way that our culture thinks about what it means to be a man. Rather, we should think about what it means to be a man in light of what the Bible teaches us about God (Eph. 3.15). His sacrificial love shows us what a man should be like (Eph. 5.25).

God as the Triune God

Even though God is one, the Bible teaches us that he is also three. Around 200 CE, the Church Father Tertullian coined the term "Trinity" to explain that God is one and three at the same time. This word does not occur in the Bible, but the idea is there. It is not until the New Testament that God reveals that he is three persons, but the Old Testament contains several hints that the one God is also more than one. When God created humankind, he used a plural form to refer to himself: "Let us make humankind in our image, according to our likeness" (Gen. 1.26; see also 3.22). But the context in the book of Genesis does not explain why God uses the forms "us" and "our," so we must wait for the revelation in the rest of the Bible to understand it.

Another indication is the fact the Old Testament distinguishes between different divine characters. The creation account introduces the Spirit of God (Gen. 1.2; see also Job 33.4; Ps. 104.30). A more mysterious character is the Angel of the Lord. In Zechariah 1.12, the Angel of the Lord speaks to the Lord of hosts, so he must clearly be a character that is distinct from God. But in several Old Testament passages, the distinction between the two is not clear. We see a good example in Gideon's encounter with the Angel of the Lord under the oak at Ophrah. The Angel talks to Gideon and Gideon responds (Judg. 6.11-15). But suddenly the one who speaks with Gideon is no longer the Angel, but God himself (Judg. 6.16). In a similar way, the Angel of the Lord and the Lord himself talk to Abraham (compare Gen. 22.11 and 22.12), Hagar (compare Gen. 16.7, 9, 10, 11; and 16.13), and Moses (compare Exod. 3.2 and 3.4, 5, 6, 7). The angel that God sends ahead of Israel is also closely associated with God. God's "name is in him" (Exod. 23.21). In Genesis 18, there is no mention of an angel, only three men who came to visit Abraham (Gen. 18.2). But the one who talked with Abraham was the Lord (Gen. 18.1, 13). The Angel of the Lord appears to be both identified with God and distinguished from him. But the Old Testament does not explain how this is possible.

Some texts in the Old Testament also make a distinction between God and his wisdom (Prov. 8.22-36). When God's wisdom speaks, this is poetic use of language. It does not mean that God's wisdom is separate from God. But the New Testament develops this language further, to explain that Jesus is at the same time both identical with God and distinguished from him (ch. 8).

The New Testament brings more clarity to the understanding of God as one, yet three. Both Jesus Christ and the Holy Spirit are distinguishable persons who are also one with God (chs 8 and 11).

God is therefore both one and three. In a few important passages, the New Testament uses what we might call a "Trinitarian formula." The Father, Son, and the Holy Spirit are mentioned together in such a way that we understand that they are one and yet three. We find the most important of these formulas in the Great Commission, where Jesus instructs his disciples to "go and make disciples of all nations, baptizing them in the name of the Father and of the Son and of the Holy Spirit" (Mt. 28.19). It is important to note that Jesus does not say "into the names of the Father, Son, and the Holy Spirit." He does not refer to three names, only one. The Father, the Son, and the Holy Spirit share one name. In the Bible, the name stands for a person's essence or nature. The Father, the Son, and the Holy Spirit are one.

In a similar way, the apostle Paul shows that spiritual gifts come from the Spirit, the Lord (Jesus), and God (1 Cor. 12.4-6). When the same apostle pronounces God's blessing, this blessing consists of "the grace of the Lord Jesus Christ, and the love of God, and the fellowship of the Holy Spirit" (2 Cor. 13.14).

When John greets the churches in Revelation 1.4-5, he blesses them with "grace and peace to you from him who is, and who was, and who is to come, and from the seven spirits before his throne, and from Jesus Christ, who is the faithful witness the firstborn from the dead, and the ruler of the kings of the earth." The one "who is, and who was, and who is to come" is God the Father. The number seven is a symbolic number that represents the perfect God. In the book of Revelation, "the seven spirits" is therefore a symbolic name for the Holy Spirit (ch. 11). Revelation 1.4-5 is another Trinitarian formula in the New Testament.

God and Evil

Because God is the only creator, he is in control of everything that happens in the world. Every living thing depends on God for everything they need to live and exist. He "gives everyone life and breath and everything else" (Acts 17.25). "For in him we live and move and have our being" (Acts 17.28; see also Job 12.10; Dan. 5.23). That all life is in God's hand is a source of great comfort for Christians. It means that we can trust him to provide for us in every way. Jesus assures his disciples that they should not worry about their life. "Look at the birds of the air; they do not sow or reap or store away in barns, and yet your heavenly Father feeds them. Are you not much more valuable than they?" (Mt. 6.26).

But if God controls everything, does he cause all the evil that happens in the world? The Bible makes it clear that God both "[brings] prosperity and [creates] disaster" (Isa. 45.7; see also Amos 3.6). He "[puts] to death and [brings] to life" (Deut. 32.39; see also 1 Sam. 2.6-7). Sometimes he brings evil upon people because he punishes them for their sins (Gen. 19.13; Num. 16.30-33; Acts 5.1-11 etc.). But many times evil happens even though there is no specific sin that has caused it. The book of Job describes the sufferings of an innocent man. His situation is so difficult because he knows that God is behind what happens to him (6.4; 9.17; 16.11-14). In the end, God does not explain why the bad things happened to Job. But he teaches Job that he is God and that what he does is more than Job can understand (42.2-6).

However, the readers of the book are given more information. We learn that God is not directly behind the bad things that happen to Job. It is Satan who causes Job's children and servants to be killed, his possessions to be lost, and Job himself to be stricken with painful sores (1.12-19; 2.7). God is able to stop Satan from doing these things, but he allows them to happen (1.12; 2.6). He is therefore indirectly behind them.

The book of Job also shows us the reason why God allowed Job to suffer. He wanted Job to demonstrate that he truly loved God. Job got the opportunity to show that he did not only love God because of the good gifts he received (1.8-12; 2.3-6). God wanted Job to demonstrate that God was worth loving because of who he is, not just because of his gifts.

But the children of God do not always gain insight into the reasons for their suffering. Sometimes they are left with no answers to the questions that the psalmist was asking: "Awake, Lord! Why do you sleep? Rouse yourself! Do not reject us forever. Why do you hide your face and forget our misery and oppression?" (Ps. 44.23-24).

Nevertheless, the Bible teaches that the suffering of the children of God will not exceed the measure that he has determined beforehand (Job 1.12; 2.6). And even though we cannot understand all of his ways, God's children can be assured that he uses even their sufferings to accomplish his glorious design. "For those who love God all things work together for good, for those who are called according to his purpose" (Rom. 8.28 ESV).

God's Knowledge

As the creator and ruler of the universe, God knows everything (Ps. 147.5; 1 Jn 3.20). He also knows what human beings are thinking (Ps. 139.1-2, 23; Rom. 8.27) and what they will do in the future (Ps. 139.4, 16). Isaiah explains that God is the only true God because he is the only one who can predict the future (Isa. 41.22-23; see also 46.9-10).

Because he knows everything, he has no need to change his mind (1 Sam. 15.29). Nevertheless, the Bible gives us several examples that God changed his course of action. In some cases, we even read that God "regretted" what he had done or what he had planned to do. Two of the most striking examples are Genesis 6.6 and Exodus 32.14. In the generation of Noah, human sinfulness had become so great that "the Lord regretted that he had made human beings on the earth, and his heart was deeply troubled" (Gen. 6.6). When Israel worshiped the golden calves at Sinai, God told Moses that he would destroy the people (Exod. 32.10). But after Moses had prayed for them, we read: "the Lord changed his mind about the disaster that he planned to bring on his people" (Exod. 32.14 NRSV).

However, these statements do not mean that God has changed. God has not realized that what he had said or done earlier was a mistake.

The Bible often speaks about God with language that we normally only use about human beings. For example, we read that God breathed (Gen. 2.7), walked (Gen. 3.8), smelled (Gen. 8.21), and laughed (Ps. 2.4). He has eyes and ears (1 Pet. 3.12). This way of speaking about God is called anthropomorphism (from the Greek words *anthropos*, which means "human being," and *morphe*, which means "form"). It must not be taken literally, but is a way of speaking about God that makes it easier for human beings to understand.

When the Bible says that God regretted, the point is that he reacted to what human beings had done. God is always the same, but human beings change. When they do, God changes the way he responds to them, so that he always acts in accordance with who he is.

Summary

The Bible describes God as a God who relates to others and interacts with them. This is essential to who God is, as the one who is one and yet three. God makes himself known to human beings through his acts of salvation, and shows that he is the only one we can trust to control the future.

Further Reading

Das, A. Andrew, and Frank J. Matera, eds. *The Forgotten God: Perspectives in Biblical Theology: Essays in Honor of Paul J. Achtemeier on the Occasion of His Seventy-Fifth Birthday*. Louisville: Westminster John Knox, 2002.

Hurtado, Larry W. *God in New Testament Theology*. Library of Biblical Theology. Nashville: Abingdon, 2010.

Wright, Christopher J.H. *Knowing God the Father through the Old Testament*. Downers Grove: IVP, 2007.

Introducing Biblical Theology

Review Questions

What does the name YHWH reveal about God?

How does the Bible show that God is one, yet three?

What would you say to someone who thinks that Christians should not have to suffer in this world?

2

Obedient and Rebellious Subjects

Angels and Demons

Chapter Outline

Angels	17
Satan	19
Satan's Fall in Sin	19
Demons	20
Angels of the Nations	21
Spiritual Beings and Human Institutions	23
Demons Occupying Human Beings	24
Exorcism	25
Summary	25

There is no other God besides the Lord. All other beings are created by God and subject to him.

Angels

Angels are spiritual beings created by God (Ps. 148.2, 5; Heb. 1.7, 14). They are personal beings, and they have a responsibility to act morally. The angel that showed John his visions at Patmos was "a fellow servant" with him and exercised his moral responsibility when he warned John not to worship him (Rev. 22.9).

Normally angels are invisible, but sometimes God enables human beings to see them (Num. 22.31; 2 Kgs 6.17). The Bible does not give us a complete description of what the angels look like; they often appear in white clothes (Mk 16.5; Acts 1.10 etc.) and surrounded with great light (Mt. 28.3; Acts 12.7 etc.). They inspire fear (Mt. 28.1-8; Lk. 1.11-12), but should not be worshiped (Rev. 19.10; 22.8-9). Their knowledge is considerable (Mk. 13.32), but they are not all-knowing and they lack insight into God's plan of salvation (1 Pet. 1.12).

Angels surround the heavenly throne where they worship God and Christ (Heb. 1.6; Rev. 5.8-14). They occasionally serve as messengers that God sends to individuals (Lk. 1.13-20, 26-38; Acts 8.26). They were involved when God gave the law to Moses (Acts 7.53; Gal. 3.19), they carry out God's punishment (Acts 12.23), and they will accompany Jesus at the final judgment (Mk 8.38; 2 Thess. 1.7-8). The Bible makes it clear that there is a large group of angels (Deut. 33.2; Mt. 26.53; Rev. 5.11), but the numbers in these accounts should not be taken literally.

In the book of Revelation, we meet seven angels that stand before God (Rev. 8.2). The angel Gabriel introduces himself as one of these angels (Lk. 1.19). God sometimes sends him to people as his messenger and interpreter (Dan. 8.15-26; Lk. 1.11-20). Later Christian tradition has identified him as the archangel in 1 Thessalonians 4.16 (see also Mt. 24.31). The only angel that is named and called an archangel in the Bible is Michael (Jude 9).

Jesus told his disciples that the believers have "their angels in heaven [who] always see the face of [his] Father" (Mt. 18.10). Elsewhere, the Bible teaches that God sends angels to serve and protect his people (Ps. 91.11; Acts 12.11; Heb. 1.14). But that is not the point that Jesus makes here. Instead, he explains that every believer has an angel who serves as his or her spiritual representative before God. Just as every believer has privileged access to God's throne (Eph. 2.18; 3.12; Heb. 4.16), so does this angel always see the face of God. According to Jewish belief, God assigned individual angels to individual human beings. These angels did not stand in God's presence. Only the highest angels were granted this special privilege. But Jesus teaches that every believer's own angel is as favored as the highest angels. Jesus shows that his disciples, even "the little ones," enjoy the highest favor with God.

Satan

When God created the angels, they were good; everything God created was good (Gen. 1.31; 1 Tim. 4.4). But as moral beings, they are capable of doing evil. Many of them have fallen away from God and become evil. The ruler of the evil angels is Satan. His name comes from a Hebrew word that means "adversary" or "accuser." In the New Testament, he is often called the devil (Mt. 4.1; Jn 8.44; 1 Pet. 5.8). This name comes from the Greek word *diabolos*, which means "slanderer." Other names that are used for Satan include Beelzebul (Mk 3.22), Beliar (2 Cor. 6.15), and the accuser (Rev. 12.10). He is not named in the book of Genesis, but the serpent that tempted Adam and Eve to fall in sin (Gen. 3.1-7) is a symbolic representation of the devil (Rev. 12.9).

Satan is a powerful being, but he is also created by God. He therefore has no power on his own, only as much as God allows him to have. The book of Job shows us that Satan can never do anything unless God lets him do it (Job 1.12; 2.6). In his supreme power, God even uses the devil and the evil spirits for his own good purposes (2 Chron. 18.18-22; 1 Cor. 5.5; 2 Cor. 12.7). Unlike God, who knows what is in the hearts of human beings (1 Sam. 16.7; 1 Kgs 8.39), Satan did not know what was in Job's heart (Job 1.8–2.10). He is not all-knowing.

Satan's Fall in Sin

The Bible does not tell the story of how Satan fell in sin. However, it is possible to understand Isaiah 14.12-15 as an account of Satan's fall. The prophet exclaims:

> How you have fallen from heaven, morning star, son of the dawn! You have been cast down to the earth, you who once laid low the nations! You said in your heart, "I will ascend to heaven; I will raise my throne above the stars of God; I will sit enthroned on the mount of assembly, on the utmost heights of Mount Zaphon. I will ascend above the tops of the clouds; I will make myself like the Most High." But you are brought down to the realm of the dead, to the depths of the pit.

In the context of the book of Isaiah, this prophecy concerned the Babylonian empire (Isa. 13.1). But in the book of Revelation, John describes "a star that had fallen from the sky to the earth" (Rev. 9.1; see also Rev. 8.10). In Revelation 12.9, he also explains that Satan "was hurled to the earth" (see also Lk. 10.18). Both of these verses allude to Isaiah 14.12, but John refers to the devil. In other words, John read Isaiah 14.12 as a description of Satan. Behind the enemies of God's people stand God's cosmic enemies (see below). Since Babylon was the main enemy of God's people, Babylon is the earthly counterpart to Satan. Isaiah's picture of Babylon is therefore also a picture of Satan. Satan's (and Babylon's) sin was that he wanted to take God's place.

In many other ways, the book of Revelation also shows that Satan tries to be like God. The ungodly alliance consisting of the dragon (12.3), the beast from the sea (13.1), and the beast from the land (13.11) is an attempt at imitating the Trinity. In the book of Revelation, the dragon appears with seven crowns (Rev. 12.3), because he tries to take the place of Jesus, who is the king of kings and who rightfully bears many crowns on his head (Rev. 19.12). It is therefore characteristic of Satan that he tempted Eve with the false promise that she and Adam would be like God (Gen. 3.5).

Demons

Satan was not the only angel that fell; he was accompanied by many others (2 Pet. 2.4; Jud 6). These evil angels are usually called evil spirits or demons. There are different levels among these evil spirits; some are more evil than others (Mt. 12.43-45; Mk 9.29). Satan is the head of all of them; he is the ruler of the demons (Mk 3.23-27).

As spiritual beings, the demons have knowledge about Jesus that is often hidden from human beings. They know that he is the Son of God (Mk 1.24; 5.7). For them, this knowledge is only a source of fear (Mt. 8.29; Mk 1.24; see also Jas 2.19).

The goal of Satan and his army is to lead people away from God. Satan tries to scare and threaten (1 Pet. 5.8), but he can also appear as an angel of light, in order to deceive people (2 Cor. 11.14). He tempted Jesus to avoid the way of the cross (Mt. 4.1-11), and he continues to tempt believers to sin and fall away from God (1 Cor. 7.5; 1 Thess. 3.5). He can work through people (Lk. 22.3; Jn 13.27), even disciples (Mt. 16.23). Satan and his demons try to deceive the people of God with false prophecy (2 Chron. 18.18-22) and false teaching (Col. 2.8; 1 Tim. 4.1). Because the inspiration to sin comes from Satan, Jesus can say that those who sin are children of the devil (Jn 8.44; 1 Jn 3.8, 10). This should not be understood literally. The word "son" or "child" can be used for disciples and for those who have learned from and been inspired by their master (2 Kgs 2.3 ESV; Amos 7.14 ESV). To be sons or children of the devil therefore means to do the works of the devil.

In 1 Peter 3.20, there is a reference to the spirits that "were disobedient long ago when God waited patiently in the days of Noah while the ark was being built." At the time of Noah, human wickedness had become very great (Gen. 6.5). Peter associates this wickedness with the activity of evil spirits. Jewish interpreters from the time between the Old and the New Testaments were even more specific (see especially *1 Enoch* 6–16). They thought the "sons of God" in Genesis 6.2 were the fallen angels and they understood the same verse as a description of their sin: "the sons of God saw that these daughters were beautiful, and they married any of them they chose." As a result, the giants were born (Gen. 6.4). However, Peter does not say that the evil spirits married human women, and there is no reason to think that he agreed with this Jewish interpretation. Jesus explains that angels do not marry (Mk 12.25). In the book of Genesis, there is no clear mention of angels in the context of chapter 6. The point of the passage is to explain why God's judgment fell on human beings (Gen. 6.3) not on angels. It is therefore better to understand the "sons of God" in Genesis 6.2 as human beings. They could be human rulers (Ps. 82.1, 6-7) or, more likely, godly human beings (Deut. 14.1; 32.5-6), the righteous descendants of Seth (Gen. 4.25-26; 5.3-32).

Angels of the Nations

The Old Testament sometimes describes God's victory over Pharaoh as his killing the monster in the sea (Ps. 74.13-14; Isa. 51.9-10). Daniel portrays a fourth beast with ten horns (Dan. 7.7). This beast stands for the Greek kingdom, which would become a terrible enemy of God's people. These images form the background for John's portrait of Satan as "an enormous red dragon with seven heads and ten horns and seven crowns on its heads" (Rev. 12.3). In other words, when John gives us his picture of Satan, he is inspired by poetic portrayals of Israel's enemies in the Old Testament. This means that the chief spiritual enemy of God's people and their earthly enemies are closely related. What happens on earth corresponds to spiritual realities in heaven.

The nations on earth have their spiritual counterpart in spiritual beings in heaven. Israel's representative angel is Michael. He was engaged in spiritual battles with the prince of Persia and the prince of Greece (Dan. 10.13, 20-21; 12.1). This battle corresponds to the earthly conflict between Israel and these nations.

It is possible that Moses also refers to angels that stand as spiritual representatives of nations. There are good reasons to conclude that the original text of Deuteronomy 32.8 should be translated: "When the Most High assigned the nations their heritage, when he parceled out the descendants of Adam, He set up the boundaries of the peoples after the number of the sons of God" (NAB). "Sons of God" is another term for angels (Job 1.6; 2.1). The meaning of Deuteronomy 32.8 may therefore be that there is a designated angel for every people in the world.

These angels or demons have led the peoples astray into idolatry. Since God is the only God, the gods that the nations worship are not real gods (Isa. 44.9-17; Jer. 10.3-11; 1 Cor. 8.4). But the powers that cause people to worship them are real (Deut. 32.17; 1 Cor. 10.19-21). Some Christians refer to these demons as territorial spirits, but that is a misleading term. They are not associated with specific territories, and they do not gain power over people in a certain territory. They are spiritual beings who gain control over people through spiritual deception. Their power does not lie in physical objects. When they use physical objects, it is the spiritual deception that gives them power (1 Cor. 8.7-8; 10.19-20).

But not all representative angels are evil angels. Michael appeared in Daniel's vision as Israel's angel (Dan. 10.13, 20-21; 12.1), and he shows up again as the spiritual representative of God's people in the book of Revelation. The battle in heaven between Michael and the dragon (Rev. 12.7-9) corresponds to the conflict between the child and the dragon on earth (Rev. 12.1-6). This child stands for Christ, who is the embodiment God's people, and the dragon is another name for Satan.

The book of Revelation also teaches us that churches have angels that represent them (Rev. 1.20; 2.1). (Some interpreters think that the angels in Rev. 2.1 etc. are elders of the churches, but that is unlikely. The word "angel" always refers to actual angels in Revelation.)

Spiritual Beings and Human Institutions

The Bible uses many different words for angelic powers, such as "ruler," "dominion," "authority," "power," and "throne." Sometimes it is difficult to know whether spiritual or human authorities are meant (1 Cor. 15.24; Eph. 1.21; Col. 1.16). Perhaps the best way to understand this is to realize that human and spiritual powers are related to each other. Spiritual powers stand behind the power structures of this world. This is why these structures often tend to take on a life of their own, as we can observe in such phenomena as corporate greed and corrupt politics. These evils manifest themselves through human beings, but they exist independently of specific individuals. We can also think of expressions such as "team spirit" and "mob spirit." The New Testament describes the spiritual powers as working through human beings (2 Cor. 11.3-4; Eph. 2.2) and especially through the social and religious structures in this world (2 Cor. 6.14-16; Rev. 2.13-14).

In the book of Revelation (17.5 etc.), Babylon stands as a symbol for the cultural, social, religious, and especially economic aspects of Rome and other empires that oppress the people of God. These aspects of the empire represent demonic forces, as Babylon "has become a dwelling for demons and a haunt for every evil spirit" (Rev. 18.2). The beast is another symbol in Revelation. It represents the political and military power of the evil empire. The beast receives its authority from Satan, the dragon (Rev. 13.2). In this way, the book of Revelation shows us that there are spiritual forces that stand behind the powers in this world.

But the book of Revelation also shows us that the power of the evil spirits is very limited. Christ's power of redemption is much stronger than all the powers of evil (Rev. 12.11). In Christ, Christians have therefore been given the means to defeat their spiritual enemies (Eph. 6.10-20). But we must not think of this battle with Satan as a battle that takes place in isolation from the physical realities in this world. Spiritual forces express themselves through human beings, even disciples (Mk 8.33). We defeat them when we help others and ourselves not to disobey God (2 Cor. 10.3-6).

It is not spiritual to be too concerned with spiritual beings. Paul has to warn the Colossians against this error. In Colossians 2.18, he mentions people who delight "in false humility and the worship of angels." This probably does not mean that these false teachers actually worship the angels, but that they focus too much on what is going on in heaven, where the angels worship God (Rev. 5.11-12). Perhaps they thought that they would gain some spiritual powers if they had detailed knowledge of the angels' worship. But Paul tells them that their focus should be elsewhere (see also Heb. 1.5–2.9). They should focus on him who is "the head over every power and authority," Jesus Christ (Col. 2.10, 19). He is supreme over all the spiritual beings (Col. 1.16-17).

Demons Occupying Human Beings

From the Old Testament, we learn that spiritual beings may influence human beings in a negative way (1 Sam. 16.14-15; 18.10; 2 Chron. 18.18-22), but it is only the New Testament that describes demons occupying human beings.

The New Testament uses a variety of expressions for demons that make human beings suffer. The Greek word *daimonizomai* is often translated "to be possessed by a demon," but this translation is misleading. This Greek word does not convey the idea of possession. We should also not think that demons possess or own human beings. God is the creator of human beings, and he is their rightful owner. When demons cause suffering to human beings, they are making an unrightful claim on them. A more accurate term may therefore be "occupied by a demon." A demon may occupy a person, but that does not mean that the demon owns the person.

The New Testament authors were able to distinguish clearly between demon occupation and sickness, also sickness that involved disturbed behavior (cf Mk 1.32; Lk. 7.21). Matthew makes a distinction between people that "were shaking wildly" and people that "were controlled by demons" (Mt. 4.24 NIrV).

The evangelists presuppose that anyone is able to make this distinction. When a woman comes to Jesus and complains that her daughter is occupied by an evil spirit (Mk 7.25), there is no question whether her diagnosis is correct. There is no discussion in the New Testament, therefore, of what distinguishes demon occupation from sicknesses that cause people to change behavior.

However, the Gospels include three accounts with detailed descriptions of demon occupation: the demoniac in the synagogue in Capernaum

(Mk 1.23-28; Lk. 4.33-37); the Gerasene demoniac (Mk 5.1-20; Mt. 8.28-34; Lk. 8.26-39); and the boy with a deaf-mute spirit (Mk 9.14-29; Mt. 7.14-21; Lk. 9.37-43a).

From these accounts, we can see the characteristics of demon occupation. People occupied by a demon are dominated by the evil spirit, so that the spirit's personality manifests itself in their behavior. The demon can cause violent behavior (Mk 5.1-5), muteness (Mt. 9.32), deafness (Mk 9.25), self-destructive behavior (Mt. 17.15), and characteristics of epilepsy (Lk. 9.39).

Exorcism

There are many accounts of exorcism from the ancient world, both from Jewish and Greco-Roman sources. These exorcism accounts typically include a description of the techniques that were necessary to cast out demons. In the Jewish writing Tobit (written between 250 and 175 BCE), we read about how the smell of a fish's liver and heart could chase away a demon (Tobit 8.1-3). The Jewish historian Josephus (ca 37–100 CE) mentions a man named Eleazar, who had a ring that had the same effect (Josephus, *Antiquities of the Jews* 8.45-49). The most common technique was to use magical formulas.

When we compare with these accounts, we realize that Jesus' exorcisms are very different. He does not need such techniques to cast out the demons (Mt. 8.32) for he has sovereign authority over them. His coming to earth marks the ultimate defeat of the evil powers (Mt. 12.25-29; see also chs 8 and 9). At the time of his death, he proclaimed his complete victory over the evil spirits (Col. 2.15; 1 Pet. 3.19-20). He can therefore give his disciples the authority to participate in his work in defeating the demons (Lk. 9.1-2; 10.17-20).

Summary

The Bible describes both good and evil spiritual beings. God created them all, and when he created them, they were good. Led by Satan, some of these spiritual beings have fallen away from God and become evil. These spiritual beings may have great power, but never more than God allows them at any given time. The position as the crown of God's work belongs to other creatures, as we shall see in the next chapter.

Further Reading

Arnold, Clinton E. *Powers of Darkness: Principalities and Powers in Paul's Letters.* Downers Grove: IVP, 1992.

Wink, Walter. *Naming the Powers: The Language of Power in the New Testament.* Philadelphia: Fortress, 1984.

Review Questions

What are the differences between God and Satan?

How does the Bible describe the relationship between spiritual and worldly powers?

How do God's people resist evil powers?

3
Made for Fellowship
Human Beings as Created

Chapter Outline
The Image of God	28
Flesh	30
Body, Soul, and Spirit	30
Heart	31
Conscience	32
Summary	32

When God created human beings they were good (Gen. 1.31). They were created last and brought his creation to perfection (Ps. 8.5-6). God created them to live in a harmonious relationship with the earth, with each other, and with himself. God put the man he had created "in the Garden of Eden to work it and take care of it" (Gen. 2.15). The human beings ruled over the fish, the birds, and all living creatures (Gen. 1.28; see also 2.19-20). They enjoyed the fruit of the plants and the trees in the garden (Gen. 1.29; 2.16).

Man was created in such a way that it was not good for him to be alone (Gen. 2.18). For God's creation to be complete in goodness, it was necessary for God to create human beings as man and woman. God created them as equals in the sense that they were both the crown of his creation. Both the man and the woman were created in the image of God (Gen. 1.27). God created them to be different in the sense that they would complement each other. The woman is "a helper suitable for" the man (Gen. 2.18). God created the man and the woman to enjoy a relationship where they are united together in marriage (Gen. 2.24; see also Mk 10.6-8).

All creatures came into being through the word of God (Gen. 1.3 etc.). But God did not speak directly to any of them, only to Adam and Eve (Gen. 1.28-30). Only Adam and Eve were in communion and relationship with God. They enjoyed his presence and his blessing (Gen. 1.28). There was nothing that separated them from God, they had an open relationship with him, and they felt no shame (Gen. 2.25).

Human beings were created so that they could make genuine, moral choices. "The Lord God commanded the man, 'You are free to eat from any tree in the garden; but you must not eat from the tree of the knowledge of good and evil, for when you eat of it you will certainly die'" (Gen. 2.16-17). Human beings were offered the choice between obeying and disobeying God.

The Image of God

Human beings are unique because they alone are created in the image of God. The creation account in Genesis gives special attention to the creation of human beings:

> God said, "Let us make human beings in our image, in our likeness, so that they may rule over the fish in the sea and the birds in the sky, over the livestock and all the wild animals, and over all the creatures that move along the ground." So God created human beings in his own image, in the image of God he created them; male and female he created them. God blessed them and said to them, "Be fruitful and increase in number; fill the earth and subdue it. Rule over the fish in the sea and the birds in the sky and over every living creature that moves on the ground." (Gen. 1.26-28)

There is a close connection between the creation of human beings in God's image and the commandment to rule over all the rest of creation. To be created in God's image is therefore to rule the world on his behalf. In antiquity, rulers often put up statutes of themselves around their empire. When those who lived in the empire saw these statutes, they were reminded of who their ruler was. The statues, or images, served as an extension of the ruler's authority. In the same way, to be created in God's image means to extend God's rule throughout the earth. An assault on any human being is therefore an assault on God himself (Gen. 9.6).

In order to extend God's rule throughout the world, it was necessary for Adam and Eve to "be fruitful and increase in number" so that they could "fill the earth" (Gen. 1.28). The creation of human beings as male and female was therefore a part of what it meant to be created in God's image. To fulfill this destiny, Adam and Eve's task was to become a family, have children, and increase in number.

In Psalm 8, the psalmist reflects on the significance of God's creation of the human being in the image of God. He refers to the same idea of the human beings as the ruler of creation: "You made him ruler over the works of your hands; you put everything under his feet: all flocks and herds, and the beasts of the field, the birds of the air, and the fish of the sea, all that swim the paths of the seas" (Ps. 8.6-8 NIV). This shows how great the human being is: "what is man that you are mindful of him, the son of man that you care for him? You made him a little lower than the heavenly beings and crowned him with glory and honor" (Ps. 8.4-5 NIV).

But human beings failed at their mission to extend the rule of God throughout the world (ch. 4). Human beings did not fulfill their purpose as God's image. To fulfill the great destiny that the psalmist describes, God sent a new Adam. The letter to the Hebrews explains that Psalm 8 reaches its ultimate fulfillment in Jesus Christ (Heb. 2.6-9). Jesus came and brought the kingdom of God (Mk 1.15; Lk. 11.20; 17.21). He came as the perfect image of God (2 Cor. 4.4; Col. 1.15). It is therefore only in Jesus Christ that human beings can become what they were created to be. In Jesus Christ, we are renewed into the image of God, the image of his Son (Rom. 8.29; 2 Cor. 3.18). This means that it is Jesus Christ who teaches us what it means to be a human being. The way that Jesus exercises his rule teaches us how we are destined to rule on God's behalf.

The New Testament does not repeat God's commandment to "be fruitful and increase in number." In the New Testament, we do not expand the rule of God or the kingdom of God through childbearing. Instead, we spread it through the gospel. When people come to faith in Jesus Christ, God manifests his rule. Several New Testament passages therefore use the phrase from Genesis 1.28, to "be fruitful and increase," when the gospel breaks new ground (Acts 6.7; 12.24; Col. 1.6, 10). Through the missionary activity of the church, God's creation reaches its goal. When this mission has reached to all the nations and people groups in the world, God's creation reaches its destiny. In Revelation 5.9-10, God's people sing about this: "with your blood you purchased for God members of every tribe and language and people and nation. You have made them to be a kingdom and priests to serve our God, and they will reign on the earth."

God enters into relationship with human beings and entrusts them with the task of bringing his creation to its goal. But this does not mean that human beings are at the same level as God. The Bible underscores the tremendous difference between God and human beings: "God is in heaven and you are on earth" (Eccl. 5.2).

Flesh

In the Bible, the word "flesh" draws attention to this difference. The word "flesh" describes human beings in their weakness and mortality. It emphasizes that they are dependent upon God. "All flesh is grass, and all its beauty is like the flower of the field. The grass withers, the flower fades when the breath of the Lord blows on it" (Isa. 40.6-7 ESV). The apostle Paul also uses the word in a more specific way. He sees the flesh as the seat of sin (Rom. 8.3). But Paul can also refer to Jesus' flesh (Col. 1.22; see also Rom. 1.3; 9.5). His meaning therefore cannot have been that the flesh in itself is sinful.

Body, Soul, and Spirit

The Bible uses several other terms to describe various aspects of the human being, such as "body," "soul," and "spirit." But it is not biblical to understand human beings as divided into two or three different parts or to think that they have a body, a soul, and a spirit. A person is body, soul, and spirit. The Bible views a human being as a unity, and these different terms are used to describe a person from different viewpoints. We may compare this to how a person may be a woman, an Ethiopian, and a student. These terms describe the same person from different perspectives. But we will not say that this person has "womanness," "Ethiopianness," and "studentness."

There is only one instance where the Bible refers to human beings as "body," "soul," and "spirit" (1 Thess. 5.23), and the two terms "body" and "soul" only occur together twice (Prov. 16.24 NRSV; Mt. 10.28). More commonly, the Old Testament refers to human beings as "heart" and "flesh" (Ps. 73.26; Ezek. 44.7, 9), and the New Testament uses "body" and "spirit" (1 Cor. 7.34; Jas 2.26). But the point is not to say that these are two or three parts of the human being. The expressions emphasize that both the inward and outward aspects of the person are in view.

In the New Testament, the term "body" focuses on the outward aspects. It describes human beings in the way they interact with the world (Mt. 6.22-23; Rom. 6.12; 12.1; Heb. 10.5). A better translation might perhaps be "embodiment" (or almost "person"). Many times, "body" might be translated "I" (Rom. 6.12-13, 16, 19; Phil. 1.20).

The original meaning of the Hebrew (*nefesh*) and Greek (*psuche*) words for "soul" was probably "breath." These words are therefore closely associated with life itself, as we see in the creation account: "the Lord God formed man of the dust of the ground, and breathed into his nostrils the breath of life; and man became a living soul" (Gen. 2.7 KJV). This is the background for Genesis 9.4, where the Hebrew text says that the soul (translated "life") is in the blood. Because of the association with breath and throat, the word "soul" can also mean simply "desire," both for food (Deut. 23.24 [Hebrew]) and more generally (Deut. 21.14 [Hebrew]; Ps. 35.25 [Hebrew]). The "soul" can also represent a human being's capacity for desire and longing. In these passages, the meaning of the word comes close to the meaning of "soul" in modern English (Ps. 42.1-2; Rev. 18.14 NRSV). More broadly, the "soul" refers to a person as capable of emotion and thought (Josh. 23.14; Ps. 6.3; Mk 14.34). In the Bible, "soul" is the word that comes closest to our word for "person" (Exod. 16.16; Acts 27.37 KJV). To devote oneself fully and wholeheartedly to a task is therefore to do something with one's soul (Deut. 6.5; Mk 12.30). Because it represents a person's life, the soul is of the very highest value (Mk 8.36-37). Since the gift of salvation is the ultimate gift of life, the "soul" is the object of salvation (1 Pet. 1.9).

The term "spirit" (Hebrew: *ruach*; Greek: *pneuma*) can also mean "wind" (Isa. 7.2 [Hebrew]; Jn 3.8 [Greek]). Like "soul," it refers to the inward aspects of the human being (Isa. 57.15; Mt. 5.3), and it is used for human beings as they relate to God (Ezek. 11.19; Rom. 1.9; 8.16). The Greek culture considered the mind to be the noblest part of a human being. But the Bible places a higher value on human beings as spirit. It is their ability to be in a relationship with God, not their capacity for rational thought, that gives human beings their special value.

Heart

The word "heart" is closely related to the term "spirit." These two words can be used as synonyms (Ps. 51.17; Ezek. 36.26). In modern English, the "heart" is associated mostly with our feelings (Exod. 4.14; Prov. 14.10; Rom. 9.2). But in the Bible, the heart is also the seat of our thoughts, our attitudes, and our will (1 Kgs 8.17; Acts 5.3; Heb. 4.12).

Conscience

In Paul's letters, the conscience (Greek: *suneidesis*) is the ability to pass a moral judgment. The conscience functions as an internal tribunal that defends or condemns one's actions (Rom. 2.15). Its verdict is not always correct; it may be wrong (1 Cor. 4.4; see also 10.28-30). The Greek word *suneidesis* may also be translated "self-awareness" as it refers to one's capacity to reflect upon one's own actions. Those who have a weak conscience or self-awareness tend to follow the example of those who are stronger, without critical self-reflection (1 Cor. 8.7, 10).

Summary

Human beings are the crown of God's creation. It is possible for them to enjoy God's presence and to be in a relationship with him. They are created in his image, in order that they may exercise his rule over all the earth. As we shall see, however, they have not lived up to their great purpose.

Further Reading

Green, Joel B. *Body, Soul, and Human Life: The Nature of Humanity in the Bible*. Grand Rapids: Eerdmans, 2008.

Middleton, J. Richard. *The Liberating Image: The Imago Dei in Genesis 1*. Grand Rapids: Brazos, 2005.

Wolff, Hans Walter. *Anthropology of the Old Testament*. Translated by Margaret Kohl. Philadelphia: Fortress, 1974.

Review Questions

What does it mean to be created in God's image?

What is the goal of being human?

Explain this statement: A person does not have a spirit, a soul, and a body, but a person is spirit, soul, and body.

4
Breaking the Relationship
Human Sin

Chapter Outline

Adam and Eve's Sin	33
Sin in Human History	35
Sin and Pride	35
Sin and God's Law	37
Idolatry	38
Sin Is against God	38
Sin and Uncleanness	39
Sin and Shame	40
Sin and Judgment	41
Paul	41
The Gospels	44
Revelation	45
Summary	46

God created human beings to live in a perfect relationship with him, with each other, and with the world. Sin ruins all these relationships.

Adam and Eve's Sin

The story of Adam and Eve shows us the nature of sin as well as its destructive effects. It began when the serpent asked: "Did God really say, 'You must not eat from any tree in the garden'?" (Gen. 3.1). In this way, he cast doubts upon whether God is good. When she answered the serpent, Eve said: "We may eat fruit from the trees in the garden, but God did say, 'You must not eat fruit from the tree that is in the middle of the garden, and you must not touch it, or you will die'" (Gen. 3.2-3). When Eve quoted God's commandment, she made it sound restrictive rather than liberating. God had said that Adam and Eve were "free to eat from any tree in the garden" (Gen. 2.16), but Eve omitted the words "free" and "any" (Gen. 3.2). She also added a new commandment when she said that God had told them not to touch the tree (Gen. 3.3).

When the serpent had succeeded in making Eve look at the commandment in this way, he proceeded with a false promise, so characteristic of the temptation to sin (Mt. 4.9). "'You will not certainly die,' the serpent said to the woman. 'For God knows that when you eat of it your eyes will be opened, and you will be like God, knowing good and evil'" (Gen. 3.4-5). Satan's temptation shows us that sin means above all that human beings want to be like God and take his place. Instead of depending on him for everything, they want to be their own god and trust in themselves.

After distrust in God, the next step is desire. Now Eve "saw that the fruit of the tree was good for food and pleasing to the eye, and also desirable for gaining wisdom" (Gen. 3.6). The act of disobedience then comes as a direct consequence (Gen. 3.6b; see also Jas 1.15).

Adam and Eve's sin destroyed their relationship with God, so that they felt shame (Gen. 3.7). Now they were afraid of God (3.10), and Adam even blamed God for what had gone wrong (3.12). Their relationship to each other was also broken. Adam turned against his wife and put the blame on her (3.12).

The gift of life comes from God (Gen. 3.22). When the relationship with God was broken, a natural consequence was that creation comes under the power of death (Gen. 2.17). Death entered the world through sin (Rom. 5.12; see also 6.23).

After the fall, God let Adam and Eve feel the effects of their own sin. Eve had led Adam to sin, and now her "desire will be for [her] husband, and he will rule over [her]" (Gen. 3.16). Adam was destined to live through trust in God. God would then give him everything he needed in abundance. But now, he would eat his food "through painful toil" all the time he would live on earth (Gen. 3.17). In Paul's letter to the Romans, God's judgment means that he gives people over to their own sin (Rom. 1.24, 26, 28). They are left in the power of sin, their sinful lifestyle runs its course, and they give into sinful desires that only become stronger and stronger, but can never really satisfy them. The seals in the book of Revelation make a similar point. When the first three seals are broken, the world suffers the consequences of human sin: violence and greed (Rev. 6.1-6).

Sin in Human History

After Adam and Eve's fall, sin became more severe and human relationships became more brutal. Cain murdered his brother Abel (Gen. 4.8). Lamech "killed a man for wounding [him]" and avenged himself 77 times (Gen. 4.23-24). Before the flood, human wickedness had become so great that "every inclination of the thoughts of the human heart was only evil all the time" (Gen. 6.5).

Some time later, human beings committed an act of ultimate arrogance and tried to build a tower that reached to heaven, so that they could make a name for themselves (Gen. 11.4). The biblical story explains that God would be the one who makes people's name great (Gen. 12.2). When the people attempted to build the tower, they therefore attempted to do the works of God and to be like him (Gen. 3.5). Instead of trusting in God, human beings tried to take God's place.

After the judgment at Babel, God chose Abraham and his descendants to be his people. The people of Israel were meant to belong to God and trust in him. Because they belonged to God and enjoyed a special relationship with him, God also called this people to account in a unique way. He told them: "You only have I chosen of all the families of the earth; therefore I will punish you for all your sins" (Amos 3.2). In many ways, the history of Israel tells the story of how God's people failed to live up to their responsibility. They destroyed their relationship with their God, and therefore also their relationship with one another (ch. 5).

Sin and Pride

Both Adam and Eve and the people of Babel put themselves in God's place. Their stories show that pride is the root of sin. In the Old Testament, human pride mostly takes the form of pride in one's own power and wealth. Those who take pride in themselves do not acknowledge that all power belongs to God. When they were about to take possession of the promised land, Moses warned the people against the dangers of wealth. When they become rich, they must be careful not to think that they have themselves to thank for their good fortune. They must not forget that everything is a gift from God (Deut. 8.11-18). Psalm 10 explains that such pride is characteristic of the wicked. They trust in their own strength and oppress the weak. They have no concern for God and think that he will never judge them (Ps. 10.2-13).

World powers, such as the Assyrians and Babylonians, provide the best examples of this kind of pride. In Isaiah 37.21-29, the prophet pronounces judgment on King Sennacherib of Assyria. God will punish Sennacherib because he believed that his own power had enabled him to conquer the land from Lebanon to Egypt. In a similar way, Isaiah also describes the arrogance of the Babylonian king (Isa. 14.3-21). This king had such faith in his own might that he thought he could "make [himself] like the Most High" (Isa. 14.14).

In the book of Daniel, we learn about the Babylonian king Nebuchadnezzar and his dream. He saw a tree that was visible throughout the earth, but a messenger came down from heaven and said that the tree would be cut down. Daniel explained that the tree stood for Nebuchadnezzar himself, whose "dominion extends to distant parts of the earth" (Dan. 4.22). Because he did not give honor to God, he "will be driven away from people and will live with the wild animals" until he realizes "that the Most High is sovereign over the kingdoms on earth and gives them to anyone he wishes" (Dan. 4.25).

In his picture of the king of Tyre, the prophet Ezekiel draws clear parallels to the story of Adam and Eve in the Garden of Eden (Ezek. 28.11-19). God created the king perfect, "full of wisdom and perfect in beauty" (Ezek. 28.12). But instead of giving credit to God, the king's "heart became proud on account of [his] beauty" (Ezek. 28.17). As a consequence, God judged him and "reduced [him] to ashes on the ground" (Ezek. 28.18).

But God's judgment against pride does not concern only world rulers. "All the proud and lofty" (Isa. 2.12) everywhere, also among the people of Israel, "will be brought low" (Isa. 2.9) on the day when God will visit the earth (Isa. 2.6-22).

The New Testament also condemns rulers who take pride in their own power. When the people praised King Herod as a god, an angel of the Lord struck him down because he did not give honor to God (Acts 12.21-23). The apostle Paul anticipated the coming of the lawless one, who would proclaim himself to be God (2 Thess. 2.3-4).

Sin and God's Law

The Hebrew word that is usually translated "sin" (*hata*) originally meant "miss the mark." It was therefore natural to use this word to describe an error or an action that fails to meet expectations. In the context of expectations for human behavior, to sin (*hata*) means to violate a norm or to disobey a law (Gen. 31.36 NRSV). Such violations destroy relationships between human beings (Gen. 42.22).

The relationship between God and Israel was regulated through covenant (ch. 5). But Israel sinned by breaking the commandments of this covenant (Neh. 9.29; Dan. 9.11). Sin is so serious because it affects the relationship with God. As a willful act of disobedience, it is rebellion against him (Deut. 1.26; Ps. 107.11; Isa. 1.2).

God's first commandment was: "You shall have no other gods before me" (Exod. 20.3). God's relationship with the people requires that they do not give their worship and obedience to anyone or anything other than him. They must not worship any other gods.

When God spoke to Moses on the mountain, Moses "heard the sound of words but saw no form; there was only a voice" (Deut. 4.12). Therefore, Israel must not make any image to worship (Deut. 4.15-19). God is the creator, the eternal "I AM." He is above all creation, and he must not be confused with it.

But while Moses was still on the mountain, Israel broke this commandment. They made "an idol cast in the shape of a calf" (Exod. 32.4). Their intention was not to turn away from God and worship the calf instead. The calf was meant as a visible representation of God. When the calf was made, they said: "This is your God, O Israel, who brought you out of the land of Egypt" (Exod. 32.4 NAB). (In many translations, this verse reads: "These are your gods." The Hebrew word is *elohe*, which is in the plural form. Since the plural form is used both for "God" and for "gods," both translations are possible. But the context shows us that the translation "This is your God" is the best. In v. 5, Aaron announces a festival to the Lord.)

Israel's sin was therefore not that they openly and directly rejected the Lord, but that they worshiped him in a way that he had forbidden. When they did that, however, they no longer worshiped the true God. They preferred their own representation of God to the God that had revealed himself to them. They did not worship the invisible God, but an image they had made for themselves.

Idolatry

Israel's first act of rebellion against God was idolatry, a violation of his first commandment (Exod. 20.3; Deut. 5.7). Idolatry continued to be their chief sin. When the northern tribes broke away from Judah, their king Jeroboam repeated the sin of the wilderness generation. He made two golden calves that he set up in Bethel and Dan. "He said to the people, 'It is too much for you to go up to Jerusalem. Here are your gods, Israel, who brought you up out of Egypt . . .' And this thing became a sin; the people came to worship the one at Bethel and went as far as Dan to worship the other" (1 Kgs 12.28, 30).

When the people made a visible representation of God and worshiped it, they committed idolatry. This shows us that even God's own visible gifts could become objects of idolatry. When God placed the Midianites in the hands of Gideon and his men, they took a great plunder of gold earrings. Gideon made this gold into an ephod, like the garment of the high priest, and placed it in Ophrah. But Israel committed idolatry with this ephod. "All Israel prostituted themselves by worshiping it there, and it became a snare to Gideon and his family" (Judg. 8.27).

Sin Is against God

Since sin is a violation of God's covenant, all sins are sins against God. When David had committed adultery with Bathsheba and murdered Uriah, he confessed to God: "Against you, you only, have I sinned" (Ps. 51.4).

Sin affects every aspect of human life. Even at their best, human beings are sinful. "Indeed, there is no one on earth who is righteous, no one who does what is right and never sins" (Eccl. 7.20). "Who can say, 'I have kept my heart pure; I am clean and without sin'?" (Prov. 20.9). The holiest man in Israel, the high priest, had to make atonement for his own sins (Lev. 16.6, 11). Even Israel's worship of God was not free from sin. Therefore, Aaron had to have a plate of pure gold on his forehead, engraved with the words "holy to the Lord." This plate would "bear the guilt involved in the sacred gifts the Israelites consecrate, whatever their gifts may be" (Exod. 28.38).

The prophets describe very vividly how sin destroys the relationship with God. Hosea saw the basic sin of the people as lack of faithfulness to the Lord. With the metaphor of Israel as the Lord's bride, he likened their sin to adultery (Hos. 2.2-8). To Isaiah, sin was first and foremost arrogance and self-exaltation (Isa. 2.11). The prophet Jeremiah rebuked the people for their falsehood; even their repentance was not sincere (Jer. 3.10).

As Israel's political leaders failed to trust in God, they turned elsewhere for security. When Judah and Israel threatened each other, both states tried to form an alliance with Assyria. When Judah later faced the threat of Assyria, they turned to Egypt for help. The prophets saw very clearly that these political dealings were an expression of the people's lack of trust in the Lord. Instead of relying on him, they pinned their hopes on unreliable alliances with world powers (Hos. 5.13; Isa. 30.2; 31.1).

The sins of the people affected not only their relationship to God, but also their relationship to one another. Those who have no respect for God are also ready to oppress the poor. "Whoever oppresses the poor shows contempt for their Maker" (Prov. 14.31). The prophets saw clearly that the lifestyle of the upper classes depended on their oppression of the poor. Their very lifestyle, not only specific offenses, was therefore sinful (Amos 6.4-7; Hos. 7.5). No individual could claim to be without responsibility for the sins of the people. Each individual shared in the responsibility for the people's sins. When Isaiah met the Lord in his holiness, he knew that he was ruined, both because of his own sins and because of the sins of his people. "'Woe to me!' [he] cried. 'I am ruined! For I am a man of unclean lips, and I live among a people of unclean lips, and my eyes have seen the King, the Lord Almighty'" (Isa. 6.5).

Sin and Uncleanness

When Isaiah confessed his sins, he described his sins as uncleanness (Isa. 6.5). The concept of cleanness and uncleanness is a powerful metaphor that shows how sin affects the relationship with God. In this respect, Israel's laws are quite detailed. Serious sins cause uncleanness (Lev. 18.30; Num. 35.33; see also Ps. 51.2), which cannot be tolerated in the presence of God. God is holy, and those who approach him must be holy. Most Israelites were not holy, but common or clean, which is a state between holiness and uncleanness. One must be clean to be in Israel's camp. Those who become unclean must be cleansed (Lev. 5.1-6) or stay outside the camp (Num. 5.2-3). This is necessary in order to ensure that nothing unclean comes into contact with something holy. If it does, it results in God's judgment (Lev. 10.1-2; 22.3).

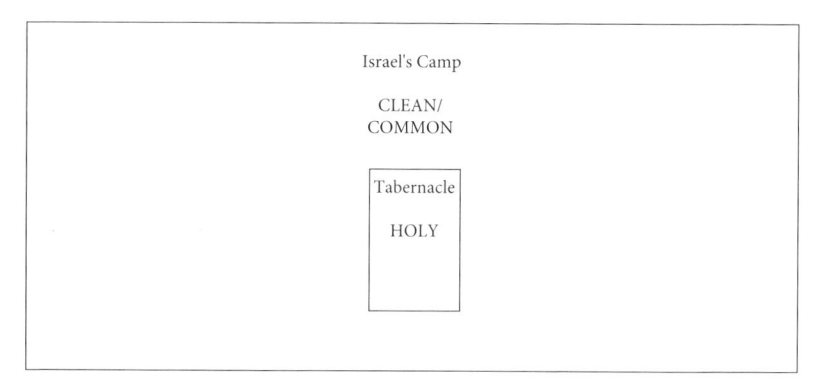

40 Introducing Biblical Theology

```
                    Israel's Camp
                    CLEAN/
                    COMMON

                    ┌─────────┐
                    │Tabernacle│
                    │         │
                    │  HOLY   │
                    │         │
                    └─────────┘


                      UNCLEAN
```

Figure 4.1 Cleanness and uncleanness in Israel's camp

Those who sacrifice their children to Molek cause God's sanctuary to become unclean (Lev. 20.2-3). Such a sin is a terrible offense against the presence of God in Israel. The prophets Jeremiah and Ezekiel explain that Israel's idolatry is just such a sin: it has defiled the sanctuary of the Lord (Jer. 7.30; Ezek. 5.11) and the land (Jer. 2.7; Ezek. 36.17-18). As a consequence, God must withdraw his presence from them (Ezek. 10.4, 18-19).

The prophets use uncleanness as a metaphor to explain the seriousness of Israel's sin (Zeph. 3.1-2). No one in Israel is clean, says Isaiah: "All of us have become like one who is unclean, and all our righteous acts are like filthy rags" (Isa. 64.6). According to Jeremiah, the uncleanness is so ingrained that it cannot come out: "Although you wash yourself with soap and use an abundance of cleansing powder, the stain of your guilt is still before me" (Jer. 2.22).

Sin and Shame

Sin is to fail to live up to God's expectations. Sin therefore causes shame, both as a subjective experience (Ezra 9.6; Jer. 31.19) and as objective humiliation (Ps. 53.5; Isa. 42.17). It is characteristic of the unrighteous that they know no shame (Jer. 3.3; 6.15; 8.12; Zeph. 3.5). But God will put them to shame (Ps. 6.10; Obad. 10). The prophet Ezekiel compares Jerusalem to a young woman and describes her idolatry with a graphic metaphor: "you poured out your lust and exposed your nakedness in your promiscuity with your lovers"

(16.36). God will judge her in kind: "I am going to gather all your lovers, with whom you found pleasure, those you loved as well as those you hated. I will gather them against you from all around and will strip you in front of them, and they will see all your nakedness" (Ezek. 16.37). Jerusalem has been unfaithful to the Lord. She has given her devotion to other gods and trusted in idolatrous nations to protect her. She will be shamed when God delivers her into the hands of these nations.

Sin and Judgment

In Leviticus 26 and Deuteronomy 28, God explains how he will judge the people if they break the covenant. The most serious punishment is that Israel will be conquered by other nations and go into captivity (Lev. 26.27-39; Deut. 28.25-57). God fulfilled this when Jerusalem was destroyed by the Babylonians and the people were led into exile (2 Kgs 25.8-12). This judgment came over Israel because God had withdrawn his presence (Ezek. 39.23). He was therefore no longer protecting them (Jer. 7.12-15). The real judgment for sin is therefore that God has rejected Israel (Ps. 78.59; Jer. 7.29). They are no longer his people (Hos. 1.9), and his dwelling is no longer among them. God has divorced his unfaithful wife (Isa. 50.1; Hos. 2.2). He responds to the people with silence (Ezek. 20.3, 31; Amos 8.12). Their prayers will not be heard (Jer. 11.11; 14.11-12). Instead, God fights against them "with an outstretched hand and a mighty arm in furious anger and in great wrath" (Jer. 21.5).

Paul

The Old Testament shows us clearly that sin is more serious than occasional mistakes. It is rebellion against God. Paul emphasizes this idea even more strongly in his letters. He uses the word "sin" in a very characteristic way. Most of the time, Paul does not refer to "sins" in the plural, but to "sin" in the singular. For him, sin is not primarily individual wrong actions, but a power. Sin "entered the world" (Rom. 5.12), "reigned in death" (Rom. 5.21), reigns in a person (Rom. 6.12, 14), and seizes "the opportunity afforded by the commandment" (Rom. 7.8). Paul can compare sin to an employer who pays wages (Rom. 6.23) and to a slave master to whom slaves are sold (Rom. 7.14).

Paul gives his most detailed discussion of the power of sin in Rom. 1.18-3.20. The effects of sin are false religion (Rom. 1.21, 23, 25) and misplaced trust (Rom. 2.17-29). Human beings did not worship the invisible God (Rom. 1.20-21). Instead, they put their trust in visible things, such as idols made by human beings (Rom. 1.23). This basic sin comes to expression in many different ways. People may rely on their own accomplishments (1 Cor. 1.19-25). Or they may put their trust in visible signs that they are elected by God. Many Jews looked to the signs of God's election: their circumcision and their membership in the Jewish nation (Rom. 2.25-29; 2 Cor. 11.22; Phil. 3.5). Many also relied on their own obedience of his law (Phil. 3.5-6). These are different ways in which people exalt themselves. They are not content to depend completely upon God and let him alone be exalted (1 Cor. 1.29, 31; 2 Cor. 10.17).

People that trust in themselves fail to be true representatives of God, and are not genuine bearers of God's image. Paul therefore explains that all people "fall short of the glory of God" (Rom. 3.23). "The glory of God" is another term for the image of God.

The root of sin is that people trust in something or someone other than God. All other sins are a consequence of that. In Romans 1.18-3.20, Paul explains that the sin of false religion is followed by other sinful acts. When God judges the sinners, he gives them over "in the sinful desires of their hearts" (Rom. 1.24). Instead of seeking to honor God, they seek their own honor and the satisfaction of their own appetites. Sexual sins are one illustrative example (Rom. 1.24-27).

Besides sexual immorality, greed is the individual sin that Paul mentioned most frequently (e.g. Rom. 1.29; 1 Cor. 5.10-11). The reason is probably that Gentile Christians found it particularly difficult to stay away from these sins. With respect to greed, Paul goes so far as to call it idolatry (Eph. 5.5; Col. 3.5). Persons who are greedy have put money in the place of God. They give their love, service, and trust to money instead of giving it to God (Mt. 6.24).

Paul also says about the sinners that "their god is their stomach" (Phil. 3.19). They have no higher goal than their own pleasure, which has taken the place that should have belonged to God.

Our sin makes us seek our own good rather than the good of others. Paul therefore often warns his churches against sins that cause conflict within the community, such as anger, slander, jealousy, selfish ambition, dissensions, factions, and envy (Gal. 5.20-21; Eph. 4.31).

Human sinfulness shows itself in rebellion against God. God's law reveals the nature of this rebellion. The law reveals how the desire of humans runs directly contrary to the will of God (Rom. 8.5; Gal. 5.17). In Romans 7.7-14, Paul explains how sin uses the law as an opportunity for itself. When the law describes what God forbids, sin does exactly what the law has forbidden. "For I would not have known what coveting really was if the law had not said, 'You shall not covet.' But sin, seizing the opportunity afforded by the commandment, produced in me every kind of coveting" (Rom. 7.7-8). The problem is not that the law is evil, for the law is good (Rom. 7.7, 11-12). But the law brings out the nature of sin and lets sin show its true face. "In order that sin might be recognized as sin, it used what is good to bring about my death, so that through the commandment sin might become utterly sinful" (Rom. 7.13).

In Romans 7.15-24 Paul continues to explain that the power of sin is so great that he is unable to free himself from it. He is "sold as a slave to sin" (Rom. 7.14), and unable to do what he wants to do. Instead he does what he hates (Rom. 7.15). Therefore, he knows that "good itself does not dwell in [him], that is, in [his] sinful nature" (Rom. 7.18).

Sin is so deep-rooted in human beings that Paul can refer to the human flesh as the place of sin (Rom. 8.3). For this reason, modern translations often render the word "flesh" (*sarx*) as "sinful nature." The flesh stands in direct opposition to the Spirit of God (Rom. 8.6; Gal. 5.16-17; Phil. 3.3).

Sinfulness is therefore characteristic of all people, as Paul explains in Romans 3.9-19 by quoting several passages from Scripture. In their original contexts, the passages that Paul quotes do not refer to human beings in general. They refer to especially wicked people. For example, in Romans 3.10-12 Paul quotes from Psalm 14.3: "there is no one who does good, not even one." But Psalm 14 is about the fools, those who "say in their hearts, 'There is no God'" (Ps. 14.1). When he quotes this Psalm and says that it applies to all human beings, Paul makes a radical point. All human beings are as wicked as the fools described in this Psalm. What the Old Testament says about the "fools" and the "evildoers" is true about all human beings.

Regarding the ultimate origin of sin and evil, Paul does not provide an explanation. He simply says that "sin entered the world" through Adam (Rom. 5.12). In Paul's time, most Jews knew that Adam and Eve were the first sinners, but they did not think that other people's sin was a direct result of what Adam and Eve had done. Instead, they believed the problem was that all human beings follow in Adam's footsteps and repeat what he did (*4 Ezra* 7.118; *2 Baruch* 54.19). But Paul saw it differently. Adam is the forefather of humanity, and what he did has direct consequences for all of us. His sin is the direct cause of death for all human beings and it brought condemnation on all people (Rom. 5.12-13; see also 1 Cor. 15.22).

Most English translations render Romans 5.12 "death came to all people, because all sinned." But the New Testament scholar Joseph Fitzmyer has shown that it is better to translate it: "death came to all people, with the result that all sinned." This translation fits better with Paul's logic in Romans 5.12-21. The passage describes the positive effects of Jesus' work, compared to the negative effects of Adam's work. In v. 15 Paul adds that "the many died by the trespass of the one man," and in v. 18 he says that "one trespass resulted in condemnation for all people." In other words, Adam's sin led directly to the death and the condemnation of all of Adam's descendants. All human beings are therefore born as sinners. For this reason, Paul concludes that "we were by nature deserving of wrath" (Eph. 2.3). Theologians refer to this idea as the doctrine of original sin.

The Gospels

Jesus also teaches that sin sits deeply in human beings, so deeply that he can simply refer to the disciples as "evil" (Mt. 7.11). The problem is deeper than individual actions because our sinful acts come from the heart (Mk 7.21-23). When he sharpens the commandments of the Mosaic law, Jesus explains that sin is not merely what we do. Sin is the attitude of our hearts (Mt. 5.21-22, 27-28). Moses taught that adultery was sin, but Jesus says that "anyone who looks at a woman lustfully has already committed adultery with her in his heart" (Mt. 5.28).

But sin is first and foremost to turn away from God. The Gospels therefore show the sin of the people in their rejection of Jesus. Jesus was the one whom God had chosen. But Israel's leaders had a long history of rejecting God's messengers, and now their stubbornness climaxed in their rejection of Jesus (Lk. 13.34-35; 19.44; Jn 1.10-11).

When the people do not receive Jesus, they show that their hearts are hardened (Mt. 13.13-15). Like Pharaoh, they have become insensitive to the truth of God. Now, God judges them by allowing them to become even more hardened. "In them is fulfilled the prophecy of Isaiah: 'You will be ever hearing but never understanding; you will be ever seeing but never perceiving. For this people's heart has become calloused; they hardly hear with their ears, and they have closed their eyes. Otherwise they might see with their eyes, hear with their ears, understand with their hearts and turn, and I would heal them'" (Mt. 13.14-15).

Even Jesus' disciples are so blind that they cannot see clearly who Jesus is. Mark is the evangelist that describes the failure of the disciples most clearly. At one point, "Jesus asked them: 'Why are you talking about having no bread? Do you still not see or understand? Are your hearts hardened? Do you have eyes but fail to see, and ears but fail to hear?'" (Mk 8.17-18). Here Jesus speaks to the disciples in the same way that he spoke about the outsiders in 4.11-12. In their failure to understand the truth about Jesus, the disciples run the risk of placing themselves outside the kingdom of God.

Even though Peter was a leader among the twelve, Peter's example shows us how strongly sin can influence even a follower of Jesus. When Jesus predicted his own death, Peter "took him aside and began to rebuke him" (Mk 8.32). In this way, he acted as a spokesperson for Satan (Mk 8.33). The night before Jesus was arrested, Peter promised him that he would rather die than disown him (Mk 14.29, 31). But when a servant girl later asked him, he denied even knowing Jesus. He even "began to call down curses, and he swore to them, 'I don't know this man you're talking about'" (Mk 14.71).

In the Gospel of John, evil is seen as pervading the whole world, and the term "world" is frequently a negative term. The world does not receive the revelation of God (1.10), but remains in darkness (12.46) because they are evil (3.19; see also 7.7). John traces sin back to the devil, with whom human beings are connected as a race (Jn 8.44; see also 1 Jn 3.8).

Revelation

In the book of Revelation, sin is first and foremost to fail to show loyalty to Christ alone. The churches in the province of Asia probably suffered persecution if they refused to participate in the worship of the emperor in Rome (Rev. 13.4-17). It may have been tempting to think that it was possible to compromise with this form of idolatry. Some Christians may have thought that they could participate both in the emperor worship and in the church's worship of Christ (Rev. 2.14).

In this situation, the book of Revelation makes it clear that Christ requires our undivided loyalty. God's judgment fall on those who have failed to give God their full commitment. Those who have taken the mark of the beast are thrown in the lake of fire (Rev. 19.20; see also 20.4). The mark of the beast stands as a symbol of the kind of loyalty that only God can require (ch. 15).

The book of Revelation also focuses on the corporate nature of sin. The prostitute in chapters 17 and 18 is a symbol of the economic power of Rome and its capacity to lure people away from Christ. In their luxury (Rev. 17.3-4), the Romans had become so proud that they had put themselves in the place of God (Rev. 18.7).

Summary

Sin leads directly to a broken relationship with God. This shows itself in that human beings no longer trust God and worship him as God. Instead, they try to take God's place. They trust in themselves and in objects of God's creation. This is idolatry. As a consequence of a broken relationship with God, our relationships with one another and with the earth are also broken. The story of the Bible will show us how these relationships can be restored.

Further Reading

Beale, Gregory K. *We Become What We Worship: A Biblical Theology of Idolatry*. Downers Grove: IVP, 2008.

Biddle, Mark E. *Missing the Mark: Sin and Its Consequences in Biblical Theology*. Nashville: Abingdon, 2005.

Blocher, Henri. *Original Sin: Illuminating the Riddle*. New Studies in Biblical Theology. Grand Rapids: Eerdmans, 1997.

Gowan, Donald E. *When Man Becomes God: Humanism and Hybris in the Old Testament*. Pittsburgh Theological Monograph Series 6. Pittsburgh: Pickwick, 1975.

Review Questions

How does the Bible show that to sin is to want to take God's place?

Explain how different manifestations of sin are also different manifestations of a ruined relationship with God.

Why is it possible to say that the apostle Paul has the most radical view of sin among the biblical authors?

5

God Makes It Personal

God's Interaction with His People in the Old Testament

Chapter Outline

Covenant	47
The Covenant with Noah	48
The Covenant with Abraham	49
The Sinai Covenant	51
Israel's Relationship with God	52
The Presence of God	58
The Covenant with David	60
The New Covenant	62
Summary	65

God's creation did not reach its intended goal because of human sin. Human beings broke their relationship with God, with each other, and with creation. Even though the human beings were at fault, God took the initiative towards restoration. The Old Testament shows that God constantly reaches out to human beings. "Many times and in various ways" (Heb. 1.1), he has taken the initiative to enter into relationship with human beings once again.

Covenant

In the Bible, the formal way of entering into a relationship is through covenant. A covenant is a solemn agreement between two parties. Sometimes these parties are equal in rank and power. Other times, one is superior to the other, such as when a sovereign king enters into a covenant with a subordinate king. A covenant may be either mutual or one-sided. In a mutual covenant, both parties promise something, whereas in a one-sided covenant, only one party makes a promise.

When God created the world, human beings had a free and open relationship with him. There was no need to regulate this relationship with a covenant. There is therefore no mention of a covenant in the first chapters of Genesis. It was the growth of evil in the world that made it necessary for God to establish covenants with human beings.

The Old Testament refers to four major covenants between God and human beings: between God and Noah (Gen. 6.19-21; 9.8-17), God and Abraham (Gen. 15.1-21; 17.1-22), God and Israel (Exod. 19.3-6; 24.7-8; Deut. 29.1-29), and God and David (2 Sam. 7.8-16; Ps. 89.3-4).

Many scholars have compared these covenants to Ancient Near East covenants that a sovereign king would make with smaller kings that were subject to him. These scholars compare God to a powerful king who promises to protect these vassal kings and who expects obedience from them. It may be true that there are some stylistic similarities between the book of Deuteronomy and such Ancient Near Eastern covenants, but other studies have shown that such covenants provide a poor model for understanding God's relationship with his people. God's care of his people does not compare to the tyranny of such kings. His covenants should instead be compared to covenants that regulate family relations, such as marriage and adoption. The Bible describes God as a husband (Jer. 2.2; Ezek. 16.8) and a father (Ps. 103.13; Jer. 3.4, 19) to his people.

The Covenant with Noah

God's first covenant is with Noah. The evil of human beings had become so great that "the Lord regretted that he had made human beings on the earth" (Gen. 6.6). He therefore said: "I will wipe from the face of the earth the human race I have created—and with them the animals, the birds and the creatures that move along the ground—for I regret that I have made them" (Gen. 6.7). But God made a covenant with Noah. He was going to save him, his family, and two of every kind of living creature (Gen. 6.18-20).

After the flood that destroyed all life on earth, God renewed the blessing he had given to human beings when he created them (cf. Gen. 1.28). He "blessed Noah and his sons, saying to them, 'Be fruitful and increase in number and fill the earth'" (Gen. 9.1). He also promised that he would never again "destroy all living creatures" (Gen. 8.21).

God made this promise into a formal covenant with Noah and his descendants. The covenant ensured that God would never again send a flood to destroy the earth. The rainbow was a sign of this covenant (Gen. 9.8-17).

The covenant with Noah shows that God is committed to his creation. Even though the wickedness of human beings had become great (Gen. 6.5), God would not destroy them. Instead, he continued his relationship with select individuals and remained determined to bring his creation to its intended goal: to bless human beings and exercise his rule over all the earth through them. God's covenant with Noah also teaches us that judgment and salvation cannot be isolated from each other. Noah was saved when God judged the whole world with a flood (cf. 1 Pet. 3.20).

The covenant with Noah was one-sided. Even though God was the superior party, God was the only one who made a promise. He promised to save Noah, and he promised never again to destroy all living creatures (Gen. 6.18-20; 9.11). But that does not mean that Noah had no obligations. Noah had to build the ark and enter it (Gen. 6.14-16, 18-21). He could only be saved when he obeyed this commandment.

The Covenant with Abraham

God's second covenant followed another incident when human evil was particularly great. Human beings had rejected God and did not depend on him. Instead, they relied on themselves. They wanted to build a tower that reached to heaven, so that they could make a name for themselves (Gen. 11.4).

After God had punished them and confused their language (Gen. 11.5-9), he chose one human being, Abram. He called Abram to leave his people, so that God could make him into a great nation (Gen. 12.1-3). In this new nation, God would complete his commitment to his creation. He would fulfill the promise he made to Adam and Eve and renewed to Noah (cf. Gen. 1.28; 9.1, 7); he would make Abram fruitful and numerous (Gen. 17.2, 6; cf. 15.5). God says "I will make you into a great nation, and I will bless you; I will make your name great, and you will be a blessing" (Gen. 12.2). Abram "will be the father of many nations," and his "name will be Abraham," which means "father of many" (Gen. 17.4-5). God also gives him and his descendants the land of Canaan as an everlasting possession, and promises that "I will be their God" (Gen. 17.8).

God's promise to Abraham also takes the form of a covenant. The Lord told Abram to bring him a heifer, a goat, and a ram. Abram cut these animals in two and placed the halves across from each other (Gen. 15.9-10). Afterwards, God came down in the form of "a smoking firepot with a blazing torch" and "passed between the pieces" (Gen. 15.17). The meaning of this ritual was to make a solemn promise and say something like: "may I be cut in two like these animals if I break this promise" (cf. Jer. 34.18). God's covenant with Abraham is also a one-sided covenant. God is the only one who makes a promise, and he is the only one who passes between the pieces of the animals.

But God's covenant with Abraham also involves an obligation on Abraham's part. God commands him to keep the covenant and to circumcise every male among his descendants (Gen. 17.9-14).

God's covenant with Abraham has a more clearly relational character than his covenant with Noah. God not only promises to keep Abraham's descendants alive, but he enters into a personal relationship with Abraham and his descendants. He promises to be their God (Gen. 17.8). Abraham also responded to God by trusting him (Gen. 15.6) and obeying him (Gen. 17.23-27; 21.4; cf. 22.1-18).

Many events in Abraham and Sarah's lives seemed to make it impossible for them to have any descendants (Gen. 12.10-20; 20.1-18; 22.1-18), but God showed that nothing could prevent him from keeping his promise. Abraham and Sarah had their son Isaac (Gen. 21.1-5), and God repeated his promise to him (Gen. 26.3-4). Isaac had two sons, Jacob and Esau. Of the two, God chose Jacob and gave him Abraham's blessing (Gen. 28.13-15; 35.11-12; cf. Mal. 1.2-3). God gave him the name Israel (Gen. 32.28) and made him the ancestor of God's chosen people.

The story of Jacob shows clearly that God did not choose Jacob because he was a good person. Esau and Jacob were twins, and Esau was the firstborn. But even though God had chosen the younger brother before the twins were born (Gen. 25.23), Isaac wanted to give the blessing to Esau, who was the firstborn (Gen. 27.1-4). Jacob showed himself to be a deceiver who lied to his father so that he could receive his father's blessing (Gen. 27.5-29). But Jacob's deceit and lies did not bring him God's blessing. In God's time, God gave Abraham's blessing to Jacob (Gen. 28.13-15; 35.11-12). In this way, God showed that his choice was based on his own sovereignty and grace, not on Jacob's goodness (cf. Rom. 9.10-13).

The Sinai Covenant

God made his covenant with Noah after an act of both judgment and salvation. In a similar way, God saved his people through an act of judgment before he made the Sinai covenant with them. The people of Israel had been in slavery in Egypt, and God came down to deliver them. Afterwards, he told them: "You yourselves have seen what I did to Egypt, and how I carried you on eagles' wings and brought you to myself. Now if you obey me fully and keep my covenant, then out of all nations you will be my treasured possession. Although the whole earth is mine, you will be for me a kingdom of priests and a holy nation" (Exod. 19.4-6). This covenant means that God upholds his choice of Israel as his people.

The Sinai covenant was different from the covenants with Noah and Abraham. Those covenants were one-sided, but the Sinai covenant involved a promise both from God and from the people. God promised that he would be their God (Exod. 6.7; 29.45-46), and the people promised that they would obey him (Exod. 19.8; 24.3, 7).

God's promise at Sinai is also different from the promises he gave to Noah and Abraham. God made no conditions when he made his promises to Noah and Abraham. He did not say "if you do this, I will do that." But at Sinai, God's promise was conditional. There was a condition Israel had to meet for God to fulfill his promise: "Now if you obey me fully and keep my covenant, then out of all nations you will be my treasured possession" (Exod. 19.5).

Some scholars argue that there is no such fundamental difference between the Sinai covenant and the other covenants. They argue that all the covenants involve both promises from God and obligations for the people to keep. We must distinguish, however, between obligations and conditions. All the covenants contained obligations, in the sense that they included duties that the people should do. But God's promises were unconditional. God did not make these duties a condition that had to be met for him to fulfill his promises. Only the Sinai covenant was conditional, in the sense that God's promises would be fulfilled only if the people fulfilled their duty.

The prophets frequently repeated the basic idea of the Sinai covenant. If the people obey God and his commandments, they will live and prosper. But if they disobey, they will be judged and taken into captivity. When Jerusalem was threatened by Babylon, the prophets made it clear that the people still had a choice: they could repent and obey the Lord. If they did, he would save them. If they did not, he would judge them and let the Babylonians take their land. Jeremiah assured the people that God would bless them if they wholeheartedly turned back to him (Jer. 4.1-2; 7.5-7). Ezekiel appealed specifically to the laws of Moses and said that "people will live if they obey them" (Ezek. 20.11, 13).

The Sinai covenant involved a heavy responsibility. Moses explains this responsibility in the blessings and curses in Leviticus 26 and Deuteronomy 28. If Israel obeys the Lord, he will bless them with peace and prosperity (Lev. 26.1-13; Deut. 28.1-14). God will also give them the blessing he gave to Adam and Eve at creation (Gen. 1.28), the blessing he renewed to Noah and Abraham (Gen. 9.1; 17.2, 6). He says: "I will look on you with favor and make you fruitful and increase your numbers" (Lev. 26.9). But if they disobey him, he will curse them. Their enemies will destroy them and drive them from their land (Lev. 26.14-39; Deut. 28.15-68).

This responsibility is so great that Joshua has to warn the people against it. When Israel entered the promised land and came to Shechem, they renewed the Sinai covenant (Josh. 24.1-28). But Joshua told them what the consequences would be: "You are not able to serve the Lord. He is a holy God; he is a jealous God. He will not forgive your rebellion and your sins. If you forsake the Lord and serve foreign gods, he will turn and bring disaster on you and make an end of you, after he has been good to you" (Josh. 24.19-20).

The prophetic books show us that this was precisely what happened. If Israel had obeyed God, they would have prospered in the land (Isa. 48.18-19). But Israel did not obey. They did not experience the covenant blessings, but suffered the curses (Isa. 24.5-6; Jer. 11.2-13). Eventually, they lost their land and had to go into exile (Jer. 25.9-11; Ezek. 12.11).

But even if God has to punish his people, he will not destroy them completely. He will remember the covenant he made with Abraham. Because of the one-sided covenant with Abraham, God cannot completely reject his people (Lev. 26.40-46).

Israel's Relationship with God

The covenants that God made with Israel show us some important differences between Israel's relationship with God and the religious practices of their pagan neighbors. Pagans typically thought of their gods as powers that could be controlled if they used the right rituals. Their approach to the gods can be characterized as magic. This approach is nonethical and nonrelational. It is not concerned with actions that in themselves are good or evil, but with words and items that in themselves are ethically neutral. These words and items are in turn thought to wield supernatural power, either for good or for evil. Those who engage in such practices do not enter into a relationship with these powers; they are not accountable to these powers or gods for the way they live their lives. When they perform the magic ritual correctly, the desired results follow. If they fail to perform the ritual or perform it incorrectly, there are negative consequences.

The Bible condemns magical practices, and makes no distinction between magic used for good or for bad (Deut. 18.10-11). Israel's relationship to their God is profoundly different from magic. Through the covenants, God has entered into a personal relationship with the people. Because God and Israel are in such a relationship, the people of Israel are personally accountable to God. Their life and actions affect God directly.

The nature of this relationship is that Israel is God's chosen people and he is their God. When God made the covenant at Sinai, he said: "Now if you obey me fully and keep my covenant, then out of all nations you will be my treasured possession. Although the whole earth is mine, you will be for me a kingdom of priests and a holy nation" (Exod. 19.5-6). That they are a kingdom of priests means that they are God's representatives in the world and that they are the world's representatives before God. The other nations do not know God. Only Israel does. God does not reveal himself to the other nations the way he does to Israel. He is present among them and dwells with them. Israel is set apart for God as a holy nation, a nation that belongs to him in a unique way.

Like his choice of Israel's ancestors, Abraham, Isaac, and Jacob, God's choice of Israel is based only on his grace. Israel did not demonstrate any qualities that made God choose them. Moses explains: "The Lord did not set his affection on you and choose you because you were more numerous than other peoples, for you were the fewest of all peoples. But it was because the Lord loved you and kept the oath he swore to your ancestors that he brought you out with a mighty hand and redeemed you from the land of slavery, from the power of Pharaoh king of Egypt" (Deut. 7.7-8). God chose Israel in spite of who they were, not because of who they were. He chose them as his people because of who he was, because he loved Israel, and because he was faithful to his own promise, the promise he had given to Abraham.

Later, when Israel experienced the lowest point in their history, their exile in Babylon, God would renew his election of them. Through the prophet Isaiah, he spoke to the exiles and assured them: "But you, Israel, my servant, Jacob, whom I have chosen, you descendants of Abraham my friend, I took you from the ends of the earth, from its farthest corners I called you. I said, 'You are my servant'; I have chosen you and have not rejected you. So do not fear, for I am with you; do not be dismayed, for I am your God. I will strengthen you and help you; I will uphold you with my righteous right hand" (Isa. 41.8-10). God's election is always based on his grace. He does not choose his people because they are attractive, but he looks to those who are small and weak.

The Bible describes the relationship between God and his people with many metaphors. One of these metaphors is that Israel is the Lord's bride (Jer. 2.2; Ezek. 16.8). This metaphor shows us the deep love that God has for his people and that God is not a distant God. He is near, and he enters into an intimate relationship with his people, a relationship as intimate as that of husband and wife.

Another metaphor is that of Israel as the adopted son of God (Exod. 4.22-23; Hos. 11.1). This metaphor also shows the love God has for his people. It also reminds us that God has expectations of his people, and he will discipline them if they fail to meet his expectations.

Several other metaphors also emphasize that Israel belongs to God as his possession and that he cares for them: Israel as God's vineyard (Isa. 5.5-7; Ezek. 19.10-12), Israel as the servant of the Lord (Isa. 41.8-9; 43.10), and Israel as God's sheep (Isa. 40.11; Ezek. 34.11-31; Ps. 100.3).

It is a great privilege for Israel to be God's chosen people. It means that God promises to protect them from harm and to care for them (Deut. 32.9-14). Israel experienced this protection as a nation, and faithful Israelites experienced God's protection in their lives (Prov. 10.30; 12.21). David experienced time and again that God kept him safe from danger. As a man that was familiar with warfare in the mountains, David knew the value of a rock as a hiding-place. For him, God was a "rock of refuge" (Pss 31.2; 71.3). His testimony was that "the Lord is my rock, my fortress and my deliverer; my God is my rock, in whom I take refuge, my shield and the horn of my salvation, my stronghold" (Ps. 18.2).

Israel's special relationship with God also involves a very big responsibility. They must live a life that is worthy of who they are as God's people. In Leviticus 19.2, God explains the nature of this responsibility: "Be holy because

I, the Lord your God, am holy." When God chose Israel and set them apart as his people, he made them holy (Exod. 19.6; Deut. 14.2). The very meaning of "holy" is that God has set them apart (cf. further ch. 12). Now that God has set them apart, they have a responsibility to live their lives so that they show what God has done. Because God has made Israel a holy people, Israel has a responsibility to be holy.

God gave Israel very specific instructions for how they should be holy. Through Moses, he gave all the laws that we find in the Pentateuch. If they obeyed these laws, Israel would demonstrate that they were a people that belonged to the Lord (cf. Deut. 14.1-2). Then Israel would indeed be a people that was different from the other peoples, a people that was holy to the Lord. When Israel obeyed the Lord in this way, they would fulfill their responsibility as a kingdom of priests. Through the way they lived, they would proclaim the greatness of God. Through their holiness, they would announce the holiness of God. In this way, they would fulfill the mandate that was given to human beings when God created them in his image (cf. ch. 3). They would extend his kingly rule in the world.

But the history of Israel is to a large extent the history of their failure to meet God's expectations. It began when they were camped at Mount Sinai. They rejected God and made golden calves to worship (Exod. 32.1-4). They complained to God and distrusted his provision in the wilderness (Exod. 16.3-9). They did not believe that God would be able to lead them into the promised land (Num. 13.31–14.10). As a consequence, God punished that generation and made them die in the desert (Num. 14.20-35).

The negative consequence of Israel's responsibility as God's people is that he will punish them for their disobedience. Because they are his people, God expects more of Israel than of the other nations. He will therefore also punish them more severely. Through the prophet Amos, he announces: "You only have I chosen of all the families of the earth; therefore I will punish you for all your sins" (Amos 3.2).

This means that Israel cannot take God's protection for granted just because they are his people. But that was exactly what they did. The prophet Jeremiah describes how the people thought they were safe because God's temple was in their midst, even if they did not obey him (Jer. 7.3-6).

Because of Israel's repeated failure to live up to their calling as God's people, God rejected them (Hos. 1.9). The prophets announced to them that God would no longer protect them as his people. As a consequence, the people of the northern kingdom were exiled by the Assyrians and the southern kingdom by the Babylonians. But because of God's promise to Israel's ancestors, this rejection will not be the last word. God will again show his mercy to Israel and once again make them his people (Hos. 2.23; cf. Isa. 41.8-10).

God will bring Israel back from captivity (Isa. 43.1-7). When he does, they will be witnesses of his salvation. Israel's function as witness in the Old Testament does not mean that they make a proclamation to the nations. Their function as witness is directed towards themselves. They have put their trust in other gods and in alliances with secular powers (Isa. 30.2; 31.1). But now they will experience God's acts of deliverance, and they will be God's witnesses: God, and no one else, has the power to save (Isa. 43.10, 12; 44.8). He is the one who is worthy of their trust. When they see God's mighty acts of salvation, God calls them to respond by trusting and believing in him (Isa. 43.10; cf. 7.9; Exod. 14.31).

The prophets compare God's relationship with Israel to a marriage, and they describe Israel's sin as adultery (Jer. 5.7; Hos. 4.12). The people have been unfaithful to the Lord, and the result is divorce (Isa. 50.1; Hos. 2.2). But in his great mercy, God will take Israel back (cf. Hos. 3.1).

In allegorical form, Ezekiel 16 tells the story of Israel's election as the story of an unwanted child that was left for dead (vv. 3-5). God found this child, cared for her (vv. 6-14) and made her his own (v. 8). But as she grew up, Israel was unfaithful to the Lord (vv. 15-34). Therefore, God punished her and divorced her (vv. 45-58). But in the end, God will once again care for Israel (vv. 59-63).

The prophetic writings explain that God's judgment is necessary, so that God can prepare for himself a people that are truly committed to him. Through this judgment, a remnant of Israel will emerge, a group of people that are faithful to God. The prophet Isaiah announces: "In that day the remnant of Israel, the survivors of the house of Jacob, will no longer rely on him who struck them down but will truly rely on the Lord, the Holy One of Israel. A remnant will return, a remnant of Jacob will return to the Mighty God. Though your people be like the sand by the sea, Israel, only a remnant will return. Destruction has been decreed, overwhelming and righteous. The Lord, the Lord Almighty, will carry out the destruction decreed upon the whole land" (Isa. 10.20-23). With these words, the prophet condemns those who put their trust in secular alliances in order to keep Israel safe. The phrase "him who struck them down" (v. 20) probably refers to the dominating world power at the time, the Assyrian empire. When Judah (the southern kingdom) was threatened by Israel (the northern kingdom) and Syria, they believed they could be kept safe if they struck a deal with the Assyrians. But Assyria turned against them (2 Chron. 28.19-21). Isaiah's message is that God's salvation will not come to those who put their trust in someone other than God, but only to those who "truly rely on the Lord" (v. 20). They are the "remnant of Israel," the "remnant of Jacob [that] will return to the Mighty God" (v. 21). This is the remnant that will be saved in the end.

When the prophet Zephaniah holds out hope for salvation, this salvation is also specifically for the remnant, for the "humble of the land, [those] who do what he commands" (Zeph. 2.3). When God will judge Israel, he promises: "I will leave within you the meek and humble. The remnant of Israel will trust in the name of the Lord" (Zeph. 3.12).

Israel's relationship to the land is in many ways a mirror of their relationship to God. The land belongs to God (Lev. 25.23), and he gives it as a gift to Israel (Deut. 1.20-21). God first gave his promise regarding the land to Abram, when Abram was a homeless wanderer in the land of Canaan (Gen. 12.7). Later, when Israel was in captivity in Egypt, God repeated the promise of land. Speaking to Moses from the burning bush, God promised to deliver Israel from slavery and "bring them up out of that land into a good and spacious land, a land flowing with milk and honey" (Exod. 3.8). This land will evidently be very fertile, and makes us think of the garden of Eden.

Israel is God's son (Exod. 4.22-23; Deut. 8.5), and the land is their inheritance (Deut. 4.38; Ps. 135.12). Each tribe and each family has been allotted a part of the land by God (Num. 26.53; 36.2). This part of the land belongs to them by virtue of their relationship with God. It must therefore never be taken away from them permanently (Lev. 25.23-28; Num. 36.6-8). For this reason, the Lord provides for a year of Jubilee. In the year of Jubilee, all land will be given back to their original owners (Lev. 25.13).

Through the Sinai covenant, the gift of the land is tied to Israel's obedience. If Israel obeys God's commands, they will enjoy fertility and peace in the land. God will dwell among them, he will be their God, and they will be his people (Lev. 26.3-13). However, if Israel does not obey, not only the land's fertility but also the land itself will be taken away from them (Lev. 26.14-39).

Since God's presence and Israel's relationship to him were connected to the land, it was a disaster for the people to be sent into exile. It meant not only that they lost their home and were displaced, but that they had lost their access to the Lord (cf. Ps. 137.4). When God's word of salvation comes to the exiles, it is therefore in the form of a promise of restoration to their land (Isa. 27.12-13; Jer. 24.5-7; Amos 9.14-15). In the restoration, the people will once again enjoy the fertility of the land. It will "become like the garden of Eden" (Ezek. 36.35).

The Presence of God

Israel's land was the place of God's dwelling (Exod. 15.17). Because of their special relationship with God, Israel enjoyed his presence in a special way. Even though God is present everywhere (Jer. 23.24; cf. Ps. 139.7-12), all people do not enjoy his gracious presence. But Israel experienced God's presence in this way; he was present to protect and bless them. Aaron, the high priest, was to bless the Israelites with these words: "The Lord bless you and keep you; the Lord make his face shine on you and be gracious to you; the Lord turn his face toward you and give you peace" (Num. 6.24-26). When God is graciously present with his people, he makes them prosperous and keeps them safe. God looks favorably on them (he turns his face toward them and his face shines). He gives them grace (favor) and peace (harmony and completeness in all areas of life).

God was present in this special way with Adam and Eve in the garden of Eden. He "was walking in the garden" (Gen. 3.8). The form of the Hebrew word that is used here is the same that we later find in connection with God's presence in the tabernacle (Lev. 26.12). But God banished Adam and Eve from the garden and from God's presence because of their sin (Gen. 3.23).

When God revealed himself to Israel's ancestors, he let them once again enjoy his gracious presence. After God had spoken to him, Abram "went on toward the hills east of Bethel" ("Bethel" means "house of God") and built an altar to the Lord (Gen. 12.8). In a dream, Jacob saw a stairway reaching to heaven (Gen. 28.12). The Lord spoke to him from above the stairway and promised that he would be with him (Gen. 28.15). Afterwards, Jacob called the place "Bethel" (Gen. 28.19). When they had experienced the presence of God, Israel's ancestors responded by building altars to him (Gen. 12.7; 26.25; 35.7).

At Sinai, God came near to Moses in a cloud (Exod. 24.15-18). The cloud, which had led Israel on their way through the wilderness (Exod. 13.21-22; Deut. 1.33 etc.), represents God's heavenly glory (cf. Exod. 16.10; Ezek. 1.4). Later, the pillar of cloud came down to the tent of meeting (Exod. 33.9) and the tabernacle, and "the glory of the Lord filled the tabernacle" (Exod. 40.34; cf. Lev. 9.23).

More specifically, God promised to meet Israel "above the cover between the two cherubim that are over the ark of the covenant law" (Exod. 25.22). The ark of the covenant represented the presence of God. The Old Testament therefore portrays this ark as God's footstool (1 Chron. 28.2; Lam. 2.1) since he is enthroned above it (1 Sam. 4.4; 2 Sam. 6.2). We can of course not take these descriptions literally. King Solomon, for example, knew that "the heavens, even the highest heaven, cannot contain you. How much less this temple I have built!" (1 Kgs 8.27). When the Bible says that God is "enthroned between the cherubim" (1 Sam. 4.4), the point is that his presence is with Israel in a special way.

However, the placement of the ark of the covenant also shows that there is a distance between God and the people. The ark was kept in the Most Holy Place, where no one could enter. Only the high priest could approach the ark of the covenant once a year, when he had made the necessary sacrifices (Exod. 30.10; Lev. 16.2-34). If anyone else came close to the ark, they were met with God's judgment (1 Sam. 6.19; 2 Sam. 6.6-7).

The ark of the covenant was also the place where the Ten Commandments were kept (Exod. 25.16; 40.20; Deut. 10.2, 5). God's presence was therefore closely tied to the ethical requirements of the covenant. The presence of the ark of the covenant did not guarantee God's gracious presence (cf. 1 Sam. 4.3-11; Jer. 7.4). His presence depended on Israel's faithfulness to him and to his commandments (Lev. 26.3-13; Deut. 28.1-14). God's relationship with Israel is not of a magical, but of an ethical nature. If the people did not repent and genuinely turn to God, the sacrifices they presented to God could not help them. Unrepentant sinners that came with offerings to God would only experience judgment (Jer. 14.12; Amos 5.21-22).

Even though God had instituted sacrifices (cf. ch. 6), what he ultimately looked for was a repentant heart. David explains: "My sacrifice, O God, is a broken spirit; a broken and contrite heart you, God, will not despise" (Ps. 51.17).

Israel's sin creates a distance between them and God. When Moses was on Mount Sinai, they worshiped the golden calf and revealed that they were a stiff-necked people. God would therefore not be among them. If he had gone with them, he might have destroyed them (Exod. 33.3, 5).

Instead, God only allowed Moses into his presence (Exod. 33.9). Moses was closer to God than anyone else. "The Lord would speak to Moses face to face, as one speaks to a friend" (Exod. 33.11). This does not mean that Moses literally was able to see God's face. It is a metaphorical expression, and it explains that Moses enjoyed a unique level of intimacy with God. But not even Moses could enjoy full closeness to God. When Moses asked to see God's glory, God did not let him see it directly. When God's glory passed by, God covered Moses with his hand. He did not let Moses see until after he had passed by. Then, Moses saw God's back because God's "face must not be seen" (Exod. 33.23).

To be close to God and enjoy his favor is the best thing a person can ever experience. David says: "One thing I ask from the Lord, this only do I seek: that I may dwell in the house of the Lord all the days of my life, to gaze on the beauty of the Lord and to seek him in his temple" (Ps. 27.4).

Much like Moses, certain people experienced God's presence in a unique way. God was "with them." When God is with someone, the point is not simply that he is present. It means that he is there to bless (Gen. 26.3), help (Josh. 1.5), protect (Isa. 43.1-2), and save (Jer. 15.20). There is therefore no reason to fear (Deut. 31.23). God gave this special privilege only to select individuals, such as Abraham, Isaac, Jacob, Joseph, Moses, Joshua, Samuel, and David.

In the Old Testament, God's special presence was therefore not available to all. It was tied to special individuals, such as Moses and David, and to a special place, the tabernacle and the temple. Ordinary Israelites therefore depended on their leaders and upon the sanctuary for God's presence. They did not have direct access to him. For this reason, they had to make pilgrimage to the sanctuary of the Lord three times a year: at Passover, at the Festival of Weeks, and at the Festival of Booths (Exod. 23.17; 34.23; Deut. 16.16).

The Covenant with David

God's presence with his people is a central element of the covenant with David. The background for this covenant was that David wanted to build a house for the Lord. In response, God sent the prophet Nathan with the following message:

> Go and tell my servant David, "This is what the Lord says: Are you the one to build me a house to dwell in? I have not dwelt in a house from the day I brought the Israelites up out of Egypt to this day. I have been moving from place to place with a tent as my dwelling. Wherever I have moved with all the Israelites, did I ever say to any of their rulers whom I commanded to shepherd my people Israel, 'Why have you not built me a house of cedar?'"

God Makes It Personal

> Now then, tell my servant David, "This is what the Lord Almighty says: I took you from the pasture, from tending the flock, and appointed you ruler over my people Israel. I have been with you wherever you have gone, and I have cut off all your enemies from before you. Now I will make your name great, like the names of the greatest men on earth. And I will provide a place for my people Israel and will plant them so that they can have a home of their own and no longer be disturbed. Wicked people will not oppress them anymore, as they did at the beginning and have done ever since the time I appointed leaders over my people Israel. I will also give you rest from all your enemies." "The Lord declares to you that the Lord himself will establish a house for you: When your days are over and you rest with your ancestors, I will raise up your offspring to succeed you, who will come from your own body, and I will establish his kingdom. He is the one who will build a house for my Name, and I will establish the throne of his kingdom forever. I will be his father, and he will be my son. When he does wrong, I will punish him with a rod wielded by human beings, with floggings inflicted by human hands. But my love will never be taken away from him, as I took it away from Saul, whom I removed from before you. Your house and your kingdom will endure forever before me; your throne will be established forever." (2 Sam. 7.5-16)

Instead of having David build a house for him, God promised to build a house for David (2 Sam. 7.11b). However, this was not a physical house, but a family. David's house was a line of successors to his throne. In 2 Samuel 7, God's promise is not called a "covenant," but the same promise is mentioned in Psalm 89 and 2 Samuel 23, where the word "covenant" is used (Ps. 89.28; 2 Sam. 23.5).

God's covenant with David continues the covenant with Abraham. Like he had promised to Abraham, so does God promise David that he will give him offspring (2 Sam. 7.12; cf. Gen. 15.4-5), who will be a king (2 Sam. 7.12-13; cf. Gen. 17.6) forever (2 Sam. 7.13, 16; cf. Gen. 17.7). David's son will enjoy a close relationship with God. God "will be his father, and he will be [God's] son" (2 Sam. 7.14).

Table 5.1 The promise to Abraham renewed in the promise to David

Abraham	David
This man will not be your heir, but a son coming from your own body will be your heir (Gen. 15.4).	I will raise up your offspring to succeed you (2 Sam. 7.12b).
Kings will come from you (Gen. 17.6).	I will establish the throne of his kingdom forever (2 Sam. 7.13b).

Like God's promise to Noah and Abraham, the promise to David is unconditional. God makes a promise, and he does not require any promise from David in return. But fulfillment is not automatic. When David's son does wrong, God will punish him (2 Sam. 7.14).

As part of the covenant, God said that David's son would build a house for his name (2 Sam. 7.13). This promise appeared to be fulfilled through Solomon. He built a house for God's name (1 Kgs 6.1-38; 2 Chron. 3.1-17), and God came in the cloud and filled this temple with his presence and his glory (1 Kgs 8.10; 2 Chron. 7.1-3).

In the early period of Israel's history, the ark of the covenant had been in the tabernacle, which was moved from place to place. David moved the ark to Jerusalem (2 Sam. 6.12-17; 1 Chron. 15.25–16.1), and when the ark was placed in the temple, God's presence became fixed to this city. Jerusalem now represented the place that God had chosen to put his name (1 Kgs 11.36; cf. Deut. 12.5, 11).

The mountain where the temple was standing is called Mount Zion, a name that is often used for the city of Jerusalem as well. The name Zion draws attention to the promise of God's presence and refers to Jerusalem as God's chosen dwelling place (Pss 76.2; 132.13-14).

But Israel's sin continued to disrupt their relationship with God. The fact that God had chosen Zion could not prevent God's judgment from befalling Jerusalem. Jeremiah proclaimed: "Zion will be plowed like a field, Jerusalem will become a heap of rubble, the temple hill a mound overgrown with thickets" (Jer. 26.18). With their idolatry, Israel had made the sanctuary and the land unclean (Jer. 2.7; 7.30; Ezek. 5.11; 36.17-18). In a vision, Ezekiel witnessed that God withdrew his presence (Ezek. 10.4, 18-19).

Through the exile in Babylon, God taught the people that he was not bound to Jerusalem and the temple. After the people had experienced God's judgment, God would come to them and be present with them even in a foreign land (Ezek. 11.16). Once again, God shows that salvation and judgment go together. God brings salvation through judgment.

The New Covenant

Israel experienced that God's promise to David did not come to realization through Solomon and the kings that followed him. Solomon turned away from the Lord (1 Kgs 11.4-13), and Israel suffered under a series of ungodly kings after him. Because of their disobedience, Israel also failed to enjoy the blessings under the Sinai covenant. Instead, they experienced the covenant curses. Israel's prophets therefore looked towards a new covenant that God would establish with the people.

The prophet Jeremiah understood what the problem was: human beings are evil on the inside. "The heart is deceitful above all things and beyond cure" (Jer. 17.9). Even if Israel repents, their repentance is not genuine (Jer. 3.10). The sign of circumcision should symbolize a spiritual circumcision (Deut. 10.16; Jer. 4.4). Such spiritual circumcision meant to be open to God's influence in one's life (cf. Jer. 6.10 ESV). But Israel remained uncircumcised in heart (Jer. 9.26). They were stiff-necked and stubbornly resisted the word of God (2 Kgs 17.14; Neh. 9.16; Jer. 7.26).

Since the human heart cannot be cured, it is necessary that God gives the people of Israel a new heart. Through the new covenant, he would do just that. Jeremiah explains how this covenant will be different from the old covenant of Sinai: "'The days are coming,' declares the Lord, 'when I will make a new covenant with the house of Israel and with the house of Judah. It will not be like the covenant I made with their ancestors when I took them by the hand to lead them out of Egypt, because they broke my covenant, though I was a husband to them,' declares the Lord. 'This is the covenant I will make with the house of Israel after that time,' declares the Lord. 'I will put my law in their minds and write it on their hearts. I will be their God, and they will be my people. No longer will they teach their neighbors, or say to one another, "Know the Lord," because they will all know me, from the least of them to the greatest,' declares the Lord. 'For I will forgive their wickedness and will remember their sins no more'" (Jer. 31.31-34).

Like the covenants with Noah, Abraham, and David, this covenant is unconditional. It contains a one-sided promise, regarding what God will do. He will restore his relationship with the people. Once again, he will be their God and they will be his people (v. 33). This covenant will be better than the old one because it will be internal. God will not impose his will on them with a law that is written on tablets of stone and comes to them from outside. Instead, they will know God's will in their hearts. He will put his law in their minds and write it on their hearts (v. 33). In other words, God "will give them a heart to know" him (Jer. 24.7). This will be possible when God takes away all their sins and forgives them (Jer. 31.34).

Ezekiel also speaks of this covenant, which he calls "a covenant of peace" (Ezek. 34.25; 37.26; cf. Isa. 54.10; 61.8). This covenant will represent the fulfillment of the covenant with David. With a reference to the promise to David (2 Sam. 7.12-16), God says that "my servant David will be king over them" (Ezek. 37.24; cf. Isa. 55.3). At that time, God's promises to Abraham, Isaac, and Jacob will also be fulfilled. The people will be a blessing (Ezek. 37.26; cf. Gen. 12.2). They "will live in the land I gave to my servant Jacob" (Ezek. 37.25; cf. Gen. 28.14; 35.12), and their numbers will be increased (Ezek. 37.26; cf. Gen. 28.14; 35.11). God's dwelling place will also be with them, when he will be their God, and they will be his people (Ezek. 37.27). As a result, the nations will take notice and realize what the Lord does (Ezek. 37.28). In other words, God's people will then fulfill the mandate God gave to Adam and Eve when he created them (Gen. 1.28). This covenant will come into place when God makes atonement for all of Israel's sins (cf. Ezek. 16.60-63).

Table 5.2 The mandate from creation renewed

Adam and Eve	Noah	Abraham	Israel	The new covenant	The Church
God blessed them and said to them, "Be fruitful and increase in number; fill the earth and subdue it. Rule over the fish in the sea and the birds in the sky and over every living creature that moves on the ground (Gen. 1.28).	Then God blessed Noah and his sons, saying to them, "Be fruitful and increase in number and fill the earth" (Gen. 9.1).	Then I will make my covenant between me and you and will greatly increase your numbers (Gen. 17.2).	I will look on you with favor and make you fruitful and increase your numbers, and I will keep my covenant with you (Lev. 26.9).	I will make a covenant of peace with them; it will be an everlasting covenant. I will establish them and increase their numbers, and I will put my sanctuary among them forever (Ezek. 37.26).	The gospel is bearing fruit and growing throughout the whole world—just as it has been doing among you since the day you heard it and truly understood God's grace (Col. 1.6).

On that day, God's creation will be restored to its former glory. "They will say, 'This land that was laid waste has become like the garden of Eden'" (Ezek. 36.35). Once more, the people will experience God's presence. In a vision with great detail, Ezekiel sees a new temple (Ezek. 40.1–43.11). He also sees God's glory enter it (Ezek. 43.4).

With this new temple follows a new time of blessing and abundance for the land of Israel. Like the river gave water to the garden of Eden (Gen. 2.10), so will a river make the land fertile. This miraculous and life-giving river flows from the temple (Ezek. 47.1) and causes trees to bear fruit every month (Ezek. 47.12).

The other Old Testament prophets also looked forward to this day, when God's salvation would be revealed. When God restores Israel to their land, the land will be so fertile that it overflows with grain and wine (Joel 2.23-26). God "will pour out [his] Spirit on all people" (Joel 2.28). On that day, the whole world will recognize God's glorious presence (Hab. 2.14). Then, they will know that he dwells in Zion (Joel 3.17), and they will come to the mountain of the Lord, so that he may teach them his ways (Isa. 2.1-4; Mic. 4.1-3). Then, "all the kings of the earth shall praise you, O Lord" (Ps. 138.4 NRSV).

Summary

The Old Testament paints a picture of God as a God who continues to reach out to human beings in order to fulfill his purpose for his creation. His initiatives take the form of four major covenants, with Noah, with Abraham, with Israel, and with David. Through these covenants, he promises to renew the blessings that he gave to human beings when they were created.

He makes his covenant with Abraham and chooses a people that will belong to him. He confirms his choice by delivering this people from slavery in Egypt. God's covenant of Sinai gives detailed regulations for the relationship between God and his chosen people. This covenant also ensures that God's gracious presence will be in Israel's midst, so that he will look favorably upon them and bless them.

However, the people of Israel are unable to keep the Sinai covenant. As a consequence, God rejects them and withdraws his presence from them. Nevertheless, God remembers his covenant with Abraham, and renews these promises in his covenant with David. In this covenant, God gives promises regarding David's offspring, who will have an eternal kingdom.

As Solomon and the other descendants of David fail to live up to the ideals of this covenant, God's promises remain unfulfilled. The Old Testament prophets therefore look forward to a future covenant that will change the people from the inside, make possible a genuine relationship between them and God, and bring creation to its goal.

The relationship between God and human beings continues to be broken, and the question keeps coming back: How can this relationship be restored?

Further Reading

Brueggemann, Walter. *The Land: Place as Gift, Promise, and Challenge in Biblical Faith.* 2d ed. Overtures to Biblical Theology. Minneapolis: Augsburg Fortress, 2002.

Hahn, Scott W. *Kinship by Covenant: A Canonical Approach to the Fulfillment of God's Saving Promises.* The Anchor Yale Bible Reference Library. New Haven: Yale University Press, 2009.

Nicholson, Ernest W. *God and His People: Covenant and Theology in the Old Testament.* Oxford: Clarendon, 1986.

Terrien, Samuel. *The Elusive Presence: Toward a New Biblical Theology.* Religious Perspectives 26. San Francisco: Harper & Row, 1978.

Review Questions

Describe the similarities and differences between the major covenants in the Old Testament.

As a result of their special relationship with God, the people of Israel have certain responsibilities and privileges. Describe them.

Explain how the new covenant will be a better covenant.

6

Mending the Relationship with God

Restitution for Sin in the Old Testament

Chapter Outline

Sin and Death	68
The Burnt Offering	68
The Sin Offering	69
The Day of Atonement	70
Guilt Offering	70
Passover	71
The Real Value of Animal Sacrifices	71
The Suffering Servant	72
Summary	72

God constantly reached out to the people of Israel because he wanted to enter into a relationship with them, but the people constantly turned their backs on him. The Bible makes it clear that human beings have violated God's norms and broken their relationship with him. Human beings, not God, are the offending party.

In God's grace, he allows them to come back to him. He gives them the opportunity to repent for their wrongdoing and to make amends.

Sin and Death

The consequence of sin is death. When human beings first sinned, death entered the world (Gen. 2.17; Rom. 5.12). The prophet Ezekiel explains that sin and death belong together also on the individual level. Every one that sins must die (Ezek. 18.20). The institution of sacrifices lets an animal take the place of a human being. The animal dies instead of the sinner. In the laws of Moses, God has given detailed instructions for such sacrifices.

The Burnt Offering

The most important offering in the Old Testament was the burnt offering. It is the first sacrifice that is mentioned in the book of Leviticus, it required the most valuable animals, and it was the offering that always had to be burning on the altar (Lev. 6.12-13).

God promised that the animal "will be accepted on your behalf to make atonement for you" (Lev. 1.4). The Hebrew word that is translated "to make atonement" is *kipper*, but scholars have not been able to determine the original meaning of this term. It may have been either "cover over" or "wipe away." In the Bible, however, several other words are used as synonyms for "to make atonement" (*kipper*). In Isaiah 27.9, the prophet declares: "By this, then, will Jacob's guilt be atoned for, and this will be the full fruit of the removal of his sin." Jeremiah prays: "Provide no atonement for their iniquity, Nor blot out their sin from Your sight" (Jer. 18.23 NKJV). These synonyms show us that the biblical meaning of "to make atonement" is to remove or to purge. When God promises that he will accept the animal as atonement, the point is that the people's sins will be blotted out.

The people are liable to death because of their sin. The point of the sacrifice is that the animal dies in the people's place, and that God accepts the death of the animal in the place of the sinner. Those who bring the offering must lay their "hand on the head of the burnt offering" (Lev. 1.4). The meaning of this ritual is to transfer the sins to the animal (Lev. 16.21).

The purpose of the offering is that "you may be acceptable to the Lord" (Lev. 1.3). When the offering is burned on the altar, it produces "an aroma pleasing to the Lord" (Lev. 1.9).

The story of Noah shows us the effect of this aroma. After the flood, Noah sacrificed a burnt offering of some of the animals that had survived (Gen. 8.20). "The Lord smelled the pleasing aroma and said in his heart:

'Never again will I curse the ground because of human beings, even though every inclination of the human heart is evil from childhood. And never again will I destroy all living creatures, as I have done'" (Gen. 8.21). Human beings would turn out to be just as evil as they had been before the flood. But because of the pleasing aroma of the sacrifice, God decided that he would never again curse the ground because of human beings.

This example shows that the burnt offering may affect God's attitude towards human beings. It may appease him and cause his wrath to go away (see also 1 Sam. 13.12; 2 Sam. 24.21). In English, this idea is called propitiation. (Scholars often discuss whether the biblical sacrifices cause propitiation or only expiation. The difference is that expiation does something to sin, but propitiation does something to God. Expiation covers or takes away the sin, but does not say anything about God changing his attitude towards human beings.)

The Bible does not explain why the burnt offering must be burning at all times (Lev. 6.12-13), so we cannot be certain about the significance of this commandment. But since the burnt offering atones for sin (Lev. 1.4 etc.), it is natural to think that this sacrifice served as a reminder to Israel that they were in constant need of atonement.

The Sin Offering

Another important sacrifice was the sin offering. But several scholars think that the name "sin offering" is not the best way to refer to this ritual. It is clear that this offering is directly connected with individual sins (Lev. 4.2), but so are several of the other sacrifices as well. The name "sin offering" does not tell us what makes this offering distinct from the other sacrifices that also deal with sin. The Hebrew term that is used comes from the root *hata*, and this root can also be used with the meaning "to purify" (Lev. 8.15; Ps. 51.7). Some scholars therefore argue that this offering should rather be called "purification offering."

One of the consequences of Israel's sin was that the land and the house of the Lord became unclean (see above). One possible result was that God could remove the uncleanness from Israel through an act of judgment. Another possibility was that God would remove his presence from the temple and from Israel. The purpose of the sin offering (or purification offering) was to remove such uncleanness, so that Israel could be spared of these terrible acts of judgment.

When a member of the community sinned and presented a sin offering (or purification offering), the priest took "some of the blood with his finger and put it on the horns of the altar of burnt offering" (Lev. 4.25, 30). This act probably symbolized cleansing. If the high priest, a leader, or the whole people sinned, the uncleanness was more serious. In those cases, the priest had to take the blood inside the tabernacle (as opposed to the altar of burnt offering, which was outside the tabernacle). The priest then had to sprinkle the blood in front of the veil that covered the Most Holy Place (Lev. 4.6, 17). Then he had to put some of the blood on the incense altar, which was inside the tabernacle (Lev. 4.7, 18).

Like the burnt offering, the sin offering brought atonement for sin. Because of that, God could forgive the people (Lev. 4.20).

The Day of Atonement

The sins of the people as a whole brought uncleanness even to the Most Holy Place. It was therefore necessary to cleanse the Most Holy Place with a special sacrifice. The high priest presented this sacrifice once a year, on the Day of Atonement. On that day, the high priest presented one bull as a sin offering for himself and one goat as a sin offering for the people (Lev. 16.5, 6, 9). He took the blood of the bull and the blood of the goat into the Most Holy Place and sprinkled it on the atonement cover (Lev. 16.14-15). (In many translations, this lid on the ark of the covenant is called the mercy seat.) It was necessary to cleanse the sanctuary in this way, so that the people of Israel could continue to enjoy God's presence among them.

There were two goats that served as a sin offering for the people, but only one of them was slaughtered. The high priest took the other one and sent it out into the wilderness. Before he sent it out, he laid "both hands on the head of the live goat and [confessed] over it all the wickedness and rebellion of the Israelites—all their sins" (Lev. 16.21-22). The sins were transferred to the goat, and taken away to the wilderness, an unclean place.

Guilt Offering

In addition to sin offerings, God gave Israel commandments regarding guilt offerings. These offerings provided compensation for the harm that the sinner had done. For example, if someone had eaten holy food without knowing it, they had to pay for what they had eaten (Lev. 22.14). In addition to what they had taken, they had to add one-fifth of the value (Lev. 5.16). People who sinned against their neighbors also had to pay back what they had gained by stealing or cheating. They should add one-fifth of the value and present a guilt offering to the Lord (Lev. 6.1-7). The guilt offering would bring atonement and forgiveness (Lev. 5.16, 18; 6.7).

Passover

The Passover lamb reminded the Israelites of their liberation from Egypt. When they were in Egypt, they took "some of the blood and put it on the sides and tops of the doorframes of the houses where they [ate] the lambs" (Exod. 12.7). The same night, God passed through Egypt to "strike down every firstborn of both people and animals, and [to] bring judgment on all the gods of Egypt" (Exod. 12.12). But when he saw the blood on the doorframes, he passed over the Israelites. After he had experienced this awesome demonstration of God's power and judgment, Pharaoh let the Israelites leave Egypt. In the years that have followed, Israelites have sacrificed and eaten the Passover lamb to remind them of what God had done for them (Exod. 12.24-28; see also Deut. 16.1-8).

In the book of Exodus, this sacrifice is not specifically associated with sin. But in his vision of the new Jerusalem, Ezekiel refers to the Passover as a sin offering (Ezek. 45.18-20). The priest must take the blood and "put it on the doorposts of the temple, on the four corners of the upper ledge of the altar and on the gateposts of the inner court" (Ezek. 45.19). In this way, he will cleanse the sanctuary. Since the blood of the Passover lamb protected Israel from God's judgment, it is natural that Ezekiel can describe it as a sin offering or purification offering. Thanks to this offering, Israel could survive God's visitation.

The Real Value of Animal Sacrifices

From the Old Testament we understand that sacrifices do not please God if the offerer's heart is not right with God (Isa. 1.11; Jer. 6.20; Amos 5.22). In the New Testament, we learn that animal sacrifices could never truly take the place of a human being (Heb. 10.1, 4, 11). The sacrifices really did nothing more than serve as a reminder of sin and demonstrate that every transgression deserves punishment (Heb. 10.3). The animal sacrifices only pointed forward to the true sacrifice of Jesus Christ (Heb. 9.9, 11; 10.1).

The Suffering Servant

In addition to the animal sacrifices, the Old Testament also describes a human being that dies in the place of sinners: Isaiah's Suffering Servant (ch. 7). The prophet explains that "he was pierced for our transgressions, he was crushed for our iniquities; the punishment that brought us peace was on him, and by his wounds we are healed" (Isa. 53.5). This reminds us of the goat that was sent away on the Day of Atonement. This goat would "carry on itself all their sins to a remote place" (Lev. 16.22).

Isaiah also says that the Servant "was led like a lamb to the slaughter" (Isa. 53.7) as if to be a sacrifice. He explains that "the Lord makes his life a guilt offering" (Isa. 53.10 NIV). This Servant will bring compensation for Israel's sins, so that they can be forgiven.

Summary

Sacrifices such as the burnt offering, sin offering, guilt offering, Day of Atonement, and Passover served to compensate for the damage that was caused by Israel's sin. The animals died instead of the sinner. In this way, they atoned for sin, which means that they removed sin and therefore also took away God's wrath. God forgave the people's sin.

The prophet Isaiah describes a human being who will serve as a sacrifice that takes the place of sinners: the Servant of the Lord. When he dies for the people's sin, the servant restores the people's relationship to God. However, as we will see in the next chapter, he is not the only Old Testament character that brings restoration and salvation.

Further Reading

Milgrom, Jacob. *Leviticus 1–16: A New Translation with Introduction and Commentary*. Anchor Bible 3. New York: Doubleday, 1991.

Wenham, Gordon J. *The Book of Leviticus*. New International Commentary on the Old Testament. Grand Rapids: Eerdmans, 1979.

Review Questions

Explain the meaning of the term "atonement."

What are the similarities and the differences between the burnt offering, the sin offering, the Day of Atonement, the guilt offering, and Passover?

What do the Old Testament sacrifices teach us about God?

7
A New Ruler and a New Order
The Old Testament Messianic Hope

Chapter Outline

Messiah	74
The Promise to David	75
Messianic Psalms	76
The Messiah in the Prophets	77
Other Prophecies	83
The Suffering Servant	84
The Righteous Sufferer	85
The Prophet Like Moses	86
The Son of Man	86
Summary	87

As Israel failed to live up to their calling from God, the prophets looked toward a future leader who would lead the people back to God. The new leader would enjoy a unique relationship with God, and he would govern the people according to God's will. Under his rule, the people would once again enjoy the blessings of God.

Messiah

"Messiah" means the anointed one. In the Old Testament, kings (1 Sam. 10.1; 16.13 etc.), priests (Exod. 28.41; 1 Chron. 29.22), and prophets (1 Kgs 19.16; 1 Chron. 16.22) were anointed. The anointing symbolized that these people were made holy and set apart for God (Exod. 30.25-29). They were chosen by him (1 Sam. 9.16), and equipped with the Holy Spirit for the task that God had given them (Isa. 61.1).

It may come as a surprise to most Christians, but the Old Testament does not use the word "Messiah" for a future ruler, except in Daniel 9.25-26. In the time after the Old Testament, however, many Jews were looking forward to a righteous king that God would send to fulfill the promises of Israel's restoration. During this period, "Messiah" became the title that was used for this future ruler. The New Testament Gospels give us a glimpse into some of the expectations people had of this Messiah (Mk 12.35; Lk. 3.15; Jn 4.25; 7.41-42).

The Promise to David

The starting point for understanding the messianic hopes is God's promise to David (2 Sam. 7.11b-16; see also 2 Sam. 23.1-7; 1 Chron. 17.1-15). In answer to David's desire to build a house for the Lord, God made this promise:

> The Lord declares to you that the Lord himself will establish a house for you: When your days are over and you rest with your ancestors, I will raise up your offspring to succeed you, who will come from your own body, and I will establish his kingdom. He is the one who will build a house for my Name, and I will establish the throne of his kingdom forever. I will be his father, and he will be my son. When he does wrong, I will punish him with a rod wielded by human beings, with floggings inflicted by human hands. But my love will never be taken away from him, as I took it away from Saul, whom I removed from before you. Your house and your kingdom will endure forever before me; your throne will be established forever.

The house that God will build (v. 11b) does not refer to a physical house, but to a family. More specifically, it refers to a line of successors to David's throne, a dynasty. This promise therefore refers to David's descendants (not only one), and this explains that the promise is fulfilled in different stages. David's son, Solomon, built a temple for the Lord (v. 13). All the descendants of David were punished by God when they did wrong (v. 14). But they all failed to become kings forever and to receive an eternal kingdom (vv. 13, 16). When Jesus was born, he was promised "the throne of his father David" (Lk. 1.32). He would be the eternal king (Lk. 1.33).

The promised king will enjoy a very special status. God "will be his father, and he will be [God's] son" (v. 14). The whole people of Israel could also be called the son of God (Exod. 4.22-23; Hos. 11.1), and so could the angels (Job 1.6; Dan. 3.25). In itself, this title does therefore not say that the Messiah will be of divine nature. The function of the term is to assure that the king rules by divine decree. It also describes a relationship of exceptional intimacy, as 2 Samuel 7.14-15 shows. The title may therefore be used for the anointed king of Israel (Pss 2.7; 89.26-27). However, Jesus is the son of God in a more profound sense, as other texts will reveal.

Messianic Psalms

There are many Psalms that make reference to the promise that God made to David. Psalm 2 describes the universal kingship of the Davidic king (vv. 8-9) and repeats the promise that he will be God's son (v. 7). This king will put an end to the rulers that rise against God (vv. 8-12).

Jesus represents the ultimate fulfillment of the Lord's decree from Psalm 2.7: "You are my son; today I have become your father." The words from Psalm 2.7 are quoted at two important points in the Gospels. Both at Jesus' baptism (Mk 1.11) and at his transfiguration on the mountain (Mk 9.7), God addresses him with words from Psalm 2.7. The book of Revelation also describes Jesus' universal rule with allusions to Psalm 2.9 (Rev. 12.5; 19.15).

However, while this Psalm shows us that the king stands in a close relationship with God, it does not teach that he was of divine nature. The word "today" in v. 7 tells us that there was a time when the king became God's son. That time was probably the time when he became king. If he became God's son at that time, his sonship cannot mean that he was of divine nature. Rather, it means that God had given him a task that he would exercise on God's behalf. God was the real king of Israel, so the man who ruled as king was standing in God's place. In that sense, he was God's "son."

God's promise to David forms the basis for several other Psalms as well, Psalms that give ideal descriptions of the king and that find their ultimate fulfillment in Jesus Christ (Pss 18.50; 45; 72; 89.3-4, 19-37; 132). The Psalm that gives the most exalted picture of the Messiah is Psalm 110. God here calls on the Messiah to "sit at my right hand until I make your enemies a footstool for your feet" (Ps. 110.1). Once again, we see that the king's rule is an extension of God's own rule.

Jesus uses this Psalm to explain that the Messiah is greater than his forefather David, because David calls him lord (Mk 12.36). Psalm 110 is the most frequently quoted Old Testament text in the New Testament. The early Christians see the fulfillment of the Psalm in the ascension of Jesus, when he was seated at the right hand of God (Acts 2.34-35; Heb. 1.3; see also 1 Cor. 15.25). This Psalm also shows that the Messiah would be both a king and a priest. "The Lord has sworn and will not change his mind: 'You are a priest forever, in the order of Melchizedek'" (Ps. 110.4).

The Messiah in the Prophets

In the course of Israel's history, it became increasingly obvious that David's descendants did not live up to the expectations of the ideal king. David's son Solomon fell away from the Lord (1 Kgs 11.4-13), and the history of his descendants is mostly the history of disobedience and rebellion against the Lord. As a consequence, Israel suffered God's punishment. The nation was divided into a northern and a southern kingdom, and both kingdoms were oppressed by their powerful neighbors. Israel, the northern kingdom, was eventually destroyed by the Assyrians in 722 BCE. In 597 BCE, the Babylonians conquered the southern kingdom, and they destroyed Jerusalem in 586 BCE.

Amos

During this period, it seemed like God's promise to David would not be fulfilled, but the prophets announced that God would once again look upon Israel with mercy. The prophet Amos assures Israel that a day will come when God "will restore David's fallen shelter" (Amos 9.11). In other words, a new son of David will emerge as Israel's king (see also Hos. 3.5). At that time, Israel will not only be free from their enemies, but all the nations will belong to God (Amos 9.12). James explains that this prophecy was fulfilled when the Gentiles were coming to Christ (Acts 15.14-18). Amos also adds that the rule of the Messiah will be accompanied by a time when the land will enjoy a miraculous degree of fertility and abundance (Amos 9.13).

Micah

The prophet Micah adds that the promised king will be something more than an ordinary human being. His "origins are from old, from ancient times" (Mic. 5.2). The Messiah is preexistent; he has existed with God from eternity. Nevertheless, he will rise from humble beginnings, being born in Bethlehem, which "is small among the clans of Judah" (Mic. 5.2). This prophecy was fulfilled when Jesus was born (Mt. 2.6). The Messiah would be Israel's shepherd and give them peace and security (Mic. 5.4). In his days, Israel will be free from their enemies. For Micah, this meant that the Messiah would deliver them from the Assyrians (Mic. 5.5-6).

Isaiah

The most detailed portrait of the Messiah is found in the prophet Isaiah. When Judah was threatened by Syria and Israel, Isaiah announced that God would give King Ahaz a sign: "The virgin will conceive and give birth to a son" (Isa. 7.14). The prophecy refers to the destruction of Israel and Syria (v. 16), which took place soon afterwards. Most scholars therefore think the son must have been born around the time of the prophet, and many identify him as King Hezekiah. Some think one of Isaiah's own sons is in view. There has also been much discussion regarding the meaning of the Hebrew word *almah*, which the TNIV translates as "virgin," but many translations now render "young woman." The word is normally used for an unmarried girl (Gen. 24.43). Even though this word does not specifically mean "virgin," it would be unusual if an unmarried girl were anything else. In the canonical context, Isaiah's prophecy refers to the future Messiah. The Septuagint, the Greek translation of the Old Testament, uses the word *parthenos* to translate *almah*. *Parthenos* is the normal Greek term for "virgin." Matthew and Luke both make it clear that this prophecy was fulfilled when the virgin Mary was with child. Luke emphasizes that Mary was indeed a virgin (Lk. 1.34). Matthew focuses more on the significance of the name Immanuel ("God with us"; Mt. 1.23).

The son that is announced in Isaiah 7.14 is not directly associated with the promise to David in 2 Samuel 7.14, but the text indicates that he is a king. His food is curds and honey (v. 15), which represent abundance (v. 22; Exod. 3.8).

The king that will be born is mentioned again in Isaiah 9.6-7, in a prophecy about a glorious future for Israel. At that time, a child is born, who will reign on David's throne forever (v. 7). In other words, this child is the fulfillment of the promise in 2 Samuel 7.12-16. His name will be "Wonderful Counselor, Mighty God, Everlasting Father, Prince of Peace" (v. 6). These are indeed astonishing names to be given to a human being. The first half of the name "Wonderful Counselor" (literally: "wonder of a counselor") has associations of divine miracles (Ps. 78.12). It also resembles the self-identification of the Angel of the Lord (Judg. 13.18), who is indistinguishable from the Lord himself (Judg. 13.22). "Mighty God" (*el gibbor*) is a name that is reserved for the almighty God (Isa. 10.21). As the one who bears the name "Eternal Father," or "One who is eternally a Father," the child endures forever, like God (Isa. 57.15). His rule will bring perfect peace (Isa. 2.4; Mic. 5.5; Zech. 9.10). This prophecy is the clearest Old Testament witness of the divinity of the Messiah. In the context of the Old Testament, the meaning is probably that the Messiah will rule like God; his government will demonstrate divine qualities (see the discussion of Ps. 2.7 above). In Jewish interpretation, however, the prophecy is understood in a very different way. The glorious names are not understood as the names of the Messiah, but the names of God. In the New Testament, these names are not quoted, but it is clear that Isaiah's prophecy is fulfilled in Jesus' ministry in Galilee (Mt. 4.14-16; see also Lk. 1.79).

In chapter 11, Isaiah describes the rule of the messianic king. He will "come up from the stump of Jesse" (David's father), and is identified as a "Branch" (v. 1). The Hebrew word is *netser* and draws attention to the humble beginnings of the king. This prophecy is perhaps the background for what Matthew says: "He will be called a Nazarene" (Mt. 1.23). The king is uniquely qualified to rule because of his exceptional equipment with the Holy Spirit (vv. 2-3). He will therefore be a completely just ruler, as he will judge on behalf of the poor and oppressed (vv. 4-5). His rule will be so peaceful that "the wolf will live with the lamb" (v. 6). In other words, the world as we know it will disappear, and the Messiah will bring a new blissful world order.

Jeremiah

The background for Isaiah's prophecies is the corruption and injustice of Judah's rulers. That is also the case for the prophet Jeremiah, who views the people's leaders as unfaithful shepherds of God's people (Jer. 23.1). In contrast, God himself will raise up a shepherd for the people. With a name that recalls the shoot "from the stump of Jesse" (Isa. 11.1), Jeremiah identifies the new leader as "a righteous Branch, a King who will reign wisely and do what is just and right in the land" (Jer. 23.5; see also 33.14-26). His name will be "the Lord is our righteousness" (Jer. 23.6 NRSV). In Jeremiah's days, Judah's king was Zedekiah ("My righteousness is the Lord"), but he had proven himself to have nothing to do with God's righteousness. Instead, the Messiah would bring God's righteousness to his people. The apostle Paul alludes to this prophecy in 1 Corinthians 1.30.

Ezekiel

Ezekiel also looks forward to a ruler that contrasts with the kings and leaders of Israel. Israel's shepherds have failed, but God will give them another shepherd, a new David (Ezek. 34.23-24). He will bring Israel back to their land and make them obey his laws (Ezek. 37.24-25). Jesus, who is the good shepherd (Jn 10.11), fulfilled these promises.

Daniel

The only place in the Old Testament where a future ruler is explicitly called Messiah is the prophecy in Daniel 9.24-27. This prophecy describes 70 "sevens" or weeks. These 70 weeks are divided into 7 weeks, 62 weeks, and one last week. The anointed one, the Messiah, will be put to death after 7 plus 62 weeks (Dan. 9.25-26). Most scholars assume that each of these "weeks" refer to 7 years. If this were to be taken literally, the Messiah would die 483 years after "the time the word goes out to restore and rebuild Jerusalem" (Dan. 9.25). There have been many suggestions regarding what "word" Daniel has in mind. A common interpretation is that he thinks of the Persian king Artaxerxes, who issued a decree to Nehemiah to rebuild the entire city of Jerusalem (444 or 445 BCE; see also Neh. 2.1-10). But Jesus' death is dated to 30 or 32 CE, which is less than 483 years later. A better interpretation of these numbers takes them as a stylized way of writing history, much like the numbers in the Old Testament genealogies and the numbers in the book of Revelation. The meaning of the numbers would then be that Israel suffers their 70 years of punishment (Jer. 25.11; 29.10) sevenfold (Lev. 26.18).

However, it is more important to understand what would happen than to be able to calculate the time. The angel explained to Daniel that "seventy 'sevens' are decreed for your people and your holy city to finish transgression, to put an end to sin, to atone for wickedness, to bring in everlasting righteousness, to seal up vision and prophecy and to anoint the Most Holy Place" (Dan. 9.24). Most commentators believe that Daniel was referring to the post-exilic ruler Zerubbabel (Ezra 3.2; Zech. 4.6-10) or the high priest Joshua (Ezra 3.2; Zech. 6.9-14). In light of the whole Bible, however, we realize that the prophecy reaches its ultimate fulfillment in Jesus Christ. When Jesus came, he brought the complete sacrifice for sin (Heb. 7.27; 9.12; 10.14) and provided an eternal righteousness for those who believe in him (Rom. 3.22; 2 Cor. 5.21; Phil. 3.9). As he brings all prophecies to fulfillment (2 Cor. 1.20), he also brings the time of prophecy to an end. Jesus himself represents the fulfillment of the temple (Jn 2.21), and the anointing of the Most Holy Place refers to Jesus' own anointing as the Messiah (Lk. 4.18).

Zechariah

Daniel associates the Messiah with atonement for sin, and the prophet Zechariah also focuses on the priestly function of the Messiah (see also Ps. 110.4). Jerusalem's high priest, Joshua, and his associates "are symbolic of things to come," namely the Messiah, who is here called God's servant, the Branch (Zech. 3.8; Jer. 23.5). The prophecy continues: "'See, the stone I have set in front of Joshua! There are seven eyes on that one stone, and I will engrave an inscription on it,' says the Lord Almighty, 'and I will remove the sin of this land in a single day'" (Zech. 3.9). The stone with seven eyes may be the stone that will be the foundation of the new temple (Zech. 4.7-10). If so, the stone points forward to the Messiah as the foundation of the new temple of God, the church (Mt. 21.42-43; Eph. 2.20; 1 Pet. 2.6-8). As high priest, the Messiah "will remove the sin of this land in a single day" (Heb. 7.27; 9.12; 10.14).

In chapter 9, Zechariah describes the judgment of Israel's enemies. During this time, the Messiah enters Jerusalem: "Rejoice greatly, Daughter Zion! Shout, Daughter Jerusalem! See, your king comes to you, righteous and having salvation, lowly and riding on a donkey, on a colt, the foal of a donkey" (Zech. 9.9). A warrior king usually comes on a horse or in a chariot (Zech. 1.8; 6.2), but the Messiah comes on a donkey. He does not win his victory by military might; he will destroy the weapons of war (Zech. 9.10). Not with the force of arms, but with humility, "he will proclaim peace to the nations," so that "his rule will extend from sea to sea." This prophecy was fulfilled when Jesus entered Jerusalem to suffer and die (Mt. 21.5; Jn 12.15).

From the prophets Micah and Ezekiel, we have learned that the Messiah king will be a true and faithful shepherd of the people (Mic. 5.4; Ezek. 34.23). In chapter 13, Zechariah shows us the death of this shepherd: "'Awake, sword, against my shepherd, against the man who is close to me!' declares the Lord Almighty. 'Strike the shepherd, and the sheep will be scattered, and I will turn my hand against the little ones'" (Zech. 13.7). Jesus saw this prophecy fulfilled when he was handed over to die on the cross (Mk 14.27).

Table 7.1 Characteristics of the Messiah

King	When your days are over and you rest with your ancestors, I will raise up your offspring to succeed you, who will come from your own body, and I will establish his kingdom (2 Sam. 7.12).
Temple-builder	He is the one who will build a house for my Name (2 Sam. 7.13a).
Eternal kingdom	and I will establish the throne of his kingdom forever (2 Sam. 7.13b). I will establish your line forever and make your throne firm through all generations (Ps. 89.4).
God's Son	I will be his father, and he will be my son (2 Sam. 7.14). You are my son; today I have become your father (Ps. 2.7). He will call out to me, "You are my Father, my God, the Rock my Savior" (Ps. 89.26).
God's love is always with him	But my love will never be taken away from him (2 Sam. 7.15). My faithful love will be with him (Ps. 72.24).
Universal king	I will restore David's fallen shelter – I will repair its broken walls and restore its ruins – and will rebuild it as it used to be, so that they may possess the remnant of Edom and all the nations that bear my name (Amos 9.11-12). Ask me, and I will make the nations your inheritance, the ends of the earth your possession (Ps. 2.8).
Rules with justice	Of the increase of his government and peace there will be no end. He will reign on David's throne and over his kingdom, establishing and upholding it with justice and righteousness from that time on and forever (Isa. 9.7). He will not judge by what he sees with his eyes, or decide by what he hears with his ears; but with righteousness he will judge the needy, with justice he will give decisions for the poor of the earth (Isa. 11.3b-4a). "The days are coming," declares the Lord, 'when I will raise up for David a righteous Branch, a King who will reign wisely and do what is just and right in the land" (Jer. 23.5). May he judge your people in righteousness, your afflicted ones with justice (Ps. 72.2).
Rules with humility	See, your king comes to you, righteous and having salvation, lowly and riding on a donkey, on a colt, the foal of a donkey (Zech. 9.9). In your majesty ride forth victoriously in the cause of truth, humility and justice; let your right hand achieve awesome deeds (Ps. 45.4).
Brings peace	And they will live securely, for then his greatness will reach to the ends of the earth (Mic. 5.4b). The wolf will live with the lamb, the leopard will lie down with the goat, the calf and the lion and the yearling together; and a little child will lead them. The cow will feed with the bear, their young will lie down together, and the lion will eat straw like the ox. Infants will play near the hole of the cobra; young children will put their hands into the viper's nest (Isa. 11.6-8). In his days Judah will be saved and Israel will live in safety. This is the name by which he will be called: The Lord Our Righteous Savior (Jer. 23.6).

A New Ruler and a New Order   83

Table 7.1 Continued

Defeats all enemies	He will strike the earth with the rod of his mouth; with the breath of his lips he will slay the wicked (Isa. 11.4b). You will break them with a rod of iron; you will dash them to pieces like pottery (Ps. 2.9). I will crush his foes before him and strike down his adversaries (Ps. 89.23).
Brings prosperity	May the mountains bring prosperity to the people, the hills the fruit of righteousness (Ps. 72.3).
Humble origins	But you, Bethlehem Ephrathah, though you are small among the clans of Judah, out of you will come for me one who will be ruler over Israel, whose origins are from of old, from ancient times (Mic. 5.2).
Shepherd	He will stand and shepherd his flock in the strength of the Lord, in the majesty of the name of the Lord his God (Mic. 5.4a).
Born of a virgin and called Immanuel	The virgin will conceive and give birth to a son, and will call him Immanuel (Isa. 7.14).
Called with divine names	For to us a child is born, to us a son is given, and the government will be on his shoulders. And he will be called Wonderful Counselor, Mighty God, Everlasting Father, Prince of Peace (Isa. 9.6).
Endowed with the Spirit	The Spirit of the Lord will rest on him—the Spirit of wisdom and of understanding, the Spirit of counsel and of might, the Spirit of the knowledge and fear of the Lord (Isa. 11.2).
Priest	Seventy 'sevens' are decreed for your people and your holy city to finish transgression, to put an end to sin, to atone for wickedness, to bring in everlasting righteousness, to seal up vision and prophecy and to anoint the Most Holy Place (Dan. 9.24). "I am going to bring my servant, the Branch. See, the stone I have set in front of Joshua! There are seven eyes on that one stone, and I will engrave an inscription on it," says the Lord Almighty, "and I will remove the sin of this land in a single day" (Zech. 3.8b-9). You are a priest forever, in the order of Melchizedek (Ps. 110.4).
Suffers a violent death	"Awake, sword, against my shepherd, against the man who is close to me!" declares the Lord Almighty. "Strike the shepherd, and the sheep will be scattered, and I will turn my hand against the little ones" (Zech. 13.7).
Enthroned at God's right hand	The Lord says to my lord: "Sit at my right hand until I make your enemies a footstool for your feet" (Ps. 110.1).

Other Prophecies

There are many other prophecies that the Old Testament does not explicitly associate with God's promise to David. In light of the fulfillment in Jesus Christ we can understand that all these prophecies point to the one individual, Jesus Christ. Already at the time when Adam and Eve fell in sin did God promise that their enemy, the serpent, would be crushed by the woman's offspring (Gen. 3.15). This enemy is Satan (Rev. 12.9), and he is crushed underneath the people of Christ (Rom. 16.20).

In Jacob's last words, he announced that a ruler would come from Judah's tribe (Gen. 49.8-12). This king would not only rule the nation of Israel, but all the nations (v. 9). Under his rule, there would be such abundance of resources that this ruler "will tether his donkey to a vine" and wash "his garments in wine" (v. 11).

The New Testament shows that this prophecy is fulfilled in Jesus Christ. In the book of Revelation, John calls him "the Lion of the tribe of Judah" (Rev. 5.5). John's Gospel shows how Jesus brings the kind of abundance that Jacob anticipated. At the wedding in Cana (Jn 2.1-11), Jesus made water into wine.

The wicked prophet Balaam was also forced to prophesy about Israel's future king (Num. 24.17-19). This ruler was not to appear in the near future (v. 17; see also v. 14). When he would come, he would destroy the enemies of God's people (vv. 17-18). In the New Testament, both Zechariah (Lk. 1.78) and the magi (Mt. 2.2) associate the birth of Jesus with the prophecy of Balaam. In Revelation 22.16, Jesus also alludes to Numbers 24.17 when he calls himself "the bright Morning Star."

The Suffering Servant

For the authors of the New Testament, Isaiah's prophecies of the Suffering Servant are among the most important. In four songs (Isa. 42.1-9; 49.1-7; 50.4-9; 52.13-53.12), Isaiah describes a figure who would be equipped by the Holy Spirit to bring international justice (42.1). He would be "a covenant for the people and a light for the Gentiles" (42.6). He would display God's splendor (49.3), not only to bring salvation to Israel but also to the Gentiles, even to the ends of the earth (49.5-6). He suffers in the hands of evildoers (50.6-7), but is vindicated by the Lord (50.8-9). The fourth song explains that the servant's suffering was also his way to glory (52.13; Lk. 24.26). His suffering is the way in which he brings salvation to his people. He does not suffer for his own wrongdoing, but bears the sins of his people (53.4-6). "He was pierced for our transgressions, he was crushed for our iniquities; the punishment that brought us peace was on him, and by his wounds we are healed" (53.5). He was without sin (53.9), but it was God's will to make him suffer (53.10). In this way, "the Lord makes his life an offering for sin," so that he could "see his offspring" and "justify many" and "bear their iniquities" (53.10-11; see also ch. 6).

The servant is closely connected with the people of Israel, and God even addresses him as "Israel" in 49.3. In the Septuagint, the servant is also identified as Jacob and Israel in Isaiah 42.1. Many scholars have followed the Jewish translators in this interpretation. But chapter 53 shows that the servant must be distinguished from Israel, as he suffers in their place. It is therefore better to see the servant as Israel's representative, as the one God has chosen to suffer in their place and instead of them.

The New Testament makes it clear that the servant is Jesus Christ. Isaiah 53 is the most important text that the New Testament uses to explain the significance of Jesus' death (Lk. 22.37; Acts 8.32-33; 1 Pet. 2.22, 24-25). He gave his life for us, to be an offering for our sins (ch. 9).

In Isaiah 61.1-7, the Servant himself is speaking. He describes the task God has given him: to bring the good news of salvation to the poor, the brokenhearted, the captives, and the prisoners (v. 1). This is precisely how Jesus understood the nature of his ministry (Lk. 4.18-21).

The Righteous Sufferer

There are also several Psalms that portray a righteous person who is suffering. These Psalms point to their fulfillment in Jesus Christ. The psalmist may have thought about his own sufferings when he wrote these Psalms. But if he did, the Holy Spirit led him to express himself in such a way that the words he used were even more appropriate for the sufferings of Jesus. The most elaborate of these Psalms is Psalm 22, which mentions several details that were fulfilled on the cross. When Jesus suffered the ultimate judgment of being forsaken by God, he used the words of this Psalm to express it: "My God, my God, why have you forsaken me?" (Mk 15.34; Ps. 22.1). This Psalm also describes how the crowds insulted him (Mk 15.29; Ps. 22.7), how he suffered from thirst (Jn 19.28; Ps. 22.15), and how the soldiers cast lots for his clothes (Jn 19.24; Ps. 22.18). Psalm 22 gives a very vivid description of Jesus' pain, and serves as a testimony of how Jesus as a human being has become one of us. He is one of our family and calls us brothers and sisters (Heb. 2.11-12; Ps. 22.22).

Psalms about the righteous sufferer also point out that Jesus was consumed by zeal for the Lord's house (Ps. 69.9; Jn 2.17), was hated without reason (Ps. 69.4; Jn 15.25), was given vinegar to drink (Ps. 69.21; Jn 19.28-29), and was betrayed by a close friend (Ps. 41.9; Jn 13.18), whose place was later deserted (Ps. 69.25; Acts 1.20).

Other Psalms also find their fulfillment in Jesus' crucifixion and resurrection. Psalm 16.10 speaks of deliverance from the grave, and points to the resurrection of Jesus (Acts 2.25-31). Psalm 40 describes what is more pleasing to God than sacrifices: to do his will. Jesus fulfilled this when he presented his body as a sacrifice on the cross (Heb. 10.5-10).

The second most quoted Psalm in the New Testament is Psalm 118. This Psalm is about the king of Israel when he comes to Jerusalem after the Babylonian exile. He represents Israel: rejected by the world empires, but vindicated by the Lord (vv. 22-23). In this way, he points forward to Jesus, who was rejected by the Jewish leaders, but approved by God (Mk 12.10-11; 1 Pet. 2.4, 7). Jesus will be the corner stone of the new temple, the people of God.

In Psalm 118.25-26, the priests greet the king when he leads a procession of pilgrims to the temple: "Lord, save us! Lord, grant us success! Blessed is he who comes in the name of the Lord. From the house of the Lord we bless you." Their greeting is an expression of God's approval of the king as he enters the temple. The crowds in Jerusalem use this greeting to welcome Jesus as the messianic king when he enters the city (Mk 11.9-10). However, Jesus' triumph was of a very different nature than what the crowds expected. He did not enter Jerusalem to display his power, but to triumph over evil by his death and resurrection.

The Prophet Like Moses

Alongside the promises regarding the messianic king, God also promised to raise up a prophet like Moses (Deut. 18.15-19). He would speak the words of God (v. 18). Jesus is the fulfillment of this promise as well (Mk 9.7; Jn 6.14; Acts 3.22; 7.37).

The Son of Man

Another figure that becomes very important in the New Testament is the Son of Man. He is described in a way that is very different from the promises discussed above. These characters all appear on earth, but the Son of Man is a heavenly being. Daniel saw him in a vision. He came "with the clouds of heaven" (Dan. 7.13). Otherwise, it is God who comes in the clouds (Exod. 19.9;

34.5; Deut. 31.15). Daniel's Son of Man shares other attributes with God as well. He "was given authority, glory, and sovereign power," and "all nations and peoples of every language worshiped him" (Dan. 7.14). No one other than God deserves worship (Deut. 6.13; 10.20; Mt. 4.10). The Son of Man will also rule for ever. "His dominion is an everlasting dominion that will not pass away, and his kingdom is one that will never be destroyed" (Dan. 7.14). The Son of Man shares all these characteristics with God himself.

God, the Ancient of Days, later explains the vision to Daniel and tells him that "the sovereignty, power and greatness of all the kingdoms under heaven will be handed over to the holy people of the Most High" (Dan. 7.27a). In the next sentence, God refers to the ruler of this kingdom in the singular: "His kingdom will be an everlasting kingdom, and all rulers will worship and obey him" (Dan. 7.27b). This person must be the Son of Man, and most scholars therefore conclude that "the holy people of the Most High" and the Son of Man must be one and the same. On this interpretation, the Son of Man is not an individual, but a symbol for God's people. In the same way, the four beasts of Daniel's vision are symbols of the worldly kingdoms (Dan. 7.1-8, 15-28).

But there are important differences between the Son of Man and the four beasts. The Son of Man is not given an interpretation like the four beasts are. He also appears separately from them and is included in the vision of the Ancient of Days. The vision of the Ancient of Days is not merely symbolic, but is presented as a vision of God's heavenly throne. It is better to conclude that the Son of Man also is more than a symbol; he may be the heavenly representative of the people of God. When Jesus comes, he identifies himself as the Son of Man from Daniel's vision (Mk 13.26; 14.62).

Another character that has a lot in common with the Son of Man is the man dressed in linen (Dan. 10.5; 12.6-7). Daniel describes him as a very exalted heavenly figure. His appearance has much in common with the four living creatures as they appear in Ezekiel 1.5-24 (Dan. 10.6). He also has "a belt of fine gold from Uphaz around his waist" (Dan. 10.5). In John's vision of the exalted Jesus, Jesus also has "a golden sash around his chest" (Rev. 1.13). It seems, therefore, that John may have thought of the man dressed in linen as an Old Testament manifestation of the preexistent Christ.

Summary

The Old Testament describes several different characters that God will send to Israel. Through the ministry of these characters, Israel will experience peace, justice, and harmony. They will once again enjoy the blessings of a right relationship with the Lord.

The Messiah will be a savior king who will rule with peace and justice. Under his rule, Israel will be secure from their enemies. The prophet like Moses will teach the people the will of God. The Servant of the Lord will suffer in their place and die as an atoning sacrifice for the people. The heavenly figure who is called the Son of Man has an eternal kingdom.

In the New Testament we discover that all these characters point forward to Jesus Christ. As we shall see in the next chapter, however, he is even more glorious than all these characters combined. He can therefore bring even more glorious blessings.

Further Reading

Fitzmyer, Joseph A. *The One Who Is to Come*. Grand Rapids: Eerdmans, 2007.

Kaiser, Walter C. Jr. *The Messiah in the Old Testament*. Studies in Old Testament Biblical Theology. Grand Rapids: Zondervan, 1995.

Porter, Stanley E., ed. *The Messiah in the Old and New Testaments*. McMaster New Testament Studies. Grand Rapids: Eerdmans, 2007.

Review Questions

Explain the meaning of the term "Messiah" and explain how this term became associated with a future king.

What will be the work of the Messiah, according to the Old Testament?

What distinguishes the Son of Man from the Messiah?

8

God Came to Us

The New Testament Picture of Jesus

Chapter Outline

Messiah	90
A Suffering Messiah	91
God's Equal	94
Son of Man	101
Jesus as the Son of the Father	102
Wisdom Christology and Preexistence	104
Lord	110
God	111
The Last Adam	113
Other Titles for Jesus	114
Christological Development?	114
Johannine Christology	115
The Book of Revelation	120
Summary	121

Jesus of Nazareth comes as the fulfillment of the Old Testament descriptions of the Messiah, the prophet like Moses, the Suffering Servant, and the Son of Man. But none of these Old Testament expectations can do him full justice. Jesus fills these titles with new meaning. In Jesus, God himself came to earth.

Messiah

The Greek translation of the Hebrew word "Messiah" is *Christos*, which in English is written as "Christ." Modern English translations usually use the word "Messiah" when *Christos* is understood as a direct reference to the Old Testament promises, and "Christ" when it is understood as a name for Jesus. But there is no difference in the original Greek text, which uses the word *Christos* everywhere except in two instances. (Jn 1.41 and 4.25 use *Messias*, which is not a Greek word, but a transliteration of the Hebrew *Mashiach*. The effect is to draw attention to the Old Testament and Jewish hope for the Messiah.)

All the Gospels identify Jesus as the Christ/Messiah (Mt. 1.1; Mk 1.1; Lk. 2.11; Jn 1.41). However, Jesus never uses the title for himself. He approves of Peter's use of the title (Mt. 16.17). To the Samaritan woman at the well (Jn 4.25-26) and the high priest at his trial (Mk 14.61-62), he also affirms that he is the Messiah (see also Jn 10.24-25). On a couple of occasions, he refers to the master of his disciples as the Messiah (Mk 9.41; Mt. 23.10).

Jesus appears almost reluctant to be identified with this title. The Synoptic Gospels show that he often instructed people not to tell others about him (Mk 7.36; 9.9 etc.). This is known in New Testament scholarship as the messianic secret. The New Testament scholar William Wrede argued that Jesus himself never claimed to be the Messiah, but that the early Christians concluded after the resurrection that he had to have been the Messiah. When they needed to answer the question why Jesus had never publicly announced himself as the Messiah, they made up the stories where he demands secrecy about his identity.

Wrede's hypothesis has been very influential in New Testament scholarship, but the so-called messianic secret has a better explanation. Jesus did not want to be associated with some of the expectations that many Jews in the first century had to the Messiah. They waited for a Messiah that would be a political ruler. A Jewish writing from the first century BCE, known as the *Psalms of Solomon*, contains a prayer to God for the coming of the Messiah. In this prayer, the writer prays that God will "undergird him with the strength to destroy the unrighteous rulers, to purge Jerusalem from gentiles who trample her to destruction" (17.22). When the Messiah comes, "he will have gentile nations serving him under his yoke" (17.30). Many Jews understood these expectations literally, that the Messiah would be a military leader and defeat Israel's enemies. In Jesus' days, several Jews claimed that they were the

Messiah and organized a liberation army to fight against the Roman army that controlled Israel (Acts 5.36-37).

A Suffering Messiah

Jesus did not want people to think that he was such a Messiah (Jn 6.15). He was the Messiah, but not the kind of Messiah that many people expected. He was not a Messiah that would put other people to death, but a Messiah that would die in their place. The Synoptic Gospels therefore associate Jesus' Messiahship closely with his death. Peter's confession of Jesus as the Messiah is followed by Jesus' prediction of his passion and resurrection (Mk 8.31). According to the Synoptic Gospels, Jesus keeps his Messiahship a secret until he is about to enter Jerusalem in order to die. In Mark's Gospel, the first one to announce him publicly as the Messiah is the blind Bartimaeus. Jesus meets him outside Jericho when he is on his way to Jerusalem, and Bartimaeus cries out: "Jesus, son of David, have mercy on me!" (Mk 10.47). "Son of David" is a messianic title. Afterwards, as he enters Jerusalem on a donkey, the crowds also identify him as the Messiah. They greet him with the words: "Hosanna! Blessed is he who comes in the name of the Lord! Blessed is the coming kingdom of our father David! Hosanna in the highest heaven!" (Mk 11.9-10). They are quoting from Psalm 118.25-26, a text that was used to express the people's hopes for a messianic kingdom.

When he was talking with the Jewish leaders, Jesus indicated that their understanding of the Messiah was not fully correct. "While Jesus was teaching in the temple courts, he asked, 'Why do the teachers of the law say that the Messiah is the son of David? David himself, speaking by the Holy Spirit, declared: The Lord said to my Lord: Sit at my right hand until I put your enemies under your feet'" (Mk 12.35-36). With this quotation from Psalm 110.1, he explained that the Messiah must be greater than David, even though David is his forefather. Later, when the high priest questioned Jesus if he were the Messiah, he answered with an affirmation (Mk 14.62). But then he continued to describe himself with a quotation from Daniel 7.13 and Psalm 110.1: "And you will see the Son of Man sitting at the right hand of the Mighty One and coming on the clouds of heaven." The point is that the Messiah is also a heavenly being who shares God's authority.

The Gospel of Matthew emphasizes strongly that Jesus is the fulfillment of what is written in the Old Testament. Matthew stresses that Jesus is the son of David (1.1), the king of Israel (2.1-4). In Peter's confession, Matthew includes the title "the son of living God" (16.16). He thereby clarifies that the Messiah is not only David's son, but also God's Son (22.41-45).

Luke's birth narrative also shows that Jesus is the promised king who will be the fulfillment of God's promise to David (1.32-33, 69). When Zechariah praises God for the birth of Jesus, he sees him as a savior who will liberate Israel from their enemies (1.71, 74). However, the rest of Luke's Gospel explains that Jesus was not the kind of savior who came to give political liberation. Instead, he came to set people free from sin and its consequences (5.32; 19.10; 24.47).

The first time Luke uses the title Messiah (Christ) is in the angels' annunciation of Jesus' birth: "Today in the town of David a Savior has been born to you; he is the Messiah, the Lord" (2.11). Here, the term occurs together with two other titles: Savior and Lord. In this way, Luke explains the meaning of the Messiah title. Jesus is a Messiah who is also Savior and Lord. "Lord" is God's name in the Bible (ch. 1). Jesus is a Messiah who is more than a son of David. He also bears God's own name.

In his sermon in the synagogue in Nazareth (Lk. 4.16-27), Jesus quotes from Isaiah 61.1-2: "The Spirit of the Lord is on me, because he has anointed me to proclaim good news to the poor. He has sent me to proclaim freedom for the prisoners and recovery of sight for the blind, to set the oppressed free, to proclaim the year of the Lord's favor" (Lk. 4.18-19). This sermon explains the purpose of Jesus' anointing or his Messiahship ("Messiah" means "the Anointed One"). Luke has placed this sermon at the very beginning of Jesus' ministry, in contrast to both Matthew and Mark, who place it much later (Mt. 13.54-58 and Mk 6.1-6). (We must remember that the Gospels are not organized in strict chronological order, but according to topic.) By placing this sermon here, Luke shows that it has programmatic significance. It serves to define Jesus' ministry. He came for the poor and for those who were outcasts in society (4.18-19; see also 6.20-21; 7.22).

It is also important to notice what Jesus does not include when he reads from Isaiah. Jesus concludes his quotation with the words "to proclaim the year of the Lord's favor" (v. 19). When we compare with the text of Isaiah 61.1-2, we notice that Jesus stopped reading in the middle of a sentence. The prophecy from Isaiah goes like this: "to proclaim the year of the Lord's favor and the day of vengeance of our God" (61.2). When Jesus came to fulfill Isaiah's prophecy, he explained that he came to fulfill the prophecies that

God Came to Us

specifically concerned salvation. He did not come to fulfill the prophecies regarding judgment and vengeance.

The prophets were inspired by the Holy Spirit to write about what God would do when he came to the earth to bring judgment and salvation. They were able to see what God would do, but did not have full insight into the time when it would happen (1 Pet. 1.11). Their perspective can be compared to someone who is looking at a mountain range from a distance. Because of the distance, some of the mountaintops look like they are so close together that one cannot be distinguished from another. It may look like there is only one of them. But when you get closer, you may realize that there are several mountaintops behind the first one, and they may be far removed from each other. In a similar way, the prophets saw God's salvation and judgment, and to them it looked like it was all going to happen at one time. But with the different perspective we have when we see the fulfillment, we can see that the prophecies are fulfilled in two stages. The prophecies regarding salvation are fulfilled through Jesus' first coming. But the prophecies regarding judgment will be fulfilled later.

John the Baptist was the last of the Old Testament prophets (Lk. 7.28; 16.16), and his perspective was that of the Old Testament. He thought that God's salvation and judgment would come at the same time. When he announced the coming of Jesus Christ to fulfill the prophecies, he probably thought that God's judgment would come immediately (Lk. 3.9). Great was his surprise when he later found himself in prison, with the evil King Herod still in power in Israel. What became of God's judgment? When John sent messengers to ask Jesus if they should wait for someone else, Jesus

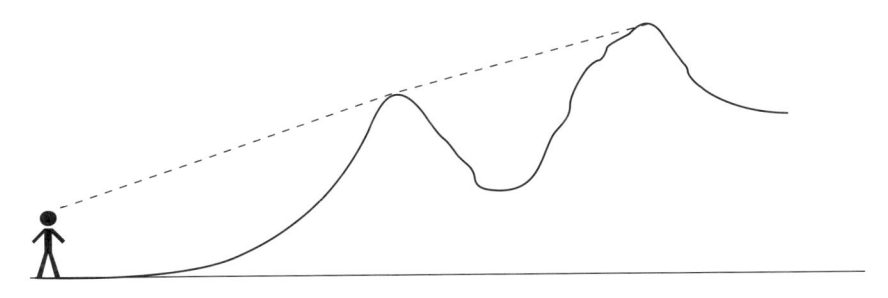

Figure 8.1 The prophetic perspective

answered: "Go back and report to John what you have seen and heard: The blind receive sight, the lame walk, those who have leprosy are cleansed, the deaf hear, the dead are raised, and the good news is proclaimed to the poor. Blessed is anyone who does not stumble on account of me" (Lk. 7.22-23). With this answer, Jesus once again made an important distinction in the way he referred to Old Testament prophecies. He alluded to several passages in Isaiah (26.19; 35.5; 61.1). All of these prophecies concern both salvation and judgment. But Jesus omitted all references to judgment, and only spoke of salvation. In this way, he explained to John that he was a different kind of Messiah than what John expected.

Jesus was a Messiah who would bring many people to salvation, not by inflicting suffering on evildoers, but by suffering himself. The work of the Messiah would bring him into great glory, but he could only enter into this glory when he walked the way that involved great suffering and death (Lk. 24.26).

God's Equal

Jesus not only fulfilled the Old Testament prophecies regarding the coming of the Messiah; what is even more astonishing is that he also came to fulfill what the Old Testament says about God's own coming to earth.

The Kingdom of God

Most importantly, Jesus claims that he came to bring the kingdom of God to earth (Mk 1.15; Mt. 10.7-8). The Greek term *basileia tou theou*, which is usually translated "kingdom of God," refers both to the territory where God rules and to God's ruling activity. The translation "kingdom of God" is not wrong, but it captures only half the meaning of the Greek term. Another translation might be: "the kingly rule of God."

In the Old Testament, God's kingdom or kingly rule is the universal kingdom of God himself. It relates to the idea that God is the king of heaven and earth, which is an idea that must be distinguished from the idea of the Messiah as the king of a renewed Israel.

The "kingdom of God" is not mentioned frequently in the Hebrew and Aramaic text of the Old Testament (only once, in 1 Chron. 28.5). But we often see the idea that God rules as king. God is the king of the entire universe. He rules over all the nations (1 Chron. 29.11-12; Ps. 99.1-5). His rule is eternal

(Ps. 145.10-13; Jer. 10.10) and reaches both to heaven and earth (Ps. 103.19). (The TNIV uses the expression "kingdom" in many of these references, where the Hebrew text refers to God ruling as king.)

Because Israel is in a special relationship with God (Exod. 19.6; Num. 23.21), God has chosen Zion as his throne (Ps. 99.1-5). He rules Israel through their king. Israel's kingdom is therefore also God's kingdom (1 Chron. 28.5), as long as the king observes God's commandments (1 Chron. 28.7).

The kings of this world are in rebellion against God and his rule (Ps. 2.1-3). God's kingdom is therefore in conflict with earthly kingdoms. This conflict is described in the book of Daniel. The four beasts of Daniel's vision symbolize four kingdoms that stand against God and his people. But they cannot stand against the power and authority of God, who gives his eternal kingdom (Dan. 6.26) to the Son of Man (Dan. 7.13-14) and to the people of the holy ones of the Most High (Dan. 7.27).

Daniel's vision is only one example of how the Old Testament prophets look forward to a time when God will establish his rule on earth. All the evil that happens in this world is a result of rebellion against God's rule. When God comes to put an end to all opposition against him, the world will experience peace and harmony. The time of salvation can therefore be described as the time when God will rule as king, on earth as he does in heaven.

The day when God comes to establish his rule is the day Israel will experience salvation (Zeph. 3.15-20). "The Lord will be king over the whole earth. On that day there will be one Lord, and his name the only name" (Zech. 14.9). That will be the day when all other powers will disappear. There will only be one name left: the name of the Lord. "On that day 'holy to the Lord' will be inscribed on the bells of the horses, and the cooking pots in the Lord's house will be like the sacred bowls in front of the altar. Every pot in Jerusalem and Judah will be holy to the Lord Almighty, and all who come to sacrifice will take some of the pots and cook in them" (Zech. 14.20-21). Nothing unholy will be left on that day. The whole land will be as holy as the temple. There will no longer be any separation between God and the people.

This will be the day when God's enemies will be defeated once and for all. "In that day the Lord will punish the powers in the heavens above and the kings on the earth below. They will be herded together like prisoners bound in a dungeon; they will be shut up in prison and be punished after many days. The moon will be dismayed, the sun ashamed; for the Lord Almighty will reign on Mount Zion and in Jerusalem, and before its elders—with great glory" (Isa. 24.21-23). That the sun and the moon will be ashamed is a metaphorical way of saying that all other powers will pale when God comes with his kingdom.

This is the time of eschatological salvation. It is the time "when the Lord Almighty will prepare a feast of rich food for all peoples, a banquet of aged wine—the best of meats and the finest of wines. On this mountain he will destroy the shroud that enfolds all peoples, the sheet that covers all nations; he will swallow up death forever. The Sovereign Lord will wipe away the tears from all faces; he will remove his people's disgrace from all the earth" (Isa. 25.6-9). That death will be swallowed up forever means that the world as we know it will be completely changed. What Isaiah describes is the new creation, the new earth.

Several Jewish writings from the time between the Old and the New Testaments tell us how the Jews understood these prophecies. They were waiting for God to come to earth, put an end to the devil, and establish his kingdom. The clearest expression of this expectation is found in the *Testament of Moses* (a Jewish writing from the first century CE): "Then his kingdom will appear throughout his whole creation. Then the devil will have an end. Yes, sorrow will be led away with him" (10.1).

When Jesus came to earth, this was precisely what he did. He announced that he had brought God's kingdom near (Mk 1.15; Mt. 10.7-8). He told the Pharisees that God's kingdom was in their midst (Lk. 17.20-21). The point is that Jesus brings the kingdom of God in his own person.

When God's kingly rule was established, the most important thing that would happen was that his enemies would no longer be able to oppose him. When Jesus came, this was exactly what happened. The evil spirits knew who Jesus was, and they knew that he had come to destroy them (Mk 1.24). Jesus himself explains why he could cast out the demons: "But if I drive out demons by the finger of God, then the kingdom of God has come upon you. When a strong man, fully armed, guards his own house, his possessions are safe. But when someone stronger attacks and overpowers him, he takes away the armor in which the man trusted and divides up his plunder" (Lk. 11.20-22). Jesus had already defeated and bound the prince of the demons, Satan himself. The flight of the demons was therefore the proof that the kingdom of God was present in Jesus. Since the coming of God's kingdom means the coming of God himself, Jesus indirectly shows that he is acting as God.

As we have seen, Jesus' fulfillment of the Old Testament promise of salvation takes place in stages. This also applies to the kingdom of God. Even though the kingdom is already present in the ministry of Jesus, it is also future. Jesus teaches his disciples to pray for the kingdom to come (Mt. 6.10), and he tells them that he "will never again drink of the fruit of the vine until that day when [he drinks] it new in the kingdom of God" (Mk 14.25).

Forgiveness of Sins

Not only Jesus' casting out of the demons, but also many other actions demonstrate that he was bringing the kingdom of God and that he himself was acting as God. When Jesus forgave sins (Mk 2.5), the teachers of the law understood what it meant. Jesus was taking God's place. That was why they accused him of blasphemy (Mk 2.7). In the Old Testament, only God could forgive sins (Ps. 103.3; Isa. 55.7; Mic. 7.18).

The Eschatological Judge

When Jesus forgave people's sins, he anticipated the eschatological judgment of God. To say that someone's sins are forgiven is to say that they will go free in God's judgment. It is therefore a natural consequence of Jesus' forgiveness that he will be the final judge of all people in the world.

Several passages in the Gospels reveal that Jesus will play a decisive role at the last judgment (Mt. 7.21-27; Lk. 12.8-10), but the clearest one is Mt. 25.31-46. Here, Jesus teaches about his second coming. He explains that all people who have lived on earth will be gathered before him, and he will pass judgment on every one of them. The Jews expected a final judgment where all people would be punished or rewarded for what they had done in this life, but the role as judge was reserved for God (Eccl. 12.14). The picture that Jesus gives of himself in Mt. 25.31-46 is therefore another example of how he took God's place.

"But I Tell You"

Jesus also talks like God. His teaching was very different from that of the rabbis. They always referred to the authority of the teachers that had gone before them. Jesus never did. His authority was even greater than that of the prophets. The prophets said "thus says the Lord" in order to explain that God stood behind their words. Jesus never did.

In the Sermon on the Mount, he gave his disciples commandments that were stricter than the commandments God had given through Moses. When Moses gave his commandments, he had his authority from God. But Jesus simply said: "but I tell you . . ." (Mt. 5.22 etc.). He spoke on his own authority. He even compared his own commandments to those God had given through Moses, and he said that his commandments were more important (Mt. 5.21-48).

This does not mean that he sat aside the authority of the law of Moses, but that he explained what this law was truly aiming at (Mt. 5.17). When he brings the ultimate revelation of the law, he speaks with an authority that is equal to that of God himself. We can easily understand why his audience was stunned (Mt. 7.28-29). His words are equally eternal as the words of God (Mk 13.31).

Absolute Demands

It was equally important to obey and serve Jesus as to obey and serve God. That is why Jesus called on people to leave everything and follow him (Mk 1.17; 10.21). The commandment to follow him was in fact more important than all other commandments, even the Ten Commandments.

One man, who wanted to follow Jesus, asked if he could go and bury his father first. To the Jews in the first century, to bury one's parents was the way to obey God's commandment: "Honor your father and your mother" (Exod. 20.12). The Jews therefore thought this duty was more important than all other religious duties. But Jesus told the man: "Follow me, and let the dead bury their own dead" (Mt. 8.22).

Jesus also told his followers that they had to love him more than they loved even their own family. "If anyone comes to me and does not hate father and mother, wife and children, brothers and sisters—yes, even life itself—such a person cannot be my disciple" (Lk. 14.26). (We must not understand the word "hate" literally. It is a very emphatic way of saying that our loyalty to Jesus is more important than our loyalty to our family.) In other words, the commandment to follow Jesus was more important than all other commandments.

Miracles

Jesus also does the works of God. Jesus performed many miracles, such as raising the dead, healing the sick, and giving sight to blind. In and of itself, this is not different from some of the things that were done by the prophets

God Came to Us

in the Old Testament, especially Elijah and Elisha (1 Kgs 17.17-23; 2 Kgs 4.18-37). But the prophets were dependent on prayer to be able to perform these miracles. Their power was not their own. It was from God. Jesus, on the other hand, did not have to pray for the miracles to happen. He performed miracles by his own powerful word (Mt. 8.8, 13). This power was so awesome that he could even control the phenomena of nature. His stilling of the storm (Mk 4.35-41) corresponds to God's own control of the sea (Ps. 107.23-30).

Table 8.1 Jesus acting in the role of God

	Jesus	God
Defeating the evil powers	But if I drive out demons by the finger of God, then the kingdom of God has come upon you (Lk. 11.20).	In that day the Lord will punish the powers in the heavens above and the kings on the earth below (Isa. 24.21).
Forgiveness of sins	The Son of Man has authority on earth to forgive sins (Mk 2.10).	The Lord . . . forgives all your sins and heals all your diseases (Ps. 103.1, 3).
Eschatological judge	When the Son of Man comes in his glory, and all the angels with him, he will sit on his glorious throne. All the nations will be gathered before him, and he will separate the people one from another as a shepherd separates the sheep from the goats (Mt. 25.31-32).	For God will bring every deed into judgment, including every hidden thing, whether it is good or evil (Eccl. 12.4).
Giving commandments	You have heard that it was said to the people long ago, "You shall not murder, and anyone who murders will be subject to judgment." But I tell you that anyone who is angry with a brother or sister will be subject to judgment" (Mt. 5.21-22).	God spoke all these words . . . "You shall not murder" (Exod. 20.1, 13).
Demanding absolute love	If anyone comes to me and does not hate father and mother, wife and children, brothers and sisters —yes, even life itself—such a person cannot be my disciple (Lk. 14.26).	Love the Lord your God with all your heart and with all your soul and with all your strength (Deut. 6.5).
Miracles	He got up, rebuked the wind and said to the waves, "Quiet! Be still!" Then the wind died down and it was completely calm (Mk 4.39).	He stilled the storm to a whisper; the waves of the sea were hushed (Ps. 107.29).

Jesus also indirectly explains that when he came to earth, God came to earth. Malachi prophesied that Elijah would come before the day of the Lord (Mal. 3.1; 4.5). The day of the Lord was the day when God himself would come, not the Messiah. Jesus identified John the Baptist as the fulfillment of Malachi's prophecy (Mt. 11.7-10). This meant that John was the forerunner of God. But John was also the forerunner of Jesus himself. That meant that Jesus' saw his own coming as the coming of God. John the Baptist saw himself as the forerunner of the Messiah (Jn 3.28), but that was because Jesus came both as God and as the Messiah.

God's Coming

The introduction to Mark's Gospel also shows us that Jesus came to earth to fulfill the promises regarding God's own coming. Even though he only refers to Isaiah by name (he was the most important), Mark begins his Gospel with a combination of three Old Testament prophecies (Exod. 23.20; Mal. 3.1; Isa. 40.3): "I will send my messenger ahead of you, who will prepare your way—a voice of one calling in the wilderness, 'Prepare the way for the Lord, make straight paths for him'" (Mk 1.2b-3). All of these prophecies concern messengers that will go before God to prepare a way for him. But Mark's Gospel continues to tell the story of how John the Baptist prepared the way for Christ. In this way, Mark indirectly makes it clear that Christ comes as God. In the following passages, Mark explains how Jesus does God's works. He does all the end time works of God as they are prophesied in Isaiah 35.5-6a: "Then will the eyes of the blind be opened (Mk 8.22-26; 10.46-52) and the ears of the deaf unstopped (Mk 7.31-37). Then will the lame leap like a deer (Mk 2.1-10), and the mute tongue shout for joy" (Mk 7.31-37).

God's Presence

Matthew structures his Gospel very carefully around his affirmations that Jesus is the presence of God. Jesus comes as the fulfillment of the prophecy in Isaiah 7.14: "they will call him Immanuel." Matthew explains that the name Immanuel means "God with us" (Mt. 1.23). This name does not represent a pious wish for the newborn son, but it means that God, who is present everywhere, is present through Jesus. Since Jesus is God's unique Son, his presence is the same as God's presence. He can therefore promise his disciples that he will be with them always and everywhere (Mt. 18.20; 28.20). We can see that this idea is very important to Matthew, as he refers to it at the very beginning (1.23) and at the very end of his Gospel (28.20). That God is present means specifically that he is present to save (Deut. 20.4; Jer. 15.20). The meaning of Jesus' name Immanuel is therefore that God's saving presence is in Jesus Christ.

The Temple

Now that God is present with his people in Jesus Christ, what use is there for the temple building in Jerusalem, God's dwelling? This building is now replaced; there is no need for it. Jesus can therefore announce that it will be destroyed (Mk 13.2; 14.58). (However, the witnesses at Jesus' trial were not truthful. Jesus had said that the temple would be destroyed, but not that he would destroy it.) Jesus himself had now taken the place of the temple (Jn 2.21).

Son of Man

The title that Jesus himself uses most frequently in the Synoptic Gospels is Son of Man. This term may mean simply "man" (Ezek. 2.1 etc.) or mankind in general (Pss 8.4; 80.17). Used in this way, the term has associations of humility and lowliness. But it can also be a reference to the heavenly being from Daniel's vision (Dan. 7.13-14), a heavenly being that shares several of God's characteristics (ch. 7). In Mark 13.26; 14.62, Jesus connects his use of the title "Son of Man" directly with Daniel's prophecy. Some Jewish writings tell us about what some Jews expected of this Son of Man. They thought he would appear at the end of history. Then he would sit on God's throne and punish the ungodly and reward the faithful (*1 Enoch* 62-63). But Jesus had a broader understanding of the Son of Man. He connected the title to Daniel's vision of the heavenly being, and also to the exalted image of the Messiah seated at God's right hand in Psalm 110.1 (Mk 14.62). But the Son of Man is not only exalted; he also has to suffer. In Mark 10.45, Jesus combines the image of the Son of Man with the picture of the Suffering Servant who would give his life in the place of many (Isa. 53.12).

When Jesus called himself the Son of Man, it was a title that not all could understand (Jn 12.34). That is probably why it never became a title the Christians used when they confessed their faith in Jesus. In the New Testament, only Jesus himself uses the title "the Son of Man" (except in Stephen's speech in Acts 7.56). Just as Jesus' message was hidden to some and revealed to others (Mk 4.11-12), so does this title both reveal and conceal who Jesus truly is. On the one hand, it draws attention to the humanity of Jesus. But on the other hand, it also reveals to those with ears to hear that Jesus is equal to God. As the Son of Man, Jesus has the authority to forgive sins (Mk 2.10), is lord of the Sabbath (Mk 2.28), and will come again to judge the living and the dead (Mk 13.26-27; Mt. 19.28; 25.31-33).

The title Son of Man is often understood as a reference to Jesus' human nature (in contrast to the title Son of God). This is not the full meaning of the title. It refers to Jesus both as a human being and as a heavenly being who shares the authority of God.

Biblical scholars have divided the Son of Man sayings in the Synoptic Gospels into three groups: (1) those focusing on his authority during his earthly life (e.g. Mk 2.10, 28; Lk. 19.10); (2) those concerning his suffering, death, and resurrection (e.g. Mk 8.31; 10.4); and (3) those focusing on his future glory (e.g. Mk 8.38; 13.26; 14.62; Mt. 19.28; 25.31). The theme that unites all the sayings is the question of authority. The earthly Jesus demonstrates his authority (1); his authority is rejected, which leads to his suffering (2); but his authority is vindicated and he returns in glory (3).

Jesus as the Son of the Father

We have seen that Jesus is so close to God that it is difficult to distinguish the two. But that does not mean that Jesus and the God of the Old Testament are one and the same. Even though Jesus takes God's place in the New Testament, he is clearly a different person. He prays to God the Father in heaven (Mk 14.36; Mt. 11.25-26) and talks about his relationship to him (Mt. 11.27). Jesus explains the nature of this relationship when he calls himself the Son of the Father (Mk 13.32; Mt. 11.27; Jn 5.19; 17.1).

The very fact that Jesus calls God Father and even the fact that he can be called God's son does not make him different from human beings who are God's people. They also pray to God as Father (Mt. 6.9; Rom. 8.15; Gal. 4.6), and they are also sons and daughters of God (Rom. 8.14; Gal. 3.26; 4.6). But the nature of Jesus' sonship is different. He explains it in Mt. 11.27: "All things have been committed to me by my Father. No one knows the Son except the Father, and no one knows the Father except the Son and those to whom the Son chooses to reveal him." The New Testament scholar Ulrich Luz comments very well on this verse: "The knowledge here spoken of is knowledge of like by like." What Jesus says here sets him apart from all other human beings. He knows God in a way that no one else does, and God knows him in a way that no one else does. Both the Father and the Son stand at a different level than human beings. No one is able to know them, except through revelation. The Son is the one who gives this revelation, just as God is the one who gives the revelation of himself in the Old Testament (Exod. 33.11-23; Num. 12.1-8). Jesus is therefore God's Son in a unique sense. All Christians have a relationship to God as sons and daughters, but only Jesus is God's Son in the sense that he is equal to God.

God himself also verifies that Jesus is his Son. At Jesus' baptism, God spoke to him from heaven: "You are my Son, whom I love; with you I am well pleased" (Mk 1.11). This sentence quotes at least three passages from the Old Testament. The first is God's words to the messianic king in Psalm 2.7: "You are my son." The second is what God says to Abraham about Isaac in Genesis 22.2, 12, 16: "your only son, whom you love." The third is God's words to the Suffering Servant in Isaiah 42.1: "my chosen one in whom I delight." By combining all these Old Testament passages, God makes it clear that Jesus is his unique Son and that he fulfills a number of Old Testament promises. He is the Messiah, the fulfillment of the promises to Abraham, and Isaiah's Suffering Servant, who suffers on behalf of his people (Isa. 53.4-5, 12).

At the transfiguration on the mountain, Peter, James, and John could see Jesus in his heavenly glory. At this event, God once again declared who Jesus is: "This is my Son, whom I love. Listen to him!" (Mk 9.7). The words resemble those from Jesus' baptism, but instead of quoting from Isaiah 42.1, God quotes from Deuteronomy 18.15. He also identifies Jesus as the prophet like Moses.

That Jesus is God's Son means that he is completely obedient to him. He put his own will completely aside, as we see in the garden of Gethsemane, when he prayed to his Father: "everything is possible for you. Take this cup from me. Yet not what I will, but what you will" (Mk 14.36).

In the New Testament, "Son of God" is one of the most important titles for Jesus. Mark's Gospel introduces Jesus as the Son of God (Mk 1.1, 11), and the whole Gospel leads up to the point when Jesus dies and the Roman officer exclaims: "Surely this man was the Son of God!" (Mk 15.39). In the context of Mark's Gospel, this officer is the first human being who makes this declaration. (God makes it at the baptism and the transfiguration, and the demons also know that Jesus is God's son; 3.11.) In this way, Mark ties Jesus' sonship to his suffering and death. It was at the cross that Jesus' sonship was revealed, even to a Gentile!

In Matthew's Gospel, the disciples come to recognize that Jesus was the Son of God when he came walking to them on the water of Lake Galilee. When they made this confession, they also worshiped him (Mt. 14.33). Since God is the only one who should be worshiped (Mt. 4.10), this event shows that Jesus' sonship is unique. He is the Son, who is equal to God and who may be worshiped like him.

Luke explains that Jesus is God's Son from his birth (Lk. 1.32). This means that Jesus' sonship is different from that of Israel's kings. The king in Israel could be called God's son because God given him a special task: to be the king of his people. But Jesus was not the son of God only because he had been given such a task. Jesus was God's Son because of who he was. He was God's Son already when he was born.

Wisdom Christology and Preexistence

Another way to explain Jesus' relationship to God is to use the Old Testament teaching about God's Wisdom. God's Wisdom is an attribute or characteristic of God. But in some poetic passages in the book of Proverbs, God's Wisdom appears to be a person. In Proverbs 8.22-36, God's Wisdom is speaking: "The Lord possessed me at the beginning of his work, the first of his acts of old" (Prov. 8.22 ESV). (Some translations render this verse: "The Lord created me . . ." but that is misleading. The Hebrew word that means create is *bara*, but that word is not used here. Instead, the Hebrew text has *qana*, which normally means "buy" or "acquire." *Qana* can also mean "possess"; Isa. 1.3.) This does not mean that God's Wisdom is a separate person from God; Proverbs 8.22-36 uses a poetic way of speaking about an attribute of God. The point of the passage is to say that creation is the work of God's Wisdom: "then I was beside him, like a master workman" (Prov. 8.30 ESV). As a poetic expression, this is a way the Old Testament makes a distinction within the Godhead: God and his Wisdom.

Jewish writings from the time between the Old and the New Testaments show a great interest in God's Wisdom. They explain how God's Wisdom represents the fullness of God's glory. "For [wisdom] is a breath of the power of God, and a pure emanation of the glory of the Almighty . . . For she is a reflection of eternal light, a spotless mirror of the working of God, and an image of his goodness" (Wisdom of Solomon 7.25, 26). The Jews thought that this Wisdom came to live in Israel by the law of Moses and in the temple (The Wisdom of Jesus Son of Sirach 24.8).

In several sayings, Jesus implies that there is a close connection between himself and God's Wisdom. In Matthew 12.42, he mentions Solomon's wisdom, and adds that "now one greater than Solomon is here." In Matthew 11.19, he claims that "wisdom is proved right by her actions." The actions he is referring to are the actions of John the Baptist and himself. When Jesus says that no one knows the Son except the Father (Mt. 11.27), it also sounds a lot like what Job says about God and his Wisdom (Job 28.20-28).

When Jesus approaches Jerusalem, he has some very striking things to say: "Jerusalem, Jerusalem, you who kill the prophets and stone those sent to you, how often I have longed to gather your children together, as a hen gathers her chicks under her wings, and you were not willing" (Lk. 13.34). Jesus' ministry was mostly in Galilee, and he had only been to Jerusalem a few times. It is therefore strange that he would say: "how often I have longed to gather your children together." These words are even more peculiar when Jesus also refers to the killing of the prophets. It seems that Jesus speaks as the one who sent the prophets to Jerusalem, even though that happened hundreds of years before Jesus was born. The saying has a lot in common with Luke 11.49, where Jesus says that God's Wisdom was sending prophets and apostles to Jerusalem.

All of these passages show that there is a very close connection between Jesus and God's Wisdom. In light of Luke 13.34 especially, one might wonder if Jesus and God's Wisdom are one and the same. But Jesus never says that he is God's Wisdom. That would be misleading. For God's Wisdom is not a person in his own right, like Jesus is. Instead, Jesus uses Wisdom language in order to explain that he is just as intimately related to God as God's Wisdom is. Just as Wisdom is inseparable from God himself, so is Jesus inseparable from God. You cannot have God without God's Wisdom. And you cannot have God the Father without his Son. The two belong together as one.

It is important to remember that the word Trinity did not exist at the time when the New Testament was written. (The first person to use it was the Latin Church Father Tertullian early in the third century CE.) Wisdom language was the language that was available to Jesus and the authors of the New Testament when they needed to talk about distinctions within the Godhead, even though God is one.

106   Introducing Biblical Theology

The apostle Paul also uses Wisdom language to explain who Jesus is. We see a good example of that in 1 Corinthians 8.6: "for us there is but one God, the Father, from whom all things came and for whom we live; and there is but one Lord, Jesus Christ, through whom all things came and through whom we live." Paul is here quoting from Deuteronomy 6.4, where Moses says: "Hear, O Israel: The Lord our God, the Lord is one." Paul takes this Israelite confession of the one God and expands it in a very remarkable way. This confession contains two names for God: Lord and God. Paul takes the second name, God, and explains it with the phrase: "the Father, from whom all things came and for whom we live." Then he takes the first name, the Lord (Yahweh), and explains it like this: "Jesus Christ, through whom all things came and through whom we live." In other words, the two major names by which God was known in the Old Testament refer to God as the Father and as Jesus Christ, respectively. Paul's confession of Jesus Christ as Lord is further explained by the use of Wisdom language. As we have already seen above, Proverbs 8.22-36 and later Jewish tradition explained that God used his Wisdom to create the world.

In Colossians 1.15-20, Paul also dwells on the idea of Jesus as God's agent in creation. In this passage, he says that "the Son is the image of the invisible God, the firstborn over all creation" (v. 15). These titles could also be used for God's Wisdom (see above), and they were therefore a way of saying that Jesus is one with God. That Jesus is the firstborn must not be understood literally, as if there was a time when Jesus was born. The word "firstborn" had a wide range of meaning. Since the firstborn was the heir and the most important child, the word "firstborn" came to be used as a term for something that is the preeminent and the best. That Jesus is the firstborn over all creation means that he is the superior one (see also Ps. 89.27). It does not mean that Jesus is part of creation, as the following verse shows: "For in him all things were created: things in heaven and on earth, visible and invisible, whether thrones or powers or rulers or authorities; all things have been created through him and for him" (v. 16). Everything was created through Jesus. Unless Jesus created himself, he can therefore not have been created. The Old Testament and Jewish tradition held that everything was created through God's Wisdom. Paul explains that this role truly belongs to Jesus, who is just as divine as God's own Wisdom.

But Paul does not say that Jesus *is* God's Wisdom. The verse where Paul comes close to saying that is 1 Corinthians 1.30: "you are in Christ Jesus, who has become for us wisdom from God—that is, our righteousness, holiness

Table 8.2 Wisdom language used to characterize Jesus

	Jesus	Wisdom
Preexistent	In the beginning was the Word, and the Word was with God, and the Word was God. He was with God in the beginning (Jn 1.1-2). He is before all things (Col. 1.17a).	The Lord possessed me at the beginning of his work, the first of his acts of old (Prov. 8.22). Before the ages, in the beginning, he created me, and for the ages I shall not cease to be" (Sirach 24.9).
Agent at creation	Through him all things were made; without him nothing was made that has been made (Jn 1.3). There is but one Lord, Jesus Christ, through whom all things came and through whom we live (1 Cor. 8.6). For in him all things were created: things in heaven and on earth, visible and invisible, whether thrones or powers or rulers or authorities; all things have been created through him and for him (Col 1.16). In these last days he has spoken to us by his Son, whom he appointed heir of all things, and through whom also he made the universe (Heb. 1.2).	When he established the heavens, I was there... then I was beside him, like a master workman (Prov. 8.27a, 30a). For wisdom, the fashioner of all things, taught me (Wisdom of Solomon 7.22a).
God's image	The Son is the image of the invisible God, the firstborn over all creation (Col. 1.15). The Son is the radiance of God's glory and the exact representation of his being, sustaining all things by his powerful word (Heb. 1.3a).	For [wisdom] is a breath of the power of God, and a pure emanation of the glory of the Almighty... For she is a reflection of eternal light, a spotless mirror of the working of God, and an image of his goodness" (Wisdom of Solomon 7.23, 26). For she is a breath of the power of God, and a pure emanation of the glory of the Almighty (Wisdom of Solomon 7.25a).
Dwelling on earth	The Word became flesh and made his dwelling among us (Jn 1.14a).	Then the Creator of all things gave me a command, and my Creator chose the place for my tent. He said, "Make your dwelling in Jacob, and in Israel receive your inheritance" (Sirach 24.8).

and redemption." But this does not mean that Jesus is wisdom, just as it does not mean that Jesus is righteousness, holiness, and redemption. Jesus is a person. The verse in 1 Corinthians 1.30 is rather a very emphatic way of saying what Jesus gives us, and that we have these gifts as long as we remain in Jesus. They are not gifts that we enjoy independently of Jesus himself, as if he could give us these gifts and then leave us alone. It is when we have Jesus that we also have these gifts.

When Paul combines the idea of Jesus as God's Son with Wisdom language (Col. 1.15), it means that Jesus as God's Son is equally eternal as God himself. "He is before all things," Paul explains in Col. 1.17. Biblical scholars refer to this idea as Christ's preexistence (see also Rom. 8.3; Gal. 4.4-5). This is an important concept in John's writings (see below). Peter's first letter also presupposes the idea that Christ is preexistent. Peter explains that Christ was active at the time of the Old Testament. It was the Spirit of Christ that was in the prophets and testified to his future sufferings (1.10-12; see also 1.20).

To Paul, Christ is God's preexistent Son, and the title "Son of God" is a very important Christological title for him. The book of Acts sums up his earliest preaching as a proclamation of Jesus as God's Son (9.20), and Paul uses it at important points in his letters (1 Thess. 1.9-10; Gal. 4.4-5; Rom. 1.3-4; Col. 1.13-20). Paul also combines the title with Wisdom language and references to Christ's preexistence. In that way, he makes it clear that Jesus was God's unique, preexistent, and eternal Son. Jesus' sonship refers to his divine nature.

The epistle to the Hebrews also uses Wisdom language to explain the significance of Jesus' sonship. Jesus was God's agent of creation (1.2), and he is "the radiance of God's glory and the exact representation of his being" (1.3). This is how the Old Testament and the Jewish tradition described God's Wisdom (see above). The author of Hebrews have combined these ideas with the conviction that Jesus' resurrection is the fulfillment of Psalm 110.1 (Heb. 1.3). In other words, Jesus is a Messiah who is one with God. Christ is therefore greater than all the servants of God in the Old Testament. Because he is the Son, he is greater than the angels (1.5-14). He is also greater than Moses, who only was a servant (3.2-6). Hebrews later compares Jesus to Melchizedek, in order to show that Jesus was God's eternal Son (5.6; 7.13, 15-17). (Melchizedek was not himself eternal. The point in the epistle to the Hebrews is that Scripture does not tell us anything about Melchizedek's ancestors, not that he did not have any.) When the epistle to the Hebrews spends so much time establishing Jesus' eternal sonship, the purpose is to explain that the salvation he has brought us is absolutely certain and perfect. It is therefore of the utmost importance that we do not reject this gift (4.14-15).

That Jesus is God's eternal and unique Son is the source of great comfort to Christians. It means that Christ, our savior, is also the one who rules as king over the entire universe (Col. 1.13-17; 1 Cor. 15.23-28). Christians therefore do not need to be afraid of any other powers, spiritual or physical. Christ is over them all.

Christ's sonship also tells us about the nature of our relationship to God. Through Christ, we have been given the same kind of relationship to God as Jesus has. We relate to him as sons, just like Jesus (Gal. 4.4-7; Rom. 8.14-17). (This does not mean that we are equal to God, as Jesus is. The correspondence between our sonship and his concerns our relationship to God; it does not concern our nature.)

We find Paul's most detailed teaching on Christ's preexistence in Philippians 2.6-8. Paul here praises Jesus as the one "who, being in very nature God, did not consider equality with God something to be used to his own advantage" (v. 6). It is here clear that Christ's preexistence is of a very different kind than for example that of the prophets. They were also preexistent in the sense that they existed in the mind of God, since God knows about everything in advance (Ps. 139.16; Jer. 1.5). But Jesus was more than a thought in God's mind. He was a person who was able to make active choices on his own. He chose not to take advantage of his position as God's equal, but made himself nothing (v. 7). Paul expresses the same idea in 2 Corinthians 8.9: "For you know the grace of our Lord Jesus Christ, that though he was rich, yet for your sake he became poor, so that you through his poverty might become rich." It was Jesus' own choice to become poor when he was rich. In Philippians 2.6, Paul explains exactly what kind of riches Jesus had. He was "in very nature God." The Greek word that here is translated "very nature" is *morfe*. This word can also be used for the heavenly appearance of God (Philo, *Life of Moses* 1.66). But the word concerns more than the outward appearance. It refers to the form that expresses the being that underlies it. In the next line, Paul uses the expression "equality with God" to explain precisely how Jesus shared God's form or nature. Jesus was equal to God in glory.

Paul's point in Philippians 2.6-8 is that Jesus did not make use of this status for his own good. He was "in very nature God," and he took "the very nature of a servant" (vv. 6-7). In many translations, the first line in v. 7 says that Jesus "emptied himself" (NRSV). Many scholars have understood this to mean that Jesus abandoned his divine attributes when he became a human being. They claim that when Jesus became a human being, he was no longer all-knowing and all-powerful like God. But Paul does not mean to say that Jesus left some of his divinity behind in heaven. His point is that Jesus did not make anything of these qualities for his own benefit. The meaning is explained in the other expressions Paul uses: "taking the very nature of a servant," "being made in human likeness," "he humbled himself," and "becoming obedient to death—even death on a cross!" (vv. 7-8).

Lord

Christ's humiliation is the way that leads to glorification. In Philippians 2.9, Paul continues: "Therefore God exalted him to the highest place and gave him the name that is above every name." The name that is above every name is the name of God himself. It is the name that God revealed to Moses, when Moses asked him to tell him his name. "God said to Moses, 'I am who I am. This is what you are to say to the Israelites: "I AM has sent me to you."' God also said to Moses, 'Say to the Israelites, "The Lord, the God of your fathers—the God of Abraham, the God of Isaac and the God of Jacob—has sent me to you"'" (Exod. 3.14-15). In the Hebrew text, God's name "Lord" is Yahweh. When the Old Testament was translated into Greek, this word was translated *kurios*, which means "Lord." Modern translators therefore render God's name Yahweh as "Lord," usually with capital letters: "LORD." In Philippians 2.11, Paul confirms that this name has been given to Jesus when he announces that "every tongue [will] acknowledge that Jesus Christ is Lord." Paul is here quoting from Isaiah 45.23, which refers to the day when "every knee will bow" before the Lord God. Through his humiliation and his suffering for our sins, Jesus has demonstrated that he is the one who bears God's own name.

"Lord" (or *kurios* in Greek) therefore becomes a very important title for Jesus in the New Testament. This word could be used as a polite way of speaking to someone (with a different form of the Greek word: *kurie*). Used in this way, the word is not very different from the English word "Sir" (Mt. 13.27; Lk. 13.8; Jn 4.11 etc.). But the form *kurios* is usually much more significant. When the Roman emperors demanded to be worshiped as God, they also used the title "Lord and God" for themselves. In the Bible, "Lord" is used as the name for God. The meaning of this name was therefore easily understood by both Jews and Gentiles. Paul could sum up his entire message as a message of Jesus as Lord (2 Cor. 4.5; Col. 2.6). The earliest Christian confession was

"Jesus is Lord" (Rom. 10.9; 1 Cor. 12.3). It means that Jesus is the one who bears God's name.

The use of this title for Jesus goes back to Jesus himself. In Mark 12.35-37, Jesus quotes from Psalm 110.1: "The Lord said to my Lord: 'Sit at my right hand until I put your enemies under your feet.'" Jesus also alludes to this verse at his trial before the Jewish Council (Mk 14.62). Psalm 110 quickly became very important to the early church because it explained what happened after Jesus' resurrection: Jesus had ascended and taken his seat at the right hand of God (Acts 2.34-35; Rom. 8.34). This Psalm lies behind all the New Testament references to Jesus sitting at God's right hand.

The insight that Jesus is truly Lord had a great influence on the way the first Christians read the Old Testament. They read many passages that originally spoke about the Lord God and understood them to be speaking about the Lord Jesus (Rom. 10.13; Phil. 4.5; 1 Pet. 2.3). In the Old Testament, the "day of the Lord" was the day when God would come and judge the world (Joel 1.15; Amos 5.18-20; Mal. 4.5). But in the New Testament, the "day of the Lord" is the day when Jesus will come again to judge the living and the dead (1 Cor. 1.8; 5.5; 1 Thess. 5.2). Because Jesus is their Lord, the first Christians could pray to him (1 Thess. 3.11; 2 Thess. 2.16-17; 3.5, 16), just as they prayed to their Father in heaven.

The name represents the nature and the character of a person. That Jesus bears God's name means that he is fully divine. Paul therefore affirms that "in Christ all the fullness of the Deity lives in bodily form" (Col. 2.9).

For Luke, "Lord" was perhaps the most important of all of Jesus' titles. In the first chapters of Luke's Gospel, he uses the title both for God (1.6 etc.) and for Jesus (1.43). What Luke says about John the Baptist is especially interesting: "He will go on before the Lord" (1.17). But who is this Lord? The words are an allusion to Malachi 3.1, which speaks of a messenger that would go before God. But, in the context of Luke's Gospel, it is clear that John goes before Jesus. This is a subtle way in which Luke shows the unity of God and Jesus. They both share the name "Lord."

God

When Jesus is called Lord, it is only a small step to call him by the name "God" (*theos*) as well. When this name is less common in the New Testament, the reason is probably that Christians usually reserved this name for the Father and used the name "Lord" for Jesus (1 Cor. 8.6). But the Father and Son are one, and the New Testament can therefore also call Jesus God. The clearest examples of this are found in John 1.1; 20.28; and Hebrews 1.8-9.

John begins his Gospel with the words: "In the beginning was the Word, and the Word was with God, and the Word was God" (Jn 1.1). As we learn from v. 14, the Word is none other than Jesus. Towards the end of his Gospel, John quotes the confession of Thomas: "My Lord and my God!" (Jn 20.28).

In Hebrews 1.8-9, we find a quotation from Psalm 45.6-7: "Your throne, O God, will last for ever and ever." The way the author of Hebrews understands this Psalm, "God" here refers to Jesus.

In 1 John 5.20, the apostle declares that "he is the true God and eternal life." From the context, this "true God" may refer either to the Father or to the Son. But the previous sentence ends with the words "his Son Jesus Christ." John most likely intends the last sentence as an explanation of who Jesus Christ is: "he is the true God and eternal life."

Titus 2.13 also refers to "our great God and Savior, Jesus Christ," and 2 Peter 1.1 mentions "the righteousness of our God and Savior Jesus Christ." The Greek grammar in both of these verses requires that the names "God" and "Jesus" do not refer to two different persons, but to one and the same: Jesus Christ.

John 1.18 is a difficult verse. The oldest and most reliable manuscripts refer to the "only God," which results in the translation: "the only God, who is at

Table 8.3 The names of God given to Jesus

Lord/Yahweh	"My Lord and my God!" (Jn 20.28b).
	There is but one Lord, Jesus Christ, through whom all things came and through whom we live (1 Cor. 8.6b).
I AM	He said to them, "I Am. Don't be afraid" (Jn 6.20 CEB).
	If you don't believe that I Am, you will die in your sins (Jn 8.24 CEB).
	I assure you," Jesus replied, "before Abraham was, I Am" (Jn 8.58 CEB).
	When he said, "I Am," they shrank back and fell to the ground (Jn 18.6 CEB).
God	In the beginning was the Word, and the Word was with God, and the Word was God (Jn 1.1).
	"My Lord and my God!" (Jn 20.28b).
	Theirs are the patriarchs, and from them is traced the human ancestry of the Messiah, who is God over all, forever praised! Amen (Rom. 9.5).
	Your throne, O God, will last for ever and ever (Heb. 1.8b).
The Alpha and the Omega	I am the Alpha and the Omega, the First and the Last, the Beginning and the End (Rev. 22.13).

the Father's side, he has made him known" (ESV). "The only God, who is at the Father's side" is such a strange expression that some of the later scribes who copied the biblical manuscripts probably thought it had to be wrong. They therefore seem to have changed it to "the One and Only Son—the One who is at the Father's side" (HCSB). But the original text almost certainly did not have the word "Son" here. Instead, it used the name "God" for Jesus.

We have a similar problem in Acts 20.28. Here, the oldest manuscripts are divided between two readings: "the church of God, which he bought with his own blood" (TNIV) and "the Church of God which he bought with the blood of his own Son" (NJB). The second reading is probably not original. If it were, it would probably not have been changed. But the first reading is strange, and the scribes may have thought the meaning was "his Son's blood." But if the original text refers to "his own blood," it means that "God" in the beginning of the sentence must refer to Jesus. Jesus, not the Father, was the one who "bought the church with his own blood."

The earliest text that most probably refers to Jesus as God is found in Romans 9.5 (from 57 CE). But this text can be interpreted in two different ways, depending on where we understand the sentence to end. The earliest biblical manuscripts did not include any kind of punctuation, so the interpreter must decide how to divide the sentences. At the end of Romans 9.5, there are two major possibilities: "from their race, according to the flesh, is the Christ who is God over all, blessed forever. Amen" (ESV) and "from them, according to the flesh, is the Messiah. God who is over all be blessed forever. Amen" (NAB). The second interpretation is unlikely because it breaks up the flow of Paul's explanation. Paul most probably meant to say that Christ is God over all.

The Last Adam

We have seen that Paul had a very strong understanding of Jesus as God. But this does not mean that he overlooked the fact that Jesus was a human being just like us. Paul explains that Christ corresponds to Adam as the last Adam (1 Cor. 15.44-49; see also Rom. 5.12-21; 1 Cor. 15.21-22). To understand what Paul says about the last Adam, we must see it in relation to Old Testament prophecies about the new creation (Isa. 65.17-24). Paul explains that these prophecies are already fulfilled in Jesus Christ (2 Cor. 5.14-17; Gal. 6.14-16). Just as Adam was the beginning of the old humanity, so is Christ therefore the beginning of the new humanity. Adam was created to enjoy life and communion with God, but he failed to attain this goal. But God restored what Adam had destroyed.

Adam was created in the image of God (Gen. 1.27), which means that he was going to rule the earth on God's behalf (Gen. 1.28). The new creation restores this image; Jesus Christ is the image of God (2 Cor. 4.4; Col. 1.15). Those who are in Christ also partake in the new creation (2 Cor. 5.17). They are therefore renewed to the same image, the image of God, which is the image of his Son (Rom. 8.29; 2 Cor. 3.18).

Other Titles for Jesus

The most important titles for Jesus are Messiah (Christ), Lord, Son of God, and Son of Man. We have also seen that he can be called God and the last Adam. Other titles that are used for Jesus include prophet and servant. Jesus is the prophet because he is the fulfillment of God's promise to Moses: "I will raise up for them a prophet like you" (Deut. 18.18; see also Mk 9.7; Acts 3.22; 7.37). Among the evangelists, Luke places the strongest emphasis on Jesus as a prophet. Like the prophets, Jesus was rejected by his own, and he had to die in Jerusalem (Lk. 4.24; 13.33).

The Gospels show that the crowds identified Jesus as the prophet (Mt. 21.11; Lk. 7.16; Jn 6.14; 7.40), but they also show that he is more than a prophet. When Luke describes Jesus as a prophet (7.11-17), he clarifies that Jesus is a prophet who is also Lord (7.13).

In the book of Acts, Jesus is also called God's servant (3.13, 26; 4.27, 30). The background is the four songs about the Suffering Servant in the prophet Isaiah (42.1-9; 49.1-7; 50.4-9; 52.13-53.12). Jesus fulfilled these prophecies in his ministry and his death (Mt. 8.17; 12.15-21; Lk. 22.37; Jn 12.38).

Christological Development?

Many scholars believe that the Christology of the early church developed from "low" to "high" Christology. When the first Christians met Jesus after his resurrection, they understood that he had to be the Messiah. Later, when they reflected on Jesus' life, they concluded that he had to have been the Messiah also during his ministry. After even more theological reflection, they saw Jesus as the Messiah already when he was born, and in the end, they realized that he had to have been God's Son from eternity, and began to refer to him as preexistent. According to these scholars, this development can be followed through various passages in the New Testament. The first stage is found in Peter's sermon in Acts 2.36, Paul's sermon in Acts 13.33, and Paul's confession in Romans 1.3-4 (which is thought to be earlier than Paul). The second stage is found in the Gospel of Mark, where Jesus is seen as God's Son at his baptism and his Transfiguration. Matthew and Luke represent the next stage, where Jesus is God's Son from his birth. The final stage is seen in John's Gospel, where Jesus is the eternal Word.

We have already seen that Jesus himself indirectly explained that he was God's equal. His preexistence is implicit in his words in Luke 13.34. There was therefore no need for a Christological "development" such as the one outlined above. But the early Christians needed to realize the full impact of what Jesus had already told them, and this realization was a consequence of their encounter with Jesus after his resurrection.

The passages that are interpreted as early Christological statements about Jesus becoming the Messiah are better understood in a different way. In Romans 1.4, Paul does not say that Jesus became God's Son, but that he "was appointed the Son of God in power." The verse refers to the position of power that Jesus entered after his temporary humiliation. Acts 2.36 says that "God has made this Jesus, whom you crucified, both Lord and Messiah." This verse must be read in light of its context. The book of Acts and the Gospel of Luke were written by the same author, who made it clear that Jesus was Lord already before he was born (Lk. 1.43). When he describes Peter's betrayal, he comments that Peter "remembered the word the Lord had spoken to him" (Lk. 22.61). This is the last time Luke uses the title "Lord" before Jesus' resurrection (24.3, 34) because this event refers to the ultimate rejection of Jesus' Lordship by human beings, even by one of his closest disciples. But God has never rejected Jesus, and the resurrection demonstrates that fact. That is the point of Acts 2.36: even though human beings rejected Jesus' Lordship and nailed him to the cross, God has verified that Jesus is both Lord and Messiah by raising him from the dead. Acts 13.33 can be understood in a similar way: in the resurrection, God has claimed Jesus as his Son.

Johannine Christology

When we turn to the writings of the apostle John, we find the most elaborate Christology in the New Testament. In contrast to the Synoptic Gospels, John begins his Gospel with a view from eternity. In his prologue (1.1-18), he makes extensive use of Wisdom language. But also John avoids identifying Jesus with God's Wisdom. Instead, he calls Jesus the Word: "In the beginning was the Word, and the Word was with God, and the Word was God. He was with God in the beginning. Through him all things were made; without him nothing was made that has been made. In him was life, and that life was the light of all people. The light shines in the darkness, and the darkness has not overcome it" (Jn 1.1-4). This Word has associations of the word that God spoke at creation (Gen. 1.3; see also Ps. 33.9) and God's Wisdom. The Word is preexistent (Jn 1.1a; Prov. 8.22), and it was present with God (1.1b-2; Prov. 8.30) as God's agent in creation (1.3; Prov. 3.19; 8.30). This Word gives life and light to people (1.4; Prov. 8.35). Human beings reject the Word (1.10-11; Prov. 1.29), but the Word gives life to those who receive it (1.12).

Most of what John says about the Word in 1.1-13 is something that many Jews could have said about God's Wisdom. But 1.14 introduces an idea that would have been much more difficult to accept: "The Word became flesh and tabernacled among us" (ISV). John here alludes to the tabernacle, when God made his dwelling with Israel in the wilderness. At that time, God dwelled among his people in a tent. But when Jesus was born, God dwelled among us in a human being: Jesus Christ. In the Old Testament, the people depended on their leaders and on the sanctuary for God's presence (ch. 5). But now, he was personally right there among them. He could be heard, seen, and even touched (1 Jn 1.1). Theologians refer to this miracle as the incarnation.

In this way, John explains that God has revealed himself to us more directly than what he did in the Old Testament. John's teaching also contrasts with what many Jews believed. The Jewish wisdom teacher named Jesus son of Sirach identified God's Wisdom with the law of Moses. He taught that God's Wisdom tabernacled in Israel (The Wisdom of Jesus Son of Sirach 24.8). But John affirms that the Word tabernacled among us by becoming flesh (1.14). Jesus is therefore able to show us who God is. In the Old Testament, the saints longed to see God's face (Pss 11.7; 42.2), and even Moses was only allowed to see him from behind (Exod. 33.20-23). But Jesus Christ is God who has become a human being, so now it is possible for us to see God. "No one has ever seen God; the only God, who is at the Father's side, he has made him known" (Jn 1.18 ESV; 1 Jn 3.2).

In many other subtle ways, John also shows that Jesus fulfills what the Old Testament has to say about God's Wisdom. He brings the perfect revelation of God. His first sign was to make water into wine (2.11), and wine was known as a symbol of God's Wisdom (Prov. 9.4-5). When he gives the living water (4.10-14; 7.37-38) and proclaims himself as the bread of life (6.35), he fulfills the function of Wisdom (Prov. 13.14; 18.4; The Wisdom of Jesus Son of Sirach 24.21). However, wisdom ideas are not fully able to explain who Jesus is. God's Wisdom is an attribute of God, but Jesus is a person in his own right.

Replacement

Jesus is the perfect revelation of God. This revelation is therefore superior to the previous revelation in the Old Testament. John explains it in this way: "For the law was given through Moses; grace and truth came through Jesus Christ" (Jn 1.17). According to John's Gospel, Jesus began his public ministry by cleansing the temple (2.13-22). John explains that he came as the replacement of the temple. God's true dwelling is Jesus himself (2.21).

Throughout John's Gospel, we see that Jesus' words and deeds take place at the Jewish festivals. The meaning is that these Old Testament festivals point forward to Jesus Christ and find their true fulfillment in him. The Sabbath was the Jewish day of rest, and Jesus comes and brings healing on the Sabbath (5.1-47). He is the one who brings true rest.

During Passover (6.1-71), Jesus explains that he is the bread of life (6.35). The Passover reminded Israel of their liberation from Egypt and of how Moses had given them manna in the wilderness. But this was not the true bread from heaven. Instead, the true bread from heaven is Jesus (6.31-35).

At the Feast of Tabernacles (Jn 7.2), the Jews celebrated with water and light ceremonies. The water ceremonies pointed backwards to the water that welled from the rock in the wilderness (Pss 78.15-16; 105.41) and forward to the water of life in the new creation (Ezek. 47.12; Zech. 14.8). During this festival, Jesus announced that he is the source of living water (Jn 7.37-38). In other words, the water in the wilderness pointed forward to him, who provides the water of the new creation. The light ceremonies reminded the Jews of the pillar of fire that had led them in the wilderness (Exod. 13.21). They also pointed forward to the light of the new creation (Zech. 14.7). When Jesus announced himself as "the light of the world" (Jn 8.12), the point is once again that he is the true fulfillment of these Old Testament ideas.

The Feast of Dedication (Jn 10.22) was celebrated in memory of the rededication of the temple. When the ruler of the Seleucid empire (centered in what is now Syria), Antiochus IV Epiphanes, invaded Jerusalem in 167 BCE, he dedicated the temple to the Greek god Zeus. He even erected a statute of Zeus in the Most Holy Place and sacrificed a pig there. Led by Judas Maccabeus, the Jews regained control of the temple in 164 BCE and rededicated the temple to God. During the Feast of Dedication, Jesus explained that he is the one "whom the Father consecrated" (Jn 10.36 ESV). He takes the place of the temple, as the dwelling of God.

Table 8.4 Jesus replaces the old revelation

The law	For the law was given through Moses; grace and truth came through Jesus Christ (Jn 1.17).
The temple	Jesus answered them, "Destroy this temple, and I will raise it again in three days." . . . But the temple he had spoken of was his body (Jn 2.19, 21).
The Sabbath	Then Jesus said to him, "Get up! Pick up your mat and walk." At once the man was cured; he picked up his mat and walked. The day on which this took place was a Sabbath (Jn 5.8-9).
Bread from heaven	Jesus said to them, "Very truly I tell you, it is not Moses who has given you the bread from heaven . . . I am the bread of life" (Jn 6.33, 35).
Water of life	On the last and greatest day of the Festival, Jesus stood and said in a loud voice, "Let anyone who is thirsty come to me and drink. Whoever believes in me, as Scripture has said, rivers of living water will flow from within them (Jn 7.37-38).
The sanctuary	The one whom the Father has sanctified and sent into the world (Jn 10.36 NRSV).

God's Name

As the perfect revelation of God, Jesus has even revealed God's holy name. When God sent Moses to Israel, he told him to say to the Israelites: "I AM has sent me to you" (Exod. 3.14). This is also the way that Jesus made himself known to his disciples when he came to them walking on the water. "He said to them, 'I Am. Don't be afraid'" (Jn 6.20 CEB). Most English translations render Jesus' words as "it is I," which is a possible meaning of the Greek phrase *ego eimi*. But there are good reasons to think that the words mean much more. Jesus is demonstrating to the disciples that he is the one who has the power to walk on water. This is the kind of power that God has (Job 9.8). Jesus is revealing to the disciples that he is "I AM"; he is the one who bears God's name.

Later on, we see the significance of this name. In John 8.24, Jesus tells the Jews: "If you don't believe that I Am, you will die in your sins" (CEB). Unless they believe that Jesus is the one who has God's name, they will not be saved. A few verses later, he says: "when you lift up the Son of Man, then you will realize that I AM" (Jn 8.28 NAB; see also 13.19). Jesus' crucifixion makes it clear that the divine name belongs to him. At the end of the conversation, Jesus uses this name once more: "before Abraham was, I Am" (Jn 8.58 CEB). He does not say "I was," which would be grammatically correct. Instead, he uses the name "I AM," which has associations of God's eternity. The eternal name of God is Jesus' name.

When Jesus is about to be crucified, we get a glimpse of the power of Jesus' eternal name. Answering the officials that came for him, Jesus told them "I AM." "When he said to them, 'I AM,' they turned away and fell to the ground" (Jn 18.6 NAB). Jesus only had to pronounce his divine name to make the soldiers fall to the ground.

John's Gospel makes it very clear that Jesus is fully God. He shares in all the glory of God. The picture that John paints of Jesus is summed up in the confession of Thomas: "My Lord and my God!" (Jn 20.28).

Son of God

We have already seen that Jesus in the Synoptic Gospels explains his relationship to God as a relationship between the Father and the Son. This is also the case in the Gospel of John, but this Gospel makes it even clearer that Jesus is God's eternal Son. As the preexistent Son, Jesus shared in the glory of the Father (17.5, 24). The Father sent him into the world (3.17; 17.18), he comes in the Father's name (5.43), and he will return to the Father (13.1-3; 16.28; 20.17).

He is therefore the Father's true representative in the world (13.20; 15.23), and he is completely obedient to the Father's will (4.34; 8.28-29). As the Son, Jesus is equal to the Father, and does the works of the Father (5.17-20): he raises the dead (5.21, 24) and judges the world (5.22, 27-29). His sonship is therefore unique; he is the Father's "one and only Son" (3.16). He is one with the Father (10.30; 17.11) and shares in his glory (1.14). He reveals this glory when he dies on the cross for our sins (Jn 17.1).

There is no contradiction between the idea that Jesus is God's equal (Jn 5.18) and the idea that he obeys the Father in everything. The equality has to do with their nature; their inequality has to do with their function. The Father and the Son are both God, but the Father is the one who sends the Son into the world (not the other way around), and the Son is the one who obeys the Father (not the other way around).

In John's epistles, we find no explanation of Jesus' divine sonship. The Johannine epistles presuppose that Jesus is God's unique Son. Because Jesus is God's Son, the salvation that Jesus has provided is fully dependable (1 Jn 5.20). In his first epistle, John explains that the ultimate test of true Christian faith is whether someone confesses Jesus as God's Son (1 Jn 4.15; 5.12). This warning is directed against a heresy that had some influence in John's churches.

These heretics probably denied the incarnation and claimed that Jesus only appeared to be a human being and only appeared to suffer.

The Book of Revelation

The most important Christological title in the Book of Revelation is the Lamb. John uses this title in a very dramatic way when he describes his heavenly vision in chapter 5. One of the elders announces the Lion of Judah (5.5), which makes us think of a powerful ruler (Gen. 49.9). But when this powerful character shows himself, John sees a Lamb, an animal that rather represents weakness. Further, this Lamb looked as if it had been slain (5.6). In this way, John shows us a paradoxical figure. This Lamb is victorious (14.10; 17.14), but its victory is not won through the demonstration of strength, but through weakness. The victory of the Lamb is won through defeat (12.11).

In the book of Revelation, Jesus also shares the name of God. One of the divine names that occur in Revelation has three different forms: The Alpha and the Omega/The First and the Last/The Beginning and the End (Isa. 41.4; 44.6; 48.12). All together, the different forms of this name occur seven times (if we do not count 2.8, where the name is an echo of 1.17). First, God is the one who bears this name (1.8; 21.6), but it also belongs to Christ (1.17), who is called by this name in all its three forms (22.13).

The book of Revelation also teaches us in a very vivid way that Christ is equal to God. God's throne is the symbol of God's majesty, and this throne is shared by God and the Lamb (22.1). The wrath of God (14.10, 19; 15.1) is also matched by the wrath of the Lamb (6.16).

Some very peculiar grammatical expressions make the same point. In 11.15, John uses the singular form of the verb ("he will reign"), but the subject is "our Lord" and "his Messiah." In 22.3-4, John refers to God and the Lamb with a pronoun in the singular. The unity between them is so complete that together they can be the subject of a verb in the singular or the referent of a singular pronoun. In this subtle way, John shows that God and the Lamb are one.

In his heavenly throne vision, John sees the heavenly host worship God (4.8-11). Immediately afterwards, he sees the Lamb being worshiped in the same way (5.9-12), and then the Lamb is worshiped together with God (5.13).

In a Jewish context, this is most remarkable. The Jews held that there was an absolute distinction between God and all his creatures. No one other than God could be worshiped (Mt. 4.10). Jewish writings that describe the angels in heaven often include warnings against the worship of these angels. The book of Revelation also has two warnings like this (19.10; 22.8-9). The reason is probably that John wants to assure his readers that he stands in the same Jewish tradition regarding worship. When he describes the worship of the Lamb, he does not mean to say that any heavenly beings other than God should be worshiped. When the Lamb is worshiped, the reason is that he and God are one.

The praise that is written down in Revelation 1.5b-6 may therefore be read as an expression of the worship that the church brings to Christ, worship comparable with the worship the angels offer him in heaven: "To him who loves us and has freed us from our sins by his blood, and has made us to be a kingdom and priests to serve his God and Father—to him be glory and power for ever and ever! Amen."

Summary

The New Testament explains that Jesus represents the fulfillment of several Old Testament characters, including the Messiah, the Son of Man, and the Servant of the Lord. But in order to explain who Jesus is, it is not enough to compare him to these Old Testament figures. Jesus also fills the role of God himself. As the Son of God, Jesus is both God's servant and God's equal.

New Testament Christology can be summarized in the confession of Thomas: "My Lord, and my God!" (Jn 20.28). Jesus is himself God and shares his name. He is the eternal, unique Son of God the Father.

God's presence is no longer in the Jerusalem temple; it is now in a person from Nazareth: Jesus. He came to earth to do what human beings were unable to do, as we shall see in the next chapter.

Further Reading

Bauckham, Richard. *Jesus and the God of Israel: God Crucified and Other Studies on the New Testament's Christology of Divine Identity.* Grand Rapids: Eerdmans, 2008.

Fee, Gordon D. *Pauline Christology: An Exegetical-Theological Study.* Peabody: Hendrickson, 2007.

Grindheim, Sigurd. *Christology in the Synoptic Gospels: God or God's Servant?* London: T & T Clark, 2012.

Hurtado, Larry W. *Lord Jesus Christ: Devotion to Jesus in Earliest Christianity*. Grand Rapids: Eerdmans, 2003.

Matera, Frank J. *New Testament Christology*. Louisville: Westminster John Knox, 1999.

Tuckett, Christopher M. *Christology and the New Testament: Jesus and His Earliest Followers*. Louisville: Westminster John Knox, 2001.

Review Questions

How did Jesus understand the Messiah title and how does this understanding shine through in the Synoptic Gospels?

How do the Synoptic Gospels show that Jesus is God's equal?

How does the New Testament use and develop the Old Testament idea of God's Wisdom?

All Christians are God's sons and daughters. How do we know that Jesus is God's Son in a unique sense?

How does John's picture of Jesus differ from that of the Synoptic Gospels?

9

What Human Beings Could Not Do

The Work of God in Christ

Chapter Outline

The Suffering Servant	123
Ransom	125
Passover	126
Victory over Satan	127
Events at Jesus' Death	128
Jesus' Death in Luke's Gospel	129
The Gospel of John	129
Paul	132
Peter	136
Summary	136

As the last Adam, Jesus represented all human beings. As God's unique Son, he also did the works of God. In him, the relationship between God and human beings could be restored. This was the reason why Jesus came to earth, and the New Testament explains how he accomplished this purpose.

The Suffering Servant

Jesus told his disciples many times that he was going to be handed over to death. After Peter's confession, "he began to teach them that the Son of man was destined to suffer grievously, and to be rejected by the elders and the chief priests and the scribes, and to be put to death, and after three days to rise again" (Mk 8.31 NJB). The Greek word that is translated here as "was destined to" (*dei*) is significant. It was God who destined Jesus to suffer, die, and rise again. God's purpose in sending Jesus to the world was to send him to die. According to the Gospels, both the Jewish and the Roman authorities in Jerusalem were responsible for Jesus' death. They convicted him even though he had "done nothing to deserve death" (Lk. 23.15). But everything the authorities did to Jesus was a part of God's plan and purpose.

Mark focuses very clearly on this purpose from the very beginning. The New Testament scholar Martin Kähler has called Mark's Gospel a passion story with a long introduction. The first indication of Jesus' early death comes already in chapter 2. When Jesus forgives the paralyzed man, the teachers of the law thought he was blaspheming (Mk 2.7). Blasphemy should be punished by death (Lev. 24.16). A little later, Jesus calls himself the bridegroom and predicts that the bridegroom will be taken from the disciples (Mk 2.20). Soon afterwards, after Jesus healed a man on the Sabbath, Mark explains that "the Pharisees went out and began to plot with the Herodians how they might kill Jesus" (Mk 3.6).

The most important Old Testament passage that explains why Jesus had to die is the fourth song about the Suffering Servant (Isa. 52.13–53.12). Matthew makes it clear that this prophecy began to be fulfilled already during Jesus' ministry in Galilee. "Many who were demon-possessed were brought to him, and he drove out the spirits with a word and healed all the sick. This was to fulfill what was spoken through the prophet Isaiah: 'He took up our infirmities and bore our diseases'" (Mt. 8.16-17). The diseases in question must be physical, not spiritual diseases, for the context is about Jesus healing physical sickness. Sin and sickness are related, but we must not think that there is a direct connection between individual sickness and individual sin (Jn 9.2-3). But on a more general level, the fact that there is sickness in the world is a result of sin. Death, and therefore sickness, came into the world because of sin (Rom. 5.12). When he healed the sick, Jesus therefore reversed the consequences of sin.

However, this does not mean that all people or all Christians can experience freedom from sickness. Jesus' miracles did not benefit all people (Lk. 4.23-37), and we know that an apostle like Paul was constantly plagued with physical infirmities (Gal. 4.13, 15; 6.11).

Matthew 8.17 does not say so directly, but the reason why Jesus could take away sickness was that he came to take away sin. This much we can understand both from the context of the fourth Servant Song (Isa. 53.5, 8, 10-12) and from the context of Matthew's Gospel (Mt. 1.21; 9.5-6).

Ransom

When Jesus talks to his disciples about the importance of serving one another, he explains: "For even the Son of Man did not come to be served, but to serve, and to give his life as a ransom for many" (Mk 10.45). This is the most direct statement we find in the Synoptic Gospels regarding the significance of Jesus' death. Jesus would give his life as a ransom. A ransom is a price that people pay to set themselves or someone else free.

The payment of a ransom or redemption served several important functions in Israel. In connection with the census, Moses commanded all Israelites to "give a ransom for their lives to the Lord, so that no plague [might] come upon them for being registered" (Exod. 30.12 NRSV). As all the firstborn belonged to the Lord, it was also necessary to bring a ransom for the firstborn children in Israel (Num. 3.45-48). When a person became poor and had to sell himself or herself as a slave, a family member could buy them free. The family member then had to pay a price for redemption (Lev. 25.48-52). When God is called a redeemer in the Old Testament, the background is the institution of paying a ransom or redemption price to set someone free. As Israel's redeemer, God delivers the people from bondage (Isa. 41.14; 43.14). That Jesus gave his life as a ransom therefore means that he died so that we could go free. He gave his life for our life.

In this saying (Mk 10.45), Jesus did not say explicitly what he came to set us free from. But when he said that he would "give his life as a ransom for many," the idea is probably based on Isaiah 53.11-12. According to these verses, the "servant will justify many" (53.11), "he poured out his life," and "he bore the sin of many" (53.12). If Isaiah 53.10-12 lies behind Mark 10.45, then the point is that Jesus' death was also "an offering for sin" (Isa. 53.10). Because he gave his life as an offering for sin, Jesus could set us free from our sin and its consequences. The words "for many" is a Hebrew expression that means "for all" (see also 1 Tim. 2.6). Jesus' death was a sacrifice for all people's sins. But this does not mean that all people are forgiven for their sins (see below).

Table 9.1 Isaiah 53.10-12 in Mark 10.45

Mark 10.45	Isaiah 53.10-12
For even the Son of Man did not come to be served, but *to serve*, and to *give his life* as a *ransom FOR MANY*.	Yet it was the Lord's will to crush him and cause him to suffer, and though the Lord *makes his life an offering for sin*, he will see his offspring and prolong his days, and the will of the Lord will prosper in his hand. After he has suffered, he will see the light of life and be satisfied; by his knowledge my righteous **servant** will justify *MANY*, and he will bear their iniquities. Therefore I will give him a portion among the great, and he will divide the spoils with the strong, because *he poured out his life unto death*, and was numbered with the transgressors. For he bore the sin *OF MANY*, and made intercession for the transgressors.

Passover

All the Synoptic Gospels describe the Last Supper as a Passover meal (Mk 14.12-16 par.). According to the tradition regarding the Passover, the head of the household would explain the meaning of the meal (Exod. 12.26-27; 13.8). But when Jesus explains the meal to his disciples, he gives it a new meaning. "While they were eating, Jesus took bread, and when he had given thanks, he broke it and gave it to his disciples, saying, 'Take it; this is my body'" (Mk 14.22 par.). In other words, Jesus' own body took the place of the Passover lamb. The meaning of the Passover lamb was that Israel was freed from slavery and death. Ezekiel understood it as a sin offering or purification offering (Ezek. 45.18-19; see also ch. 6). Jesus now explains that his body is the fulfillment of the Passover sacrifice. He gives his life for our lives so that he can set us free from sin and death.

When he had given his disciples the bread, Jesus also took the cup. "When he had given thanks, he gave it to them, and they all drank from it. 'This is my blood of the covenant, which is poured out for many,' he said to them" (Mk 14.23-24 par.). When God made the covenant with Israel on Mount Sinai, the Israelites presented burnt offerings and fellowship offerings. To seal the covenant, Moses splashed half the blood against the altar and sprinkled the other half on the people (Exod. 24.5-8). Jesus' words to the disciples allude to Exodus 24.8: "This is the blood of the covenant that the Lord has made with you in accordance with all these words." In other words, Jesus brings the Sinai covenant to its fulfillment when he gives his life as the sacrifice that seals the new covenant. According to Luke and Paul, Jesus specified that the cup was the new covenant (Lk. 22.20; 1 Cor. 11.25).

In a more general sense, Jesus' words about the cup may also be understood in light of the fourth Servant Song. When he says that his blood "is poured out for many," he fulfills the prophecy in Isaiah 53.11-12, which predicts that the "servant will justify many" (53.11), and "[bear] the sin of many" (53.12). As in Mark 10.45, the meaning is that Jesus gives his life for all.

Victory over Satan

Jesus' sacrifice is also his victory. With his ministry on earth, he establishes the kingdom of God (ch. 8) and defeats Satan. His exorcisms are the decisive proof of his victory over Satan. He explains: "When a strong man, fully armed, guards his own house, his possessions are safe. But when someone stronger attacks and overpowers him, he takes away the armor in which the man trusted and divides up his plunder" (Lk. 11.21-22). The "strong man" is Satan (Lk. 11.18). "Someone stronger" is Jesus, who has now come and overpowered him. As a consequence, "he takes away the armor in which the man trusted and divides up his plunder." This is what happens when Jesus casts out the demons. Satan has already been defeated.

This is why the demons have to flee when Jesus approaches. In Mark 1.24, a demon exclaims: "Have you come to destroy us? I know who you are—the Holy One of God!" There was only one demon present, but the demon knew what was about to happen. Not only this demon, but all demons were about to be destroyed. When Jesus cast out demons, what happened was more than an exorcism. It was the beginning of the ultimate downfall of the evil army.

There is one passage that explains the way in which Jesus establishes the kingdom of God and wins his victory over Satan. That is the passage that describes Jesus' confrontation with Satan in the most detail, the passage about the temptation in the wilderness (Mt. 4.1-11). Satan's temptations aim at the very heart of who Jesus is: the Son of God (Mt. 3.17).

If Jesus is God's Son, Satan claims, he should be able to turn stones into bread (Mt. 4.3). This test ties in with Israel's expectations regarding the Messiah and a prophet like Moses (Deut. 18.18). Many Jews believed that the Messiah would perform a feeding miracle, like Moses had done (Jn 6.14). When Satan challenged Jesus to tell the stones to become bread, he was tempting him to perform a visible sign that most Israelites would recognize as a sign of the

Messiah. By performing the sign, Jesus could have been recognized as the Messiah that Israel expected.

The nature of the second temptation is very similar. By falling down from the temple and being rescued by angels (Mt. 4.6), Jesus would have been seen by all Israel as the one whom God had chosen. If Jesus had given in to these temptations, he could have been hailed as Israel's Messiah without having to suffer crucifixion and death.

Jesus' temptation was therefore to become a glorious Messiah rather than to become a suffering Messiah. If Jesus had become a glorious Messiah, he could have been praised by all Israel, but he could not have saved them from their sins. In order to save the world, Jesus had to be a Messiah that suffered and died in our place. The Messiah of God was a Messiah that had to suffer first and then enter into his glory (Lk. 24.26).

This was Jesus' victory over the devil: he refused to enter immediately into his glory and chose the way of suffering instead. Jesus' victory was that he chose to be weak and suffer and give his life as a ransom for many (Mt. 20.28), instead of demonstrating his power and authority in an outward display of strength. Faced with this kind of power, the power of Jesus' self-sacrificing love, the devil is helpless, and he has nothing to do but to flee.

We can find this perspective on Jesus' death also in Paul's letters. Paul understands Jesus' death as his victory over all evil powers: "having disarmed the powers and authorities, he made a public spectacle of them, triumphing over them by the cross" (Col. 2.15).

Events at Jesus' Death

When Jesus died, all the Synoptic Gospels report that "the curtain of the temple was torn in two from top to bottom" (Mk 15.38). In Jewish thought, this curtain symbolized heaven. When it was torn, it showed that Jesus had opened the way to heaven. Human beings could now have access to God's presence.

According to Matthew's Gospel, the tombs were opened when Jesus died. "The bodies of many holy people who had died were raised to life. They came out of the tombs after Jesus' death and went into the holy city and appeared to many people" (Mt. 27.52-53). The background for this event is the prophecy of Ezekiel. He had seen a valley full of dead bones, and God made flesh and skin cover them and breath enter them, so that they came to life (Ezek. 37.1-10).

The meaning of the vision was that God would bring the people back from captivity and back from death (Ezek. 37.12-13). When Jesus died, he brought this prophecy to its fulfillment. The Gospels show that the most serious captivity is the captivity to sin (ch. 4). But Jesus' death has freed us from this bondage and broken the power of death.

Jesus' Death in Luke's Gospel

It is surprising that Luke has not included the clearest statement about the meaning of Jesus' death, the saying about how he gave his life as a ransom (Mk 10.45; Mt. 20.28; compare Lk. 22.27). Many scholars think the reason is that there is no room for Jesus' substitutionary death in Luke's theology. But there is a better explanation for Luke's omission. He has preferred to explain the meaning of Jesus' death through the story he tells rather than with theory.

In his story of Jesus' crucifixion, Luke tells us that the people and the rulers were watching and said: "He saved others; let him save himself if he is God's Messiah, the Chosen One" (Lk. 23.35). There is a deep irony in these words. The mockers were unaware of the profound truth they were expressing, but the audience of Luke's Gospel can understand: Jesus could not save himself, and the reason was precisely that he had saved others. One of the criminals that were crucified with Jesus hurled similar insults at Jesus (Lk. 23.39), but the other criminal had a better perspective. He said: "'We are punished justly, for we are getting what our deeds deserve. But this man has done nothing wrong.' Then he said, 'Jesus, remember me when you come into your kingdom'" (Lk. 23.41-42). Jesus' answer, "Truly I tell you, today you will be with me in paradise" (Lk. 23.43), is one of the most beautiful statements of the gospel in the whole Bible. Because Jesus died innocently, he could take the guilty criminal with him to paradise.

The Gospel of John

The Gospel of John also describes Jesus' death as a sacrifice. When he saw Jesus coming, John the Baptist identified him as "the Lamb of God, who takes away the sin of the world" (Jn 1.29). As the one who takes away the sins of the world, Jesus reminds us of the goat that was sent into the wilderness on the Day of Atonement (Lev. 16.21-22; see also ch. 6). He removed the people's sin. But John explained that the fulfillment in Jesus was greater than the preparation. The Day of Atonement took care of only Israel's sins, but Jesus took the sins of the whole world.

As the lamb, Jesus also fulfilled the prophecy of the Suffering Servant, who "was led like a lamb to the slaughter" (Isa. 53.7). But the most important background for John's words is the Passover lamb (Exod. 12.21-23). Jesus was sacrificed as a lamb to set the people free and give them life. Later, Jesus told his disciples that they have life if they eat his flesh and drink his blood (Jn 6.50-51, 53-58). The reason he could make that promise is that he was sacrificed as the true Passover lamb.

In his account of Jesus' crucifixion, John mentioned that he died on the day the Passover lamb was slaughtered (Jn 19.14). Like Moses had instructed regarding the Passover lamb (Exod. 12.46; Num. 9.12), so did Jesus die without having his bones broken (Jn 19.33-36).

The apostle John is fond of using irony, and one such instance is his report of the high priest Caiaphas' advice to the Jewish council. He told them: "it is better for you that one man die for the people than that the whole nation perish" (Jn 11.50). Even though he did not understand the true significance of Jesus' death, the high priest explained its meaning very clearly. Jesus died in his people's place.

When Jesus refers to his death in John's Gospel, he usually says that he is going back to the Father (Jn 14.12; 16.10 etc.). John's Gospel gives us the eternal perspective on Jesus' ministry, and in this perspective Jesus' crucifixion was his journey back to heaven. Jesus is the eternal Word. He has come from heaven and gone into heaven (Jn 3.13). God sent him (3.17) and he came into the world (3.19). The purpose of his journey to earth was to give life (6.33; 10.10). He accomplished this purpose by giving his own life.

Jesus' death was therefore the goal that his whole life led up to. John's Gospel frequently refers to the "hour" that is the climax of Jesus' ministry (2.4; 12.27; 13.1 etc.). This is the hour when God will glorify his Son and the Son will glorify his Father (17.1). This hour is Jesus' crucifixion.

Since Jesus' crucifixion is his glorification (12.23, 28; 17.1), Jesus also talks about his death as the time when he will be "lifted up." In his conversation with Nicodemus, Jesus says that "just as Moses lifted up the snake in the wilderness, so the Son of Man must be lifted up" (3.14). This expression has a double meaning. It refers to the time when Jesus is literally lifted up on the cross, and it also describes a metaphorical lifting up. Jesus' cross is his exaltation. It is the fulfillment of Isaiah's prophecy: "he will be raised and lifted up and highly exalted" (Isa. 52.13).

When Jesus was lifted up on the cross, he brought salvation to those who believe in him (3.14-15). But the "uplifting" of Jesus also resulted in judgment. When Jesus was lifted up, Satan was cast down (12.31-32; see also 16.11). For those who refuse to believe in Jesus, his crucifixion means judgment. Even though Jesus did not come to judge anyone (8.15; 12.47), those who do not believe bring judgment on themselves (12.48). Their judgment is that they remain in darkness. "This is the judgment, that the light has come into the world, and people loved darkness rather than light because their deeds were evil" (3.19).

Because Jesus' crucifixion was also his exaltation, his way to the cross was a victorious journey. John's Gospel paints a picture of a Jesus who is in full control of the events leading up to his execution. He laid down his life. No one took it from him. When the soldiers came to capture him, all he had to do was to pronounce his name, the divine name "I AM" (Jn 18.5 NAB). Then all the soldiers fell to the ground (Jn 18.6). Jesus went willingly to his own death. When he breathed his last, he let out a cry of victory: "It is finished" (19.30).

The book of Revelation continues the focus on Jesus' death as a victory. In John's throne vision in chapter 5, one of the elders introduces Jesus as "the Lion of the tribe of Judah, the Root of David, [who] has triumphed" (Rev. 5.5). But when this Lion appears immediately afterwards, what John sees is not a ferocious lion, but "a Lamb, looking as if it had been slain" (Rev. 5.6). Jesus has triumphed over the forces of evil because he was slaughtered as a lamb.

In chapter 12 John describes a vision of a pregnant woman. This woman symbolizes the people of God, and the child that is born represents Jesus. In this passage, John does not refer to Jesus' death directly, but says that the "child was snatched up to God and to his throne" (12.5). This is a picture of Jesus' ascension, which took place after his death. In the following verses, John explains the spiritual significance of Jesus' death and ascension. "The great dragon was hurled down—that ancient serpent called the devil, or Satan, who leads the whole world astray. He was hurled to the earth, and his angels with him" (Rev. 12.9). As a consequence of Jesus' death, Satan lost his place in heaven. Now he can no longer accuse the people of God, as he did at the time of the Old Testament (Job 1.9-11; 2.4-5; Zech. 3.1-2).

The slaughtered Lamb has already defeated Satan. When the beast and its followers gather to the final battle against Christ and his armies, the battle is over before it begins (Rev. 19.19-20; 17.14). Christ's final victory over evil is certain. The final victory of those who are faithful to Jesus is therefore equally certain (12.11; 15.2; 17.14).

Paul

The cross of Christ was at the very center of Paul's theology. He can use the term "the word of the cross" as another way of referring to the gospel (compare 1 Cor. 1.18 and Rom. 1.16).

When they explained the significance of the cross, Jesus and the evangelists used the idea of redemption through the payment of a ransom. This idea is also important to Paul.

Paul understood that human beings are slaves under sin and under the law. But through his death, Christ has bought us and redeemed us (1 Cor. 6.20; Gal. 3.13). This does not mean that we are free to do whatever we want, but that we belong to Jesus as our new master (1 Cor. 6.19-20; 7.22-23). It also means that we are no longer under the curse of the law (Gal. 3.13) and that our sins are forgiven (Eph. 1.7; Col. 1.14).

Some scholars have argued that redemption in the New Testament does not involve the payment of a price since Christ does not pay anyone to set us free. (He certainly does not pay anything to the devil, who has no rightful claim to human beings.) But this whole line of questioning is misleading. The point of the New Testament teaching on redemption is not that Jesus paid someone, but that our redemption came at a high cost. Many scholars therefore prefer to use the word "cost" rather than "price." The cost that Jesus had to pay was his own life. Jesus bought our redemption with his blood (Rom. 3.24-25; Eph. 1.7; Tit. 2.14).

Redemption

Our redemption by Jesus came at the highest cost, the giving of his life (Rom. 3.24-25; Tit. 2.14). By this redemption, we are liberated from the slavery of sin so that we belong to a new master, Jesus (1 Cor. 6.19-20; 7.22-23). Redemption also means that Jesus has freed us from the guilt that our sin has caused before God and that he has liberated us from the curse (Gal. 3.13).

The reason why Jesus had to pay this high cost was that he had to atone for our sins. Our sins put us under the wrath of God, and Christ had to suffer his wrath. In Romans 3.24-35, Paul explains that "the redemption that is in Christ Jesus" was something "God put forward as a propitiation by his blood" (ESV). The Greek word that is translated "propitiation" (*hilasterion*) can also be used for the lid on the ark of the covenant. Some translations therefore use the term "mercy seat" here. But it is doubtful that Paul meant to refer directly to the mercy seat in this verse. When the word *hilasterion* is used in this way, there is usually some indication in the context that there is a reference to the lid on the ark of the covenant. In itself this word means "a propitiatory gift or offering." ("To propitiate" means "to gain or regain the favor or goodwill of." Its synonyms are "appease" and "conciliate.") The purpose of a propitiatory gift or offering (*hilasterion*) is to make God turn away from his wrath. There is a verb that comes from the same root (*hilaskomai*). In the Septuagint, the Greek translation of the Old Testament, this verb is often used to describe how God turns away from his anger (Exod. 32.11-14, TNIV translates "relent"; Dan. 9.16, 19, TNIV translates "forgive").

In his letter to the Romans, Paul describes how "the wrath of God is being revealed from heaven against all the godlessness and wickedness of human beings" (Rom. 1.18; see also 1.18-3.20). In Romans 3.21-4.25, he explains how God's righteousness is revealed (3.21) and how it is possible to escape God's wrath. It is possible because Jesus gave his life as a sacrifice of atonement. He was a propitiatory offering, so that God could punish the sins of the world by punishing Jesus Christ. Later in Romans 3.25, Paul says that "in his forbearance [God] had left the sins committed beforehand unpunished." The implication is that they are no longer unpunished because Christ has borne the punishment.

Theologians often discuss whether we should understand Christ's death as propitiation or merely as expiation. If we understand it as expiation, the point is that Christ did something with sin, but not necessarily anything with God. That Christ expiated our sin means that he removed our sin, but it does not mean that he changed the way God feels towards us. But if we understand Christ's death as propitiation (as explained above), the idea is that Christ did something that directly affected God. When Christ died, he appeased God's anger.

Reconciliation

Since Jesus has turned away God's wrath, he has also reconciled us to God. In some key passages, Paul describes Jesus' work on the cross as reconciliation (Rom. 5.10; 2 Cor. 5.18, 19). The meaning of "to reconcile" (Greek: *katallasso*) is to change enmity for friendship. When this word is used in Jewish literature from New Testament times, God was always the logical object of the verb, never the subject. The logic is clear: human beings had sinned and therefore caused enmity between themselves and God. The human beings were the guilty party and they were therefore the ones who had to restore the relationship. They had to present the acceptable sacrifices so that God could be reconciled. It was apparently unthinkable that God would be the one who reconciled people to himself; he had nothing for which he needed to make amends.

The Jewish writing 2 Maccabees (124 BCE) quotes a letter from the Jews in Jerusalem to the Jews in Egypt. In this letter, the Jerusalem Jews express the following wish for the Egyptian Jews: "May he hear your prayers and be reconciled to you" (2 Macc. 1.5). The point is that God must hear the prayers of the Egyptian Jews and that he must consider these prayers sufficient compensation for their sins. By their prayers, the Egyptian Jews may then reconcile God. Later in the same book, a young Jewish man explains that he believes Israel's suffering is something they have to go through in order to reconcile God: "if our living Lord is angry for a little while, to rebuke and discipline us, he will again be reconciled with his own servants" (2 Macc. 7.33). Once again, the people are the ones that have to reconcile God. In this example, their suffering is the way they compensate for their sins.

Paul's understanding of reconciliation is completely different from the examples above. He also knows that human beings are the ones who have ruined the relationship with God. But he does not think that human beings can reconcile God. Instead, he explains that it is God, the offended party, who takes it upon himself to restore the relationship and bring about reconciliation: "All this is from God, who reconciled us to himself through Christ and gave us the ministry of reconciliation: that God was reconciling the world to himself in Christ, not counting people's sins against them" (2 Cor. 5.18-19). God is now the active party in reconciliation. Paul turns normal thinking upside-down and explains that human beings are being reconciled, even though they are the guilty party. "While we were God's enemies, we were reconciled to him through the death of his Son" (Rom. 5.10).

Substitution or Representation?

As it is explained above, Christ's death is a substitutionary death. That means that he has died in our place. But many scholars think that we should not use the word "substitution" to describe Jesus' death. They argue that his death does not mean that we do not have to die. The point is rather that Christ shared our death. Because of that, it is possible for us to share his death and enjoy its results: freedom from sin and judgment. These scholars therefore prefer to speak of Christ's death as representative rather than substitutionary. Christ died as our representative, but not in our place. There is an important point here: to be a Christian means to share in Christ's death (Rom. 6.3-8; Gal. 2.20; Phil. 3.10). But our union with Christ is only possible because he has taken our place. In the most fundamental sense, Jesus died so that we can trade places with him. Christ was cursed by God, so that we can go free (Gal. 3.13). He was made to be sin for us, so that we are made God's righteousness (2 Cor. 5.21; see also Rom. 5.18). We still have to die, but for us death has lost its sting. It is swallowed up into victory (1 Cor. 15.54-56).

Hebrews

The letter to the Hebrews focuses on Jesus as the eternal high priest. His death is the ultimate sacrifice that accomplishes what the Old Testament sacrifices could only illustrate. The letter to the Hebrews explains that the Old Testament sacrifices could not really bring forgiveness of sins.

The Old Testament tabernacle and its institutions are only a copy and a shadow of the heavenly reality (Heb. 8.5). Their purpose is pedagogical; they teach the people of Israel about God. The author of Hebrews calls it "an illustration for the present time" (Heb. 9.9).

These sacrifices therefore had only an outward significance. They "were not able to clear the conscience of the worshiper" (Heb. 9.9), but could only "sanctify them so that they are outwardly clean" (Heb. 9.13). In other words, these sacrifices could not take away sins (Heb. 9.4). Therefore, they had to be repeated year after year, and they served as "an annual reminder of sins" (Heb. 10.3). They showed the need for a perfect sacrifice for sin.

Christ's sacrifice is the real sacrifice. "For Christ did not enter a sanctuary made with human hands that was only a copy of the true one; he entered heaven itself, now to appear for us in God's presence" (Heb. 9.24). His sacrifice was his own blood, and with this sacrifice he could truly "do away with sin" (Heb. 9.26).

In the Old Testament, the sins of the people made the tabernacle unclean. It was therefore necessary to bring the sacrifices, so that God could continue to be present in the tabernacle (ch. 6). This points forward to the need for a spiritual, inward cleansing, so that we can be acceptable to God.

The blood of Christ provides this cleansing. His blood "[cleanses] our consciences from acts that lead to death, so that we may serve the living God" (Heb. 9.14). This cleansing is complete; it takes place once and for all

(Heb. 10.10). "For by one sacrifice he has made perfect forever those who are being made holy" (Heb. 10.14).

(The meaning of "holy" in this verse is not to be sanctified in the sense that Christians normally use that word. We think of sanctification as a constant growth where we become more and more like Christ. The letter to the Hebrews uses the word "holy" differently. It means "to be set apart for God." See also ch. 10. This happens once and for all, through Christ's sacrifice. The author of Hebrews knows that Christians are at different levels of maturity [Heb. 5.11–6.3]. But that does not change the fact that all Christians are made holy once and for all through the sacrifice of Christ.)

To the author of Hebrews, the meaning of Christ's death is that it takes away sin once and for all. Those who believe in Jesus are therefore perfect and holy in God's eyes.

Peter

To Peter, Jesus' death means above all that he suffered as the Servant of the Lord from Isaiah 52.13–53.12. Peter quotes from Isaiah 53.9 in 1 Peter 2.22, and alludes to the same passage in 1 Peter 2.24: "'He himself bore our sins' in his body on the cross, so that we might die to sins and live for righteousness; 'by his wounds you have been healed'" (Isa. 53.4, 5, 12). There is even another allusion to Isaiah 53.6 in 1 Peter 2.5 and probably to Isaiah 53.11 in 1 Peter 3.18.

As the Suffering Servant, Jesus fulfills the Old Testament sacrifices. He is the true Passover lamb, who has redeemed the Gentile Christians "from the empty way of life handed down to [them] from [their] ancestors" (1 Pet. 1.18). With his death, Christ has set the Gentile Christians free from a life in sin.

As Peter explains it in 1 Peter, the benefit of Jesus' death was that it enables us to live a new life. We are set free from sin and we have a new life with God (1 Pet. 1.3). All this is the work of Jesus. He is the righteous one who died in our place, so that he could bring us to God (1 Pet. 3.18).

Summary

The Old Testament sacrifices could only serve to demonstrate that sin had to be punished. It was impossible for human beings to repair the damage they had caused with their sin. God was the only one who could restore what was broken. He sent his Son and brought reconciliation. It is now possible for human beings to enjoy a harmonious relationship with God. Jesus has conquered evil and set us free from slavery to an alien master: sin. He has taken the just punishment for our sin and therefore freed us from God's wrath. He has taken away our sin so that we may enjoy God's favor.

However, reconciliation always involves two parties. In Christ, God is reconciled, but we must also be reconciled to him. In the next chapter we will see how that can happen.

Further Reading

Carroll, John T., Joel B. Green, with Robert E. Van Voorst, Joel Marcus, and Donald Senior. *The Death of Jesus in Early Christianity*. Peabody: Hendrickson, 1995.

Hill, Charles E., and Frank A. J. L. James, eds. *The Glory of the Atonement: Biblical, Historical and Practical Perspectives: Essays in Honor of Roger R. Nicole*. Downers Grove: IVP, 2004.

Morris, Leon. *The Apostolic Preaching of the Cross*. 3d ed. London: Tyndale, 1965.

Review Questions

How do we know from the Synoptic Gospels that Jesus died as a sacrifice for sins?

How does Jesus demonstrate his superior power and defeat the devil?

How does Paul explain that Jesus' death takes away the wrath of God?

How is Jesus' sacrifice superior to those of the Old Testament, according to the letter to the Hebrews?

10
Enjoying Favor with God
Salvation in the New Testament

Chapter Outline

The Synoptic Gospels and the Kingdom of God	138
Discipleship in the Gospel of Matthew	140
Discipleship and Faith in Luke's Gospel	141
Justification in Paul's Letters	143
James	152
Peter	153
John	154
Summary	156

Jesus came to the world as God's unique Son, so that he could repair everything that had been destroyed by sin. He brought a new eschatological reality where there once again is harmony between God and human beings. In this chapter, we will see how human beings can become a part of this new reality and enjoy God's favor. This new reality is salvation in Jesus Christ.

The Synoptic Gospels and the Kingdom of God

According to the Synoptic Gospels, the central theme of Jesus' message is the kingdom of God (Mk 1.15). The biblical term "kingdom of God" refers both to the exercise of God's rule (God's kingly rule) and the territory of this rule (the kingdom of God). The Old Testament describes a time when God will rule without opposition, and the Synoptic Gospels refer to these expectations with the term "the kingdom of God." In this kingdom, there will once again be harmony in God's creation. Sickness and suffering will no longer exist. In his person, God will bring this kingdom and all its benefits to earth (ch. 8).

The important question is then: who will take part in this kingdom and who will be allowed to enter into it? Through his teaching, Jesus answers this question. Just like God rejected the great and chose the small when he made Israel his people, so does Jesus shut the great out of his kingdom and include the small. Those who took it for granted that the kingdom belonged to them were cast outside (Mt. 8.12; 21.31). But those who were written off as impossible were included (Lk. 13.28-29). The kingdom of God turns everything upside-down: "So the last will be first, and the first will be last" (Mt. 20.16).

Jesus demonstrated the dynamics of this kingdom in the way he interacted with his contemporaries. The company he kept was not of the upper classes, but he often associated with people that were known for their sinful lifestyles. Jesus became known as "a friend of tax collectors and sinners" (Lk. 7.34). Respectable citizens tended to keep their distance from Jesus. Even those who were not openly hostile to him, such as the Pharisee Simon, were still more reserved with their affections than the social outcasts, such as the prostitute who threw herself at Jesus' feet (Lk. 7.36-50).

Jesus shows us that the kingdom of God brings a new reality. It turns the values of this world upside-down, includes the outcasts and excludes the well-to-do. Jesus' kingdom brings the presence of salvation, a salvation that is for the sinners, the poor, the sick, the lepers, the lower classes, the marginalized, those who were otherwise excluded from good society (Lk. 4.18-19; 7.22). Jesus' table fellowship with sinners (Mk 2.15-16) establishes a new community, a community that represents the presence of the kingdom of God, a kingdom based on the forgiveness of sins, freely given by Jesus himself (Mk 2.5; Lk. 7.48).

Jesus always gives the kingdom to those who are outside it. But he takes it away from those who think they are already inside and that they can keep others out. For this reason, Jesus lifts up small children as models in the kingdom. "Unless you change and become like little children, you will never enter the kingdom of heaven," he says (Mt. 18.3). Children are ready to receive the kingdom for nothing. They do not turn the focus on themselves and conclude that they have done something to deserve the kingdom or that the kingdom belongs to them more than to others. They have no idea that they have deserved to be in the kingdom of God, and others have not. They are happy to receive it as a gift.

Discipleship in the Gospel of Matthew

At the same time, Jesus makes it very clear that those who wish to enter the kingdom have to follow him and obey him. Matthew emphasizes this aspect more than the other evangelists. In his Gospel, he frequently mentions the need for good works and explains that God's final judgment will be according to works (e.g. 5.21-30; 19.16-30; 25.31-46). Matthew concludes his Gospel with the Great Commission, where Jesus sends his followers out to make disciples of all nations. As he does so, he tells his disciples to teach the new disciples "to obey everything I have commanded you" (Mt. 28.20). To be a disciple of Jesus is therefore to obey everything he has commanded.

In the Sermon on the Mount, we can read what Jesus commanded. In this great sermon on discipleship, Jesus tells us that "unless your righteousness surpasses that of the Pharisees and the teachers of the law, you will certainly not enter the kingdom of heaven" (Mt. 5.20). "The kingdom of heaven" is another term that Matthew uses for the kingdom of God. In the following verses (Mt. 5.21-48), Jesus explains what kind of righteousness is required in the kingdom. It is the kind of righteousness that not only concerns outward action ("you shall not murder"), but inward attitude ("anyone who is angry with a brother or sister"). To do good works, one must first be good on the inside (see also Mt. 12.33-35; 15.18-19). The righteousness of the Pharisees and the teachers of the law reached only to their actions (Mt. 23.1-33), but the righteousness of the disciples reaches to the heart and to their inward attitude. It is the righteousness that expresses itself through love for one's enemies (Mt. 5.44), in disciples that are perfect, like their heavenly Father is perfect (Mt. 5.48).

For whom is such righteousness possible? To understand this, we must see the bigger context within the Sermon on the Mount. Jesus begins this sermon with the Beatitudes, where he proclaims: "Blessed are the poor in spirit, for theirs is the kingdom of heaven" (Mt. 5.3). There are two words for "poor" in classical Greek. One word refers to those who are so poor that they have to work for a living, and the other for those who are so poor that they have to beg. It is the second of these that is used in Matthew 5.3. The poverty that Jesus refers to is poverty in spirit; it refers to those who are poor in their relationship to God. It refers to those who are so desperate that there is nothing they can do except come to God as beggars. The poor in spirit are painfully aware of their own shortcomings. They know very well that they fall short of the righteousness that God demands (Mt. 5.6), the perfection that Jesus describes in the Sermon on the Mount. They know that they have nothing to bring to God, nothing to show for themselves, nothing to be proud of, no righteousness that is acceptable to him. They are completely dependent upon God (Mt. 18.2-3).

The best example from the Gospel of Matthew of a person who was poor in spirit is the Syro-Phoenician woman that came to Jesus to pray for her demon-possessed daughter (Mt. 15.21-28). Initially, Jesus ignored her. When his disciples asked him to help her, he dismissed them. When she knelt before him, he rejected her with the words: "It is not right to take the children's bread and toss it to the dogs" (Mt. 15.26). Jesus has now called the woman a dog, but she does not object. Instead, she agrees with this evaluation of herself, but continues her plea: "'Yes it is, Lord,' she said. 'Even the dogs eat the crumbs that fall from their master's table'" (Mt. 15.27). This woman knows that there is only one way in which she can come to Jesus: as a beggar. She and the Roman centurion (who shows a similar attitude towards Jesus, see Mt. 8.5-10) are the only characters that Jesus commends for their great faith (Mt. 15.28).

The promise to those who come to Jesus as beggars, those who are poor in spirit, is that the kingdom of heaven is theirs. Not only will they enter the kingdom; the kingdom belongs to them. This is where discipleship begins and this is where it ends: as beggars before Jesus, as beggars to whom the kingdom of heaven belongs. Those who come to Jesus in this way and follow him are transformed through their fellowship with Jesus and become more and more like him. In this way, they come to demonstrate a righteousness that is different and far better than the righteousness of the Pharisees and the teachers of the law: a righteousness that comes from the inside, a righteousness that comes from a poor spirit. Those who have this kind of righteousness have no need to put their righteous acts on display, as the hypocrites do (Mt. 6.1-4, 16-18). It is rather a righteousness that imitates Jesus in seeking out the marginalized, the poor, the sick, and the sinners (Mt. 25.31-46).

Discipleship and Faith in Luke's Gospel

In Matthew's Gospel, Jesus addresses his first beatitude to those who are poor in spirit (Mt. 5.3). But Luke does not specify that Jesus talks about spiritual poverty. In Luke 6.20, Jesus is more direct: "Blessed are you who are poor, for yours is the kingdom of God." The difference between the two accounts is not as great as it may seem at first. In the New Testament, "poverty" is a broad concept. It concerns economic poverty, but also social poverty, which may be even more disastrous. People who do not have family or friends to help them are even worse off than those who do not have money. A poor person is therefore a person who is not able to rely on themselves or on anyone else. They are therefore completely dependent on God, which is also what it means to be poor in spirit.

Those who are poor and become Jesus' disciples also have to follow him. Jesus himself explains: "Whoever wants to be my disciple must deny themselves and take up their cross daily and follow me" (Lk. 9.23). Those who follow Jesus have to be prepared for the possibility that they may have to suffer martyrdom, but Jesus here has something else in mind. Since Jesus says we must take up our cross daily, his words cannot primarily refer to literal death. Instead, the point is that the disciples must give up all ambitions on their own behalf. When Jesus took up his cross and walked to his death, he was completely powerless and suffered the deepest humiliation. In the same way, his disciples do not put their hope in anything that belongs to this world. This is another way of saying that Jesus' followers are poor in spirit and depend on God.

This attitude of dependence upon God can also be called faith. The word "faith" can be used in different ways. In the Gospels, "to have faith" or "to believe" often means to believe that Jesus is able to perform a miracle (Mt. 8.13; 9.28). However, the goal of faith is not to receive a miracle, but to be led into a saving relationship with Jesus. Luke's Gospel shows this most clearly in the story of the ten lepers (Lk. 17.11-19). All ten lepers were healed, but only one of them was told: "your faith has saved you" (Lk. 17.19 NAB). The Greek word that is used here (*sozo*) can be translated both "save" and "heal/make well." In Luke 17.19, most English translations read: "your faith has made you well." But all the lepers were healed, so that cannot be the point of Jesus' words. The Samaritan was not only healed, he was also saved. The nine other lepers also received the gift of healing from Jesus, but they did not receive the most important gift. We see, then, that the purpose of healing is that those who are healed may enter into a relationship with Jesus, and that "to have faith" means to have such a relationship with him.

To have faith means to trust in someone or something. In the case of miracle-working faith, faith is to trust that Jesus can and will perform a miracle. In the case of saving faith, it is to trust in Jesus in a more comprehensive sense. It involves trusting in him for forgiveness, as we can learn from the story about the sinful woman in Simon's house (Lk. 7.36-50). She threw herself at the feet of Jesus, trusting that he would forgive her and accept her (Lk. 7.48, 50).

Since Jesus is the one who can forgive sins, he is also the one who passes the final judgment on all human beings (ch. 8). To be forgiven and accepted by Jesus is therefore also to be accepted at the final judgment. Luke's Gospel introduces this perspective in the parable of the Pharisee and the tax collector (Lk. 18.9-14). The Pharisee in this parable trusted that he was a good person and that God would therefore accept him. It is important to note that the Pharisee did not believe that he had accomplished this on his own. He thanked God and gave him honor for what he had done. The point is that he believed that God received him because he was a better person than the tax collector, even if this superior status was a gift he had received from God. The tax collector on the other hand did not have any ideas about his own superiority. In fact, he did not compare himself to others at all. He knew that he was standing before God and he could do nothing other than come as a beggar: "God, have mercy on me, a sinner" (Lk. 18.13). With this attitude, he was "justified before God" (Lk. 18.14).

To be justified and to be righteous (both these words come from the same root in Greek) have to do with God's final, end time judgment. When the New Testament refers to justification in the present (as in the parable of the Pharisee and the tax collector), the idea is that God's final judgment has been moved forward to the present time. Justification is therefore the anticipation of a positive verdict in God's final judgment.

Justification in Paul's Letters

The background for the New Testament language about justification and righteousness is found in the Old Testament. Unlike in English, the Hebrew and Greek words "to justify" (*tsadeq* and *dikaioo*) and "righteous" (*tsadiq* and *dikaios*) come from the same root, as these concepts are closely related. Israel's judges had to pass a verdict according to what was right and what was wrong. Those who had done right, and therefore were righteous, had to be justified. It is important to note that "to be righteous" refers to who a person is or what a person has done. "Justification" and "to justify," on the other hand, refer to the act of a judge. If the judge is honest and righteous, the judge's verdict will be in accordance with what the person has done (Deut. 25.1; see also 1 Kgs 8.32). In that case, the justification by the judge corresponds to the righteousness of the one on trial. But if the judge is wicked, he will justify the wicked and condemn the righteous (Exod. 23.7; Prov. 17.15).

One of the most important concepts in Paul's letters is the concept of God's righteousness. This concept forms the theme of the letter where Paul offers the most systematic discussion of his teaching, the letter to the Romans. Paul affirms: "I am not ashamed of the gospel, because it is the power of God that brings salvation to everyone who believes: first to the Jew, then to the Gentile. For in the gospel the righteousness of God is revealed—a righteousness that is by faith from first to last, just as it is written: 'The righteous will live by faith'" (Rom. 1.16-17). The most straightforward meaning of the term "the righteousness of God" is that God is just and fair, and that he treats everyone in the same way, as a righteous judge. Because God is just, the gospel is for all people, without distinction. God does not give special treatment to any social classes or any ethnic groups when he offers his salvation (Rom. 1.14).

However, "the righteousness of God" does not only refer to a quality of God, that he is just and fair. It may also refer to his activity. Because he is just, he acts in righteousness and saves his oppressed people. In the Old Testament, God's "righteousness" is therefore often a synonym for his "salvation" (Ps. 71.2, 15; Isa. 51.8).

When we see the context of Paul's letter to the Romans, we see that Paul also understands God's righteousness as an active righteousness. "The righteousness of God" refers not only to who God is, but also to what he does. That is why he can say that God's righteousness is revealed (Rom. 1.17), just as God's wrath (Rom. 1.18) and his activities in history are revealed (Rom. 3.21). Paul also explains that God's righteousness is related to "the power of God for salvation" (1.16), another reference to what God does.

In many passages, "God's righteousness" means almost the same as "God's saving activity," and it refers to how God intervenes in this world in order to bring salvation to his people.

Many biblical scholars see "righteousness" as a concept that primarily has to do with relationships. According to these scholars, to be righteous means to be faithful to a relationship. In 1 Samuel 24.17, we have an example where the word "righteous" belongs in the context of a relationship. Saul tells David: "You are more righteous than I . . . You have treated me well, but I have treated you badly."

God's relationship with his people is described in his covenants with Israel. If we understand his righteousness in this context, then God's righteousness means that he is faithful to his covenant. Many scholars argue that "God's righteousness" may be understood as God's covenant faithfulness. Specifically, God is faithful to his covenants when he acts to save his people.

But God's righteousness is even more fundamental than his covenant with Israel. Most basically, it is connected with the idea of God as creator. As the king and judge of the whole universe, God establishes the right order between

Enjoying Favor with God

himself and the world. This right order may be referred to as "righteousness" (Pss 7.1-17; 11.1-7; Isa. 51.1-8). Righteousness therefore has more to do with a norm than with a relationship. To act righteously or justly means to act in accordance with God's norm for his creation. "Righteousness" can therefore be explained as "conformity to God's norm" (Job 4.17; 33.12; Ps. 143.2).

Those scholars who tie the concept of righteousness closely to the idea of a relationship often argue that God's righteousness refers to his acts of salvation, not to any acts of judgment. But this understanding is also too narrow. When we see God's righteousness in the light of his role in creation, we realize that the righteous judge of the world exercises his righteousness both in salvation and in judgment (Ps. 7.11; Isa. 10.22).

In Paul's letter to the Romans, the themes of judgment and salvation are also closely linked together. As soon as Paul has introduced the concept of God's righteousness (Rom. 1.16-17), he proceeds to the revelation of God's wrath (Rom. 1.18–3.20). In order to explain the meaning of God's righteousness, he first describes God's judgment. He makes it clear that the entire world is guilty before God (3.19).

But the revelation of God's righteousness takes place in a surprising way. First of all, Paul announces that God's righteousness is not revealed through the law (Rom. 3.21). To understand what Paul means with this statement, we must clarify what he means by the term "law" (Greek: *nomos*). Sometimes this word simply refers to the five books of Moses (Rom. 3.21b; Gal. 4.21) and sometimes to the whole Old Testament (1 Cor. 14.21). But the most characteristic way that Paul uses this word is when he refers to the Sinai covenant (Gal. 3.13, 17-19) or the commandments of this covenant (Rom. 2.25; 5.13; 7.7).

The purpose of this covenant and these commandments, as Paul explains it, was to reveal human sinfulness (Rom. 3.19-20; 5.20; Gal. 3.19). This takes place when the law condemns the actions of human beings (Rom. 2.1–3.20), but also when human beings try to obey the law of God. In Romans 7.7-14, Paul explains how the law actually makes human sin even greater (ch. 4).

This does not mean that God's law failed in any way. God did not give the Sinai covenant so that human beings would gain salvation and eternal life through the law (Gal. 3.21). The purpose of the law was to reveal sin and to make it clear that the whole world is guilty before God. Paul sums it up in Romans 3.19-20: "Now we know that whatever the law says, it says to those who are under the law, so that every mouth may be silenced and the whole world held accountable to God. Therefore no one will be declared righteous in God's sight by observing the law; rather, through the law we become conscious of our sin." The law served its purpose in God's judgment. It was an instrument of condemnation and death (2 Cor. 3.6, 9). It brought people under slavery (Gal. 4.24).

When the law had this function, it served God's purpose. That is why Paul can say that the law was glorious (2 Cor. 3.7, 9-11). But this glory is overshadowed by the glory of the new covenant, which is the covenant that gives life (2 Cor. 3.8-11). God's work consists of both judgment and salvation. He does his work of judgment through the law and through the Sinai covenant.

An important passage where Paul describes the effect of the law is Galatians 3.10-12: "All who rely on observing the law are under a curse, for it is written: 'Cursed is everyone who does not continue to do everything written in the Book of the Law.' Clearly no one is justified before God by the law, because 'the righteous will live by faith.' The law is not based on faith; on the contrary, it says, 'Whoever does these things will live by them.'"

There is a lot of scholarly debate about this passage. The problem is that Paul is quoting three Scripture verses (Deut. 27.26; Hab. 2.4; Lev. 18.5), but none of these passages make the point that Paul is making: "all who rely on observing the law are under a curse." In fact, these Old Testament quotations do not bring a curse upon those who observe the law, but upon those who break it. Many interpreters have therefore suggested the following solution: Paul presupposes that the law must be kept perfectly and that no one really does keep the law in a perfect way. As long as that is the case, the law only brings a curse.

But this solution is difficult. Paul does not say that it is impossible to keep the law perfectly. In fact, in one passage Paul says that he had been blameless in the way he kept the law (Phil. 3.6). The concept of "perfect law observance" probably cannot help us understand what Paul means in Galatians 3.10-12.

It is better to look to the prophets in the Old Testament, and see how they understood the verses that Paul quotes. The prophet Jeremiah also makes reference to Deuteronomy 27.26 (Jer. 11.3), and he makes a point that is very similar to Paul's. Jeremiah explains that Israel had broken the covenant with God, and that they therefore had to suffer the curse of Deuteronomy 27.26 (Jer. 11.6-8). The reason why Israel had broken the covenant was not that they had failed to obey the law perfectly, but that they had fundamentally turned away from God.

This is the point that Paul is making, then: those who rely on observing the law have turned away from God. They are therefore under the curse. But how could Paul conclude that those who try to obey God's law have turned away from him? Because God has not provided justification through the law, but through faith (Gal. 3.11). Those who try to be justified by obeying the law are therefore disobedient in a more fundamental way: they implicitly reject God's way of justification. They fail to trust in God and to depend on his grace.

In his letter to the Galatians, Paul explains that God always intended for human beings to receive his gift through faith. The covenant with Abraham was older than the covenant with Moses, and this covenant was based on God's promise and is now fulfilled in Christ (Gal. 3.15-18).

In Romans, Paul makes a similar point: the law does not bring life, but death. It condemns all human beings, both Jews and Gentiles. Against this background, Paul affirms that the righteousness of God is not revealed through the law (Rom. 3.19-21).

Instead, God's "righteousness is given through faith in Jesus Christ to all who believe" (Rom. 3.22). In this statement, we see that the word "righteousness" takes on yet another shade of meaning. Here, it does not refer to a quality of God or to his activity. Instead, "righteousness" is something that God gives. "Righteousness" is a gift of God and refers to the status of being declared right with God (justified).

The meaning of the word "righteousness" as a righteous status before God also has its background in the Old Testament (Isa. 46.13; 62.1-2 ESV). In Romans 1.17 and Galatians 3.11, Paul quotes from Habakkuk 2.4: "the righteous live by their faith" (NRSV). In its original context, this verse also concerns human status. That Paul thinks of righteousness in this way is clear when he says that righteousness is something that is "credited" (Rom. 4.3, 5, 6, 9, 11; Gal. 3.6). This status is also a gift, as we understand from Paul's expression "the gift of righteousness" (Rom. 5.17) and from the fact that this righteousness is "from God" (1 Cor. 1.30; Phil. 3.9).

The standard that is necessary in order to stand in God's judgment, "righteousness" (see above), is now a gift. This gift is given by faith. Those who believe in Jesus Christ are given the gift of righteousness. God treats everyone in the same way. Just as both Jews and Gentiles are condemned for their sin, so are they "justified freely by his grace through the redemption that came by Christ Jesus" (Rom. 3.24). God now passes a verdict, he proclaims believers to be righteous, he justifies them. This verdict is not based on what they have done. It takes place "freely, by his grace." Paul can even go so far and say that God is the one "who justifies the ungodly" (Rom. 4.5). In other words, God lets the sinner go free and acquits the guilty.

Table 10.1 The meaning of "righteousness"

	Paul	OT background
A Quality of God	But if our unrighteousness brings out God's righteousness more clearly, what shall we say? (Rom. 3.5). He did this to show his righteousness, because in his divine forbearance he had passed over the sins previously committed (Rom. 3.25b NRSV).	He rules the world in righteousness and judges the peoples with equity (Ps. 9.8).
An Activity of God	For in the gospel the righteousness of God is revealed (Rom. 1.17).	The Lord has made his salvation known and revealed his righteousness to the nations (Ps. 98.2). I am bringing my righteousness near, it is not far away; and my salvation will not be delayed. I will grant salvation to Zion, my splendor to Israel (Isa. 46.13).
A Gift from God	This righteousness is given through faith in Jesus Christ to all who believe (Rom. 3.22a). However, to anyone who does not work but trusts God who justifies the ungodly, their faith is credited as righteousness (Rom. 4.5). How much more will those who receive God's abundant provision of grace and of the gift of righteousness reign in life through the one man, Jesus Christ! (Rom. 5.17). God made him who had no sin to be sin for us, so that in him we might become the righteousness of God (2 Cor. 5.21).	I am bringing my righteousness near, it is not far away; and my salvation will not be delayed. I will grant salvation to Zion, my splendor to Israel (Isa. 46.13). For Zion's sake I will not keep silent, and for Jerusalem's sake I will not be quiet, until her righteousness goes forth as brightness, and her salvation as a burning torch. The nations shall see your righteousness, and all the kings your glory, and you shall be called by a new name that the mouth of the Lord will give (Isa. 62.1-2 ESV).

But if God acts in this way, does he not violate his own rule: "I will not acquit the guilty" (Exod. 23.7)? If God declares the sinner to be righteous, is he not an unjust God? On the surface, it may certainly seem that way, but Paul explains that there is a more profound principle at work. The believers are "justified through the redemption that came by Christ Jesus. God presented Christ as a sacrifice of atonement, through the shedding of his blood—to be received by faith. He did this to demonstrate his justice because in his forbearance he had left the sins committed beforehand unpunished—he did it to demonstrate his justice at the present time, so as to be just and the one who justifies those who have faith in Jesus" (Rom. 3.24-26).

God did not stop being just when he justified the ungodly, Paul explains. He still punishes sin without holding back because he has made Christ a sacrifice of atonement. The Greek word that Paul uses here (*hilasterion*) may refer to the lid on the ark of the covenant, but it is also used more generally for an offering that turns away God's wrath (ch. 9).

By giving his Son as a sacrifice, God remains the just God who responds to sin with the just punishment and at the same time he is the God who lets sinners go free when they believe in Jesus Christ.

What God does can be described as the great exchange between Jesus and the believer. Jesus takes our place and we take his. He becomes sin and we become righteousness (2 Cor. 5.21). He becomes a curse and sets us free (Gal. 3.13).

In Romans chapter 4, Paul combines the language of the law court with the language of accounting. "Now to the one who works, pay is not considered as a gift, but as something owed. But to the one who does not work, but believes on Him who declares the ungodly to be righteous, his faith is credited for righteousness" (Rom. 4.4-5 HCSB).

It is as if the believer has a "heavenly bank account" and this account is credited with righteousness. This righteousness does not consist of the righteous works of the believer. In fact, it does not consist of anything the believer has done at all. Instead, it is Christ's righteousness that is credited to the believer's account, as Paul explains more directly in Romans 5.19: "through the obedience of the one man the many will be made righteous." The basis for the justification of the many believers is not their own obedience, but the obedience of the one man, Christ. Paul can therefore also say that Christ is the one "who has become for us . . . our righteousness" (1 Cor. 1.30). In 2 Corinthians 5.19-21, he explains that God is "not counting people's sins against them," but that in Christ "we might become the righteousness of God."

Those who believe in Christ are "in him" and have been given a new identity. Paul can even say: "I no longer live, but Christ lives in me" (Gal. 2.20). It is no longer our own life that counts, but Christ is our life (Col. 3.4). Those who have Christ's identity also have his status. Because of his obedience, they are righteous before God. Their union with Christ is so complete that Paul not only says that they receive the righteousness of God, but that they "become the righteousness of God" (2 Cor. 5.21). In Christ, the believers are "holy and blameless in [God's] sight" (Eph. 1.4). In God's eyes, the believers are now just as holy as his Son, and they have the same relationship to God as Jesus has. They have been given "adoption to sonship" (Eph. 1.5).

This does not mean that the believers are no longer sinners or that they no longer fall in sin. Throughout his life, Paul continues to confess that he is a sinner, even the worst of sinners (1 Tim. 1.15). The flesh is sinful for as long as the believer lives (Rom. 7.14-24; see further ch. 12).

Since the believer's righteousness is from God, it is not based on any kind of human work or accomplishment (Phil. 3.9). In fact, Paul explains that there is a contrast between a righteousness that is based on one's own work and the righteousness that comes from God. Those who wish to receive God's righteousness cannot trust in their own righteousness. According to Paul, most of his fellow Jews did not receive the righteousness of God precisely because they wished to establish their own righteousness (Rom. 10.3). Those who trust in what they are or what they have done do not submit to the righteousness of God. In Philippians 3.4-6, Paul describes his former life, when he trusted in his own righteousness. Such righteousness may be based on one's heritage and background (Paul mentions that he is "circumcised on the eighth day, of the people of Israel, of the tribe of Benjamin, a Hebrew of Hebrews") as well as one's works and accomplishments (Paul says that he is "in regard to the law, a Pharisee; as for zeal, persecuting the church; as for righteousness based on the law, faultless").

When the question is how one is justified before God, Paul rejects everything he is and everything he has done: "whatever were gains to me I now consider loss for the sake of Christ. What is more, I consider everything a loss because of the surpassing worth of knowing Christ Jesus my Lord, for whose sake I have lost all things. I consider them garbage, that I may gain Christ and be found in him, not having a righteousness of my own that comes from the law, but that which is through faith in Christ—the righteousness that comes from God on the basis of faith" (Phil. 3.7-9). The reason is not that it is wrong to be Jewish or that it is sinful to obey God's law. These are good things in themselves. But Paul does not want to trust in anything other than the gift of God in Jesus Christ. If he trusted that he would be justified by God because he belonged to God's chosen people or because he had fulfilled God's law, he would be condemned. This is how we must understand what Paul has to say about the contrast between faith and works (Rom. 3.27-28; Eph. 2.8-9).

In his letter to the Galatians, Paul is mostly concerned with specific works that were prescribed in the law, such as circumcision (Gal. 2.3; 5.2 etc.). In the letter to the Romans, circumcision is still important (Rom. 2.25-29; 4.9-12), but in that instance Paul is thinking of the law more broadly (Rom. 2.17-24; 7.7; 13.8-10). Some scholars associated with the so-called new perspective on Paul, such as James Dunn and N. T. Wright, have therefore suggested that Paul's contrast between faith and works is not between faith and good works as such, but between faith and "works of the law" (Rom. 3.20; Gal. 2.16 NRSV). According to these scholars, the problem Paul is addressing is not that some people trust in their good works. The problem is that they misunderstand the Mosaic law. This misunderstanding was that many Jews believed they enjoyed a special status with God because they were Jews. When Paul refers to "works of the law," they claim, he did not think of "good works," but of the works that made the Jews different from other nations, such as circumcision and food laws.

There is a lot of truth in this understanding of Paul's theology. Paul's teaching about justification means that no people can claim that they are better than others. But the reason why Paul rejects such thinking is not that he rejects a certain misunderstanding of the Mosaic law. The reason is that he rejects all human accomplishment when it becomes an object of trust. Paul does not teach us that a misunderstanding of the Mosaic law leads to death, but that the very law itself leads to death (2 Cor. 3.7-9).

When we compare Paul's argument in Romans and Galatians with his argument in Ephesians, we can also see that what he has to say concerns good works as such, not merely certain works of the law. In Ephesians 2.8-9, Paul makes a point very similar to that in his earlier letters: "For it is by grace you have been saved, through faith—and this is not from yourselves, it is the gift of God—not by works, so that no one can boast." But in Ephesians, the contrast to faith is not "works of the law;" it is simply "works." Paul here also emphasizes that salvation "is not from yourselves." In other words, faith means to trust in God, not ourselves. That is why there is a contrast between faith and good works (see also Tit. 3.5).

"Faith" for Paul therefore means trust. Saving faith is the opposite of placing one's confidence in the flesh (Phil. 3.3). The greatest example of a person of faith is Abraham. He trusted in God even when it seemed impossible that God would fulfill his promise. "Abraham believed and hoped, even when there was no reason for hoping, and so became 'the father of many nations.' Just as the scripture says, 'Your descendants will be as many as the stars'" (Rom. 4.18 GNB).

Abraham was the model of justification by faith. Paul finds the biblical evidence in Genesis 15.6: "Abraham believed God, and it was credited to him as righteousness" (Rom. 4.3). To Paul, it is of the utmost importance that Abraham was declared righteous before, not after, he was circumcised (Rom. 4.10). This proves that God's justification was not based on Abraham's works, but solely on his faith. Paul's understanding of Abraham's justification differs greatly from an understanding that was common among the Jews.

They would often read Genesis 15.6 in light of the story of Abraham's willingness to sacrifice his son Isaac. The author of the Jewish history book known as 1 Maccabees (ca 100 BCE) refers to this event and concludes: "Was not Abraham found faithful when tested, and it was reckoned to him as righteousness?" (1 Macc. 2.52).

When Paul so strongly emphasizes justification by faith, it is surprising that he also can refer to judgment according to works (Rom. 2.6-16, 25-29; 2 Cor. 5.10). Some scholars have therefore concluded that Paul has room for two justifications: one initial justification by faith alone, and one final justification, which is also by works. But it would be strange if Paul so strongly denied that we are justified by works if he meant that we will be justified by works one day after all.

The verses where Paul speaks of justification by works can be understood in a different way. Chapter 2 of Romans is part of an argument that leads to the conclusion that the law condemns all human beings (Rom. 3.19-20). When Paul says that "it is those who obey the law who will be declared righteous" (Rom. 2.13), his point is that it is not enough merely to have and listen to the law (Rom. 2.17-18). In order to be justified by the law, it is also necessary to keep it. What Paul explains in the rest of this section of Romans is that neither Jews nor Gentiles do (Rom. 3.9). The possibility that someone might be justified by the law is therefore purely theoretical.

In none of the other passages where Paul appears to teach that we are judged by our works (Rom. 14.10-12; 2 Cor. 5.10; Gal. 6.8; Col. 3.23-25) does he actually discuss the question of justification. The purpose of these passages is to encourage his readers not to focus on what human beings value, but on what God values. It is not the judgment of human beings that matters, but the judgment of God, and we are all accountable to him.

James

There is some tension between what Paul says about justification by faith alone and some statements that we can find in the rest of the New Testament, especially in the epistle of James. In James 2.24, he appears to contradict Paul directly: "You see that people are justified by what they do and not by faith alone." Some scholars have even concluded that James wrote his epistle in order to correct Paul's teaching about justification.

But the context for James' discussion is very different from that of Paul, and we will understand neither Paul nor James if we assume that they address the same question. It is quite possible that the epistle of James was written before any of Paul's letters. In any case, James' concern is not to discuss the basis for our justification, like Paul did. Instead, James addresses a situation where it was necessary to warn against double-mindedness and lack of wholehearted commitment to the Lord (1.7-8; 4.8). Apparently, some church members did not see any connection between their faith and good works (2.18), such as taming the tongue (1.19, 26; 3.1-12) and showing mercy to the poor (2.1-13).

When James talks about "faith" he uses the word in a completely different sense than the apostle Paul. Whereas "faith" for Paul means to trust in God (see above), James uses the word simply in the sense "to believe that something is true." (Perhaps the reason why James talked about "faith" in this way was that the people he was correcting had used the word in this sense.) James can therefore refer to the faith of the demons (2.19). When we see how Paul describes faith as putting one's hope in God (Rom. 4.18-21), it is impossible to imagine that he could have talked about the demons' faith. It is James' very different concept of faith that also makes it possible for him to use the term "dead faith" (Jas 2.17, 26), a term we do not find in Paul's letters. The way Paul understands the nature of faith, faith is always living faith. When James uses the word "faith," therefore, he does not discuss what Paul calls "faith."

James also uses the term "justification" in a different sense than Paul. For Paul, the word refers to God's verdict, but James uses the word in connection with how external testimonies demonstrate one's righteousness. James wants to explain how someone's righteous status with God can be shown and made known (Jas 2.18). For Paul, "justification" means to be declared righteous by God. But for James, the term means to be proven to be right with God.

James also knows that our salvation is the work of God and not of ourselves. God, "who gives generously to all without finding fault" (Jas 1.5), is the one who "chose to give us birth through the word of truth" (Jas 1.18). The idea that God has given us birth implies that we have done nothing in order to gain this life because no one can do anything in order to be born.

James therefore shares Paul's conviction that salvation is a gift from God. And, as we shall see later, Paul is also in agreement with James that this gift necessarily results in a transformed life.

Peter

Like James, and unlike Paul, Peter does not dwell on the question of how people are saved. His concern is to explain how those who are saved should live their lives. But he gives several clear indications of how he understands salvation because God's gift of salvation is the foundation for the new life of believers.

Peter refers to this gift of salvation as a new birth, which is the result of the resurrection of Jesus Christ and of "the living and enduring word of God" (1 Pet. 1.3, 23). The believers are who they are because of the mercy of God (1 Pet. 2.10) and because Jesus died in their place (1 Pet. 2.24; 3.18). "His divine power has given us everything we need for a godly life," and the result is that "you may participate in the divine nature" (2 Pet. 1.4). To participate in the divine nature means to be like God, reflect his glory, and become immortal. The believers share in this gift through faith in Jesus Christ (1 Pet. 1.5, 8-9; 2 Pet. 1.1), which Peter also refers to as obedience (1 Pet. 1.2, 14, 22).

For Peter, "salvation" refers first and foremost to what believers will experience when Christ comes again (1 Pet. 1.5, 9-10, 2.2). They must strive to be found obedient when he appears (1 Pet. 4.7; 2 Pet. 3.11-14). However, the salvation that will be revealed at his coming is not to be understood as a reward, but as grace to be brought to them (1 Pet. 1.13).

John

When the apostle John writes about the gift of salvation, he prefers to use the term "life" or "eternal life." John is fond of word pairs that describe stark contrasts, such as "light" and "darkness" and "life" and "death." By using such words, he shows that the gospel introduces an absolute distinction between human beings. They are either in the light and have life, or they are dead and in darkness. There is no middle ground.

When John uses the language of life and death, he also makes it clear that human beings are completely dependent upon God. Life is a gift from God (Jn 4.10), and God gives this gift through his Son, Jesus Christ (Jn 4.14; 6.27), who has life in himself (Jn 1.4; 5.26). In order to receive this life, one must be born from above (Jn 1.13; 3.3-8). The metaphor of being born from above shows very clearly that salvation is a gift from God. Just as no one can do anything in order to be born, so can human beings do nothing to be saved and be born again. Those who are children of God are therefore "children born not of natural descent, nor of human decision or a husband's will, but born of God" (Jn 1.13).

In his conversation with Nicodemus, Jesus shows that such a new birth is the work of the Holy Spirit (Jn 3.8). When Nicodemus asks how someone can be born of the Spirit (Jn 3.9), Jesus does not answer with an explanation of what it means to be born again. Instead, he refers to himself and his work. "Just as Moses lifted up the snake in the wilderness, so the Son of Man must be lifted up, that everyone who believes may have eternal life in him" (Jn 3.14-15). Jesus here alludes to the bronze snake that Moses made and put up on a pole. The Israelites that were bitten by poisonous snakes could look at this snake and save their lives (Num. 21.8-9). Jesus compares this snake to himself and his crucifixion. In the wilderness, those Israelites who trusted in God's promise and turned their eyes to the bronze snake were saved. In a similar way, people are born from above when they put their trust in Jesus Christ, whom God gave to save the world (Jn 3.16). To have eternal life is therefore to believe in God's Son, as Jesus says in his high-priestly prayer: "this is eternal life: that they know you, the only true God, and Jesus Christ, whom you have sent" (17.3; see also 1 Jn 5.12-13).

This faith is also a gift from God. It is God who makes a person come to Jesus. Jesus says: "All whom the Father gives me will come to me, and whoever comes to me I will never drive away" (Jn 6.37). People do not come to Jesus on their own, only when they are drawn by the Father (Jn 6.44, 65). When Jesus says, "The work of God is this: to believe in the one he has sent" (Jn 6.29), the meaning is probably that faith is something that God gives.

Nevertheless, people have a responsibility to seek the gifts of Jesus (Jn 6.27) and to put their faith in him. Jesus therefore commands his disciples: "Believe me when I say that I am in the Father and the Father is in me; or at least believe on the evidence of the works themselves" (Jn 14.11). In John's Gospel, Jesus' works serve as evidence that makes it possible for people to believe in him (Jn 2.11, 23; 11.15). That is why John's Gospel refers to Jesus' miracles as signs. Because the miracles are signs, they point beyond themselves, to the glory of Jesus. To believe is therefore more than to recognize the power of a miracle. It is to recognize and know who Jesus is (Jn 6.69). To believe in Jesus is to know him as the Son of God (Jn 20.31; 1 Jn 4.15). Since he and the Father are one (Jn 10.30), to know and to have fellowship with Jesus is also to know the Father (Jn 14.7; 2 Jn 9).

Those who know Jesus follow him (Jn 10.27) and obey him (1 Jn 2.3; see also 2.4-5; 3.24). His disciples are the ones who abide in his word (Jn 8.31; 15.7-11) and keep it (Jn 8.51; 14.23; 17.6).

Summary

Entrance into the kingdom of God is a free gift. Jesus gives this gift to those who are poor in spirit, those who come to him like children. They have no right to make any claim, but have to come as beggars. This process is also referred to as being born again, by the will of God, not of ourselves. When someone comes to Jesus in faith, God's final judgment is moved forward to the present time, and God lets the believer trade places with Jesus. God punishes Jesus instead of the sinner, and looks at the sinner the way he looks at Jesus.

God's free gift can be described as entrance into the kingdom of God, as justification, and as new birth and new life. It means to enjoy God's favor and therefore participate in the blessings that he gives. It means to enjoy fellowship with God in the most intimate way.

Further Reading

Bird, Michael F. *The Saving Righteousness of God: Studies on Paul, Justification and the New Perspective.* Milton Keynes, UK: Paternoster, 2007.

Klaiber, Walter. *Justified Before God: A Contemporary Theology.* Nashville: Abingdon, 2006.

Seifrid, Mark A. *Christ, Our Righteousness: Paul's Theology of Justification.* New Studies in Biblical Theology 9. Leicester: IVP, 2000.

Talbert, Charles H., and Jason A. Whitlark. *Getting Saved: The Whole Story of Salvation in the New Testament.* With other contributions by A. E. Arterbury et al. Grand Rapids: Eerdmans, 2011.

Wright, N. T. *Justification: God's Plan and Paul's Vision.* Downers Grove: IVP, 2009.

Review Questions

Who enters the kingdom of heaven?

What is the meaning of the term "the righteousness of God" in Paul's letters?

Why does Paul insist that we are justified by faith and not by works?

On the question of salvation, Paul's letters differ from the Gospel of Matthew and the epistle of James. Describe the differences and similarities between these writings.

The New Testament uses several different metaphors to show that salvation is a gift from God. Mention some of the most important of these metaphors.

11

The Most Intimate Fellowship
The Gift of the Holy Spirit

Chapter Outline

The Old Testament	157
The New Testament	158
Jesus and the Spirit	159
The Trinity	162
Believers and the Holy Spirit	162
The Holy Spirit's Work in Believers	163
The Holy Spirit and Mission	164
The Holy Spirit and Final Salvation	164
Sin against the Holy Spirit	165
Summary	165

In the Old Testament, God dwelled among his people in the temple. When Jesus came, he dwelled among them as a human being. After Pentecost, he came even closer.

The Old Testament

The Holy Spirit was given to believers on the day of Pentecost (Acts 2.4, 17-18), but he was present in the world from the beginning. The term "Holy Spirit" is not very common in the Old Testament, however; it only occurs three times (Ps. 51.11; Isa. 63.10-11). Instead, the Old Testament authors prefer to refer to the Spirit as "the Spirit of the Lord" or "the Spirit of God."

God's Spirit is at work in creation (Gen. 1.2; Ps. 33.6) and gives the power of life to all living beings (Job 33.4; Ps. 104.29-30), but the Old Testament's main focus is on the Spirit's activities in Israel. The Spirit works by putting words in the mouths of the prophets (Num. 11.25-29; Ezek. 11.5), by giving them visions (Ezek. 8.3; 11.24), and by transporting them from place to place (1 Kgs 18.12; 2 Kgs 2.16). Moses (Num. 11.17), Joshua (Num. 27.18), and other leaders in Israel (Num. 11.25-29; Neh. 9.20) have been equipped for their tasks by the Spirit. Sometimes the Spirit also came over the priests in a special way (2 Chron. 24.20). The men who prepared the tabernacle and its furnishings had been given their wisdom from God's Spirit (Exod. 31.3; 35.31). In Israel's later history, the king was anointed with the Spirit so that he could rule with justice (1 Sam. 10.1-11; 16.13).

The Old Testament shows us that the Holy Spirit is particularly involved in God's communication with this world. Beyond that, the Spirit has an important role to play in the prophets' eschatological expectations. The prophet Isaiah promises that the Messiah and the Servant of the Lord will be filled with the Spirit in a special way (Isa. 11.2; 42.1; 61.1).

Since the Spirit was involved when God created the world (Gen. 1.2; Ps. 33.6), it is not surprising that he is also involved in the new creation. God will bring the people of Israel home, and give them peace and prosperity when he pours out his Spirit on them (Isa. 32.15; 44.3). Ezekiel looks forward to the day when God will give new life to his people by his Spirit (Ezek. 36.27; 37.14). The prophet Joel paints the most vivid picture of the outpouring of the Spirit. God "will pour out [his] Spirit on all people," and they will all have the gift of prophecy (Joel 2.28-29). To learn about the fulfillment of these expectations, we turn to the New Testament.

The New Testament

The names that are used in the Old Testament are also found in the New Testament. We meet "the Spirit of God," "the Spirit of the Lord," and "the Spirit." Compared to the Old Testament, the name "the Holy Spirit" is much more common. But the most notable difference is that the Spirit is now called "the Spirit of Christ" (Rom. 8.9; 1 Pet. 1.11), "the Spirit of Jesus" (Acts 16.7; Phil. 1.19), and "the Spirit of his Son" (Gal. 4.6). The New Testament understanding of Christ as God's equal and God's Son has given us a clearer picture of the Holy Spirit, too. John refers to the Spirit with the characteristic titles "Advocate" (Jn 14.16) and "the Spirit of truth" (1 Jn 4.6).

In the book of Revelation, the Holy Spirit is symbolically called the "the seven spirits before [God's] throne" (Rev. 1.4). The number seven is the number for God. It also corresponds to the seven-fold name of God's Spirit in the Greek translation (Septuagint) of Isaiah 11.2: "the spirit of God shall rest on him, the spirit of wisdom and understanding, the spirit of counsel and might, the spirit of knowledge and godliness." Zechariah 4.2, 10 compare the work of the Spirit to seven lamps and seven eyes (Zech. 4.6). In Revelation 5.6, these seven spirits are identified with the seven eyes of the Lamb. This is Revelation's way of showing that the Holy Spirit is the Spirit of Christ.

Jesus and the Spirit

Like the prophets of the Old Testament, Jesus performs his ministry in the power of the Holy Spirit (Mt. 12.18, 28; Lk. 4.18-19). The Spirit descended on Jesus at his baptism (Mk 1.9-11). Matthew and Luke also report that Jesus' conception and birth took place by the Holy Spirit (Mt. 1.18, 20; Lk. 1.35). Luke gives special attention to the Spirit's work in Jesus' earthly life (1.80; 4.1, 14, 18; 10.21).

Jesus came to give the Holy Spirit. In fact, John the Baptist summarizes Jesus' whole ministry in this way: "I baptize you with water, but he will baptize you with the Holy Spirit" (Mk 1.8). This was fulfilled on the day of Pentecost. Jesus' disciples "saw what seemed to be tongues of fire that separated and came to rest on each of them. All of them were filled with the Holy Spirit and began to speak in other tongues as the Spirit enabled them" (Acts 2.3-4). Peter explains that what happened was a fulfillment of Joel's prophecy (Acts 2.16-21; see also Joel 2.28-32). In the time of the Old Testament the Spirit was given to kings, priests, and prophets, but in the New Testament there is a general outpouring of the Spirit on all believers. The gift of prophecy demonstrates that this outpouring has taken place.

We find the most detailed teaching about the Holy Spirit in Jesus' Farewell Discourse in the Gospel of John. Jesus tells his disciples that he and his Father will love those who obey his teaching. He also promises that he and his Father will "come to them and make our home with them" (Jn 14.23). This promise is fulfilled through the presence of the Spirit, or the Advocate, as he is called in John's Gospel. Whereas the Gospel of Matthew speaks of Jesus' continued presence with his disciples (Mt. 18.20; 28.20; see also ch. 8), the Gospel of John speaks of Jesus' continued presence through the Advocate, his Spirit.

What we learn about the Advocate in John's Gospel is that he does what Jesus does. Jesus came (Jn 5.43; 16.28), and now the Advocate will come (Jn 15.26; 16.7). Like Jesus goes out from the Father (Jn 8.42; 13.3), so does the Advocate (Jn 15.26). The Father gives him (Jn 14.16), like he gave his Son (Jn 3.16). As the Father sent his Son (Jn 3.17; 5.36), so does he send the Advocate in Jesus' name (Jn 14.26). He is called another Advocate (Jn 14.16), which implies that Jesus is the first Advocate (1 Jn 2.1).

The disciples know Jesus (Jn 14.7, 9), and they will also know the Advocate (Jn 14.17). He will live with the disciples (Jn 14.17), as Jesus had promised that he would be in them and make his home with them (Jn 14.20, 23).

The Advocate will teach the disciples all things (Jn 14.26), as Jesus had been teaching them previously (Jn 4.25-26; 6.59). He will guide them to all the truth (Jn 16.13), as Jesus is the truth (Jn 14.6). As Jesus did not testify on his own behalf (Jn 8.14), so does the Advocate testify about Jesus (Jn 15.26). He does not speak on his own (Jn 16.13). He will take what belongs to Jesus and give it to the disciples (Jn 16.14), glorify Jesus (Jn 16.14), and remind the disciples of what Jesus has told them (Jn 14.26).

Like Jesus (Jn 16.3), so is the Advocate not accepted, seen, or known by the world (Jn 14.17). Jesus testifies against the world that its works are evil (Jn 7.7), and the Advocate proves "the world to be in the wrong about sin, and righteousness and judgment" (Jn 16.8-11).

Table 11.1 Characteristics Shared by Jesus and the Holy Spirit

	Jesus	The Holy Spirit
Comes from the Father	I came from the Father (Jn 16.28).	When the Advocate comes, whom I will send to you from the Father (Jn 15.26).
Given by the Father	For God so loved the world that he gave his one and only Son (Jn 3.16).	And I will ask the Father, and he will give you another advocate to help you and be with you forever (Jn 14.16).
Sent by the Father	For God did not send his Son into the world to condemn the world, but to save the world through him (Jn 3.17).	The Advocate, the Holy Spirit, whom the Father will send in my name (Jn 14.26).
Called Advocate	We have an advocate with the—Jesus Christ, the Righteous One (1 Jn 2.1).	He will give you another advocate (Jn 14.16).
Known by the disciples	If you really know me, you will know my Father as well (Jn 14.7).	But you know him, for he lives with you and will be in you (Jn 14.17).
Lives with the disciples	My Father will love them, and we will come to them and make our home with them (Jn 14.23).	But you know him, for he lives with you and will be in you (Jn 14.17).

Table 11.1 Continued

Teaches the disciples	He said this while teaching in the synagogue in Capernaum (Jn 6.59).	But the Advocate, the Holy Spirit, whom the Father will send in my name, will teach you all things and will remind you of everything I have said to you (Jn 14.26).
Truth	Jesus answered, "I am the way and the truth and the life" (Jn 14.6).	But when he, the Spirit of truth, comes, he will guide you into all the truth (Jn 16.13).
Does not testify on his own behalf	Jesus answered, "Even if I testify on my own behalf, my testimony is valid, for I know where I came from and where I am going" (Jn 8.14).	The Spirit of truth who goes out from the Father—he will testify about me (Jn 15.26).
Not known by the world	They have not known the Father or me (Jn 16.3).	The world cannot accept him, because it neither sees him nor knows him (Jn 14.17).
Proves the world to be in the wrong	The world cannot hate you, but it hates me because I testify that its works are evil (Jn 7.7).	He will prove the world to be in the wrong about sin and righteousness and judgment (Jn 16.8).

When Jesus appeared to his disciples after the resurrection, he "said, 'Peace be with you! As the Father has sent me, I am sending you.' And with that he breathed on them and said, 'Receive the Holy Spirit'" (Jn 20.21-22). Jesus' act of breathing on the disciples reminds us of the creation account, where God "formed a man from the dust of the ground and breathed into his nostrils the breath of life" (Gen. 2.7). It also makes us think of Ezekiel's vision of the new creation, when God told him to say: "Come, breath, from the four winds and breathe into these slain, that they may live" (Ezek. 37.9). When Jesus breathes on the disciples, therefore, he shows that what he is doing is an act of creation. He is bringing the new creation when he gives the Holy Spirit to his disciples.

But how are we to understand that the disciples received the Spirit before Jesus' ascension and before Pentecost? In the book of Acts the Holy Spirit descended on the day of Pentecost, and in John's Gospel Jesus says: "Unless I go away, the Advocate will not come to you; but if I go, I will send him to you" (Jn 16.7; see also Jn 7.39; 15.26).

Some scholars have suggested that John 20.22 merely describes a symbolic giving of the Spirit and that the actual gift of the Spirit came later, on the day of Pentecost. But this interpretation does not seem to do justice to what Jesus says to his disciples: "Receive the Holy Spirit." Another suggestion is that the disciples received the Spirit twice, but this interpretation is also problematic. Jesus describes one gift of the Spirit, not two (Jn 7.39).

Questions such as these, regarding the chronology of Jesus' salvific ministry, are always very difficult to answer. The reason is that the New Testament authors were usually not interested in answering such questions. Instead, they focus on the nature of Jesus' mission and what it means for us. The account in John 20.22 is therefore an important supplement to the one in Acts 2, since it focuses on the gift of the Spirit as an act of new creation.

John's Gospel describes the Holy Spirit in such a way that he must be understood as a person. All the verbs that are used about the Advocate in John 14-16 make this clear. He is also so intimately related to Jesus that the two must be understood as one.

The Trinity

The New Testament therefore teaches that the Holy Spirit is a person who is equal to and one with the Father and the Son. This teaching led the early church to formulate the doctrine of the Trinity. The word "Trinity" is not found in the New Testament (it was coined by the church father Tertullian around 200 CE). But the idea is there (ch. 1).

Believers and the Holy Spirit

Since the Spirit is Christ's representative, those who belong to Christ also have the Spirit (Rom. 8.9-10; Gal. 2.20; 4.6). This gift is given in baptism (Acts 2.38), and all believers have received it (Gal. 3.27; Eph. 1.13). It is impossible to know and confess Jesus without the Holy Spirit (1 Cor. 12.3). All Christians therefore have the Spirit, not only in part, but in full (Jn 3.34).

The whole story of the book of Acts presupposes that genuine believers have the Spirit. If someone has the Spirit, that is the proof that they belong to Christ. A major purpose of the book of Acts is to show that Gentiles are included in the people of God. When God gives the Spirit to the Gentiles, this gift is the proof that God has included them (10.44-45; 11.15; 15.8; see also Gal. 3.1-5).

To be filled with the Holy Spirit is different than to have the Holy Spirit. The book of Acts reports that some Christians were filled with the Holy Spirit on special occasions. When that happened, they were empowered in a special way to give their testimony about Christ (Acts 4.8, 31; 7.55; 13.9).

Even though the gift of the Holy Spirit is given to every individual believer, it is not a gift that individuals enjoy alone. It is a gift to the community of believers. Paul can therefore say that "God's Spirit dwells in you" (1 Cor. 3.16 NRSV), when he refers to the whole church.

We must understand the individual spiritual gifts in this light. They are not really "individual" at all; they are given to the community of believers. Their purpose is to build up the church (1 Cor. 12.7; Eph. 4.11-13), and they must not be used to pit individuals against each other (1 Cor. 12.12-31; see also ch. 13). There is only one Spirit, and this oneness must also come to expression in the unity of the church (1 Cor. 12.4-11; Eph. 2.18; 4.3-4).

The Holy Spirit's Work in Believers

It is only through the Holy Spirit that human beings can truly understand and receive what Jesus teaches them. For Jesus' disciples, it was necessary that the Spirit remind them of what Jesus had taught them and that he guide them to all truth (see above). Paul explains that no one can understand the wisdom of God, the word of the cross, except through the Holy Spirit (1 Cor. 2.7-16).

Because they have the Spirit, believers trust God and relate to him as children. In the words of the apostle Paul, God has "sent the Spirit of his Son into our hearts, the Spirit who calls out, '*Abba*, Father'" (Gal. 4.6). When they are not even able to put their own prayers into words, the Spirit intercedes for them (Rom. 8.26).

The Holy Spirit changes a person completely. When the Holy Spirit lives in a person, he or she has a new mind, a new attitude, a new will. He or she will no longer "have their minds set on what [the sinful] nature desires," but "on what the Spirit desires" (Rom. 8.5). By the Spirit they "put to death the misdeeds of the body" (Rom. 8.13). Their lives are now characterized by the fruit of the Spirit: "love, joy, peace, patience, kindness, goodness, faithfulness, gentleness and self-control" (Gal. 5.22-23). The Spirit motivates Christians to change their lives so completely that Paul compares it to taking off one's old clothes and putting on new clothes (Eph. 4.22-24).

James does not mention the Holy Spirit by name in his letter. Instead, he refers to the gift of the Spirit as "the wisdom that comes from heaven" (Jas 3.17). The virtues of this wisdom correspond to the fruit of the Spirit in Galatians 5.22-23.

The Holy Spirit and Mission

In the Gospel of John, Jesus explains that one of the main functions of the Spirit is to give witness to the world (Jn 15.26; 16.8-11). In the book of Acts, Jesus promises his disciples that they "will receive power when the Holy Spirit comes on [them]; and [they] will be my witnesses in Jerusalem, and in all Judea and Samaria, and to the ends of the earth" (Acts 1.8). The book of Acts tells the story of how Jesus begins to fulfill this promise. It is the Holy Spirit that motivates and directs the church's mission to the world. He directs Philip to proclaim the gospel to the Ethiopian (Acts 8.29), and he instructs Peter to evangelize the Gentile Cornelius and his household (Acts 10.19; 11.12). He also calls Paul and Barnabas to embark on their missionary journey outside the land of Israel (Acts 13.2), and he gives them the power that is needed so that their work may be fruitful (Rom. 15.18-19).

The Holy Spirit and Final Salvation

The gift of the Holy Spirit is God's promise that he will complete his work of saving believers. Paul says that God "set his seal of ownership on us, and put his Spirit in our hearts as a deposit, guaranteeing what is to come" (2 Cor. 1.22). The Greek word that Paul uses is *arrabon*. This is a term that is normally used in connection with buying and selling. When someone bought something, a down payment (*arrabon*) constituted a legally binding contract. It obligated the buyer to make the full payment. Paul says that the Spirit is such a down payment or deposit. This means that God is committed to complete his work of salvation. Those who have received the Spirit as a down payment can be assured that God will stand behind his gift until their salvation reaches its completion.

In the same way, Paul calls the Spirit the first fruits (Rom. 8.23). The first fruit serves as an assurance that the full harvest will follow later. Paul's point is that the Holy Spirit gives believers assurance that God will be with them until their final salvation. The power of the Holy Spirit raised Jesus from the dead. His presence therefore assures believers that they will be raised as well (Rom. 8.11).

Sin against the Holy Spirit

In a challenging passage, Jesus states that "whoever blasphemes against the Holy Spirit will never be forgiven, but is guilty of an eternal sin" (Mk 3.29). To understand what this sin is, we must study the context. The teachers of the law and the Pharisees had accused Jesus of casting out demons by the power of Beelzebul, which is another name for Satan (Mk 3.22). Jesus' work of casting out demons was the visible proof that the kingdom of God was present (Lk. 11.20). In other words, the Pharisees and teachers of the law saw and experienced the work of God, but they called it the work of Satan. To sin against the Holy Spirit is therefore to experience compelling evidence that the Holy Spirit is working through Jesus, and then willfully to reject it.

A related question concerns those who cannot be brought back to repentance. According to the letter to the Hebrews, "it is impossible for those who have once been enlightened, who have tasted the heavenly gift, who have shared in the Holy Spirit, who have tasted the goodness of the word of God and the powers of the coming age and who have fallen away, to be brought back to repentance" (Heb. 6.4-6a; see also 10.26-31). Calvinist interpreters see here a portrayal of people who have participated in the life of the church without being born again. But it is better to understand these verses as a description of those who have had a genuine experience of the gifts of salvation. These verses do not apply to those who have followed Jesus without becoming rooted through genuine fellowship with him, but to those who have seen through genuine experience who Jesus is and what he gives. If they still turn away from him, they act in defiance of what they know and have seen. Those who willfully reject Jesus in this way have shut themselves out from his fellowship.

Summary

The New Testament explains that God's Spirit is a person in his own right. He is both the Spirit of God and the Spirit of Christ. As Christ's perfect representative, his chief function is to serve as Christ's presence in believers. Through the Holy Spirit, believers therefore enjoy an entirely new level of closeness to God. He now dwells in them. As a result, believers' lives will be completely transformed.

Further Reading

Fee, Gordon D. *God's Empowering Presence: The Holy Spirit in the Letters of Paul.* Peabody: Hendrickson, 1994.

Feldmeier, Reinhard, and Hermann Spieckermann. *God of the Living: A Biblical Theology.* Translated by Mark E. Biddle. Waco, Tex.: Baylor University Press, 2011.

Turner, Max. *The Holy Spirit and Spiritual Gifts Then and Now.* Carlisle: Paternoster, 1996.

Review Questions

What are the functions of the Holy Spirit in the Old Testament?

How does the New Testament show us that the Holy Spirit is a person in his own right?

How does the Holy Spirit work among Christian believers?

12
A Life Transformed
The New Life of the Believer

Chapter Outline

Sanctification	167
Jesus and the Gospels	169
Paul	170
The Law and the Christian	171
Jesus and the Law	172
Fulfillment of the Law	173
Other New Testament Writings	176
Summary	177

The gift of the Holy Spirit is given to all those who believe in Christ. Christians are therefore "led by the Spirit" (Gal. 5.18) and live an entirely new life, a life that is pleasing to God.

Sanctification

Today, we use the word "sanctification" for the growth that takes place in the Christian life after conversion. In the New Testament, however, the words for holiness and sanctification (Greek: *hagios* etc.) are not used in this way. Their basic meaning is to be set apart for God. The background is the distinction between the holy and the profane in the Old Testament. In order for people or objects to be acceptable in God's presence, they had to be holy. If they were not, they had to be sanctified, or made holy. Since objects, such as the articles in the temple (Exod. 39.1; 1 Chron. 22.19), could be called holy, the word "holy" is not first and foremost an ethical term. It simply refers to someone or something that is set apart for God. However, this does not mean that holiness has nothing to do with ethics. People that are set apart for God have to reflect God's holy nature, and that means to be ethically pure (Lev. 19.2; Deut. 14.1-2). But it is important to be aware of this distinction, if we wish to understand what it means to be holy in the New Testament.

In the New Testament, people are set apart and belong to God when they become believers (1 Cor. 6.11; Heb. 10.10). All Christians are therefore holy (Eph. 3.18; Rev. 8.3 NAB). Even the church in Corinth, with all its immoral members, is holy (1 Cor. 1.2; 6.11).

The fundamental idea when it comes to ethical conduct in the New Testament is this: believers must act in accordance with who they are. Since God has made them holy, they must live holy lives. In 1 Thessalonians, Paul gives many exhortations to the believers, and he explains the reason why: "For God did not call us to impurity but in holiness" (1 Thess. 4.7 NRSV). In Colossians 3.12, he insists that the believers must live "as God's chosen people, holy and dearly loved." Peter quotes Leviticus 11.45 to make a similar point: "But just as he who called you is holy, so be holy in all you do; for it is written: 'Be holy, because I am holy'" (1 Pet. 1.15-16).

While Paul makes it clear that those who believe in Christ have already been made holy or sanctified (1 Cor. 1.30; 6.11), he also admonishes believers to live in holiness. There are therefore often two main sections in Paul's letters. The first part describes the gift of God, and the second part describes the obligations for believers. The shift between the two sections often corresponds to a shift in verb moods. In the letter to the Ephesians, for example, most of the verbs in chapters 1–3 are in the indicative, referring to facts. On the other hand, most verbs in chapters 4–6 are in the imperative, expressing commands. Colossians 3.1-3 also gives us a nice illustration of Paul's logic: "Since, then, you have been raised with Christ, set your hearts on things above, where Christ is seated at the right hand of God. Set your minds on things above, not on earthly things. For you died, and your life is now hidden with Christ in God." The believers have been united with Christ's death and resurrection and they have a new life. What they should do now is to live this new life that they have been given (see also Rom. 6.3-8).

Paul's ethical instructions presuppose that there has been a fundamental change in the life of those who believe in Jesus. Characteristically, Paul refers to the "before" and the "now" of believers' lives (Rom. 6.17-19; Eph. 2.11-22).

Before, they belonged to the old order of things, and they were slaves to death, sin, and the law. But now, Christians have experienced the eschatological intervention of God, through Jesus Christ. The new creation is already a reality for those who believe in him (2 Cor. 5.17; Gal. 6.15). Their old human being is crucified with Christ, and they have put on the new human being (Rom. 6.4, 6; see also Col. 3.9-10). To put on the new human being corresponds to putting on Christ (Rom. 13.14; Gal. 3.27). This new human being is created according to the image of Christ (Rom. 8.29; 2 Cor. 3.18), and Christ is the image of God (2 Cor. 4.4). To live a new life as a Christian is therefore to imitate Christ (1 Cor. 11.1; 1 Thess. 1.6). Since Christ is the image of God, it is only in him that human beings can be what they were created to be (Gen. 1.27). Christ is therefore the goal of creation (Col. 1.16), and when human beings are transformed by him, creation fulfills its intended purpose.

Jesus and the Gospels

Paul was convinced that the new life of the believer is a direct consequence of the new eschatological reality or the new creation. This corresponds to what Jesus was preaching as well. Jesus announced that the kingdom of God was near (Mk 1.15). As a consequence, he called people to leave everything and follow him (Mk 1.17 etc.). To be a disciple of Jesus means to give up one's own life and imitate Jesus, even to the point of death (Mk 8.34-35; Mt. 10.38-39; see also ch. 10).

Jesus has given his disciples the gift of the kingdom of heaven. That means that God's saving power is at work through them, and Jesus can say that they are "the salt of the earth" and "the light of the world" (Mt. 5.13-14). Because they have this new status and on the basis of this new reality, Jesus gives the disciples the commandments in the Sermon on the Mount.

The most important commandment is to love God (Mk 12.28-31; see also Jn 13.34; 15.12), as it is in the Old Testament (Deut. 6.5). In the time of the New Testament, however, this commandment is fulfilled through commitment to Jesus. Those who wish to fulfill the commandment about love for God must now love Jesus. They must love him above everyone and everything else. Jesus demands that all other responsibilities take second place compared to following him. Even one's responsibilities towards one's family are less important than devotion to Jesus (Mk 10.21; Lk. 14.26).

But the commandment to love one's neighbor is equally important as the commandment to love God (Mk 12.28-31; see also Jn 13.34; 15.12). In his teaching, Jesus explains that there is no limitation to this love commandment. He tells the parable of the Good Samaritan (Lk. 10.29-37) to show that love knows no boundaries, and he calls his disciples to love even their enemies (Mt. 5.38-48).

Jesus' love commandment plays a fundamental role in early Christian preaching. Christians may simply be called "those who love God" (Rom. 8.28; Jas 1.12). Love of God is closely connected with love for one's neighbor, as John emphasizes in his first letter (1 Jn 4.7-10, 20). Jesus' command to love one's enemies made such an impact that it is repeated in the writings of both Peter (1 Pet. 3.8-9) and Paul (Rom. 12.14).

Paul

It is only possible to fulfill this commandment by the power of the Holy Spirit, as the apostle Paul emphasizes. Those who have the Holy Spirit have an entirely new direction for their lives. They are no longer ruled by selfish and sinful desires. Instead, the Holy Spirit motivates and empowers them to live lives that are pleasing to God (Rom. 8.5-8).

Those who are led by the Spirit, Paul explains, are not under the law (Gal. 5.18). This may come as a surprise, but Paul insists that God's commandments are unable to produce the right fruits in a Christian. These commandments do not cause a person to do good. Instead, they provoke a person to break God's law. Paul "found that the very commandment that was intended to bring life actually brought death. For sin, seizing the opportunity afforded by the commandment, deceived me, and through the commandment put me to death" (Rom. 7.10-11).

In Romans 7.14-23, Paul explains how he is powerless to obey the law. He concludes: "I do not do the good I want to do, but the evil I do not want to do—this I keep on doing" (Rom. 7.19). Over the centuries, Christians have discussed whether Paul in this passage describes his life before or after he became a believer in Christ. On the one hand, Paul makes no reference to the Holy Spirit in this passage and he has a very pessimistic view of himself (Rom. 7.19, 23-24). Many interpreters have therefore concluded that the passage could not describe a Christian believer.

On the other hand, the person in the passage can also say: "in my inner being I delight in God's law" (Rom. 7.22). It is difficult to imagine that Paul would think that this statement could be true of a nonbeliever (Rom. 8.5a, 6a,

7-8). It is therefore best to understand this passage as Paul's description of a Christian, but from a limited perspective. He describes the effect of the law in the life of a believer. That is why he does not mention the Holy Spirit.

Romans 7 and 8 may therefore be compared to the lament psalms in the Old Testament. Typically, the first part of these psalms focuses on the reasons why the psalmist is about to despair. But the perspective changes in the second part of the psalm. Now, the psalmist focuses on the faithfulness of God and the reasons for hope (e.g. see Ps. 77.7-9, 10-15). A similar shift takes place between Romans 7.24 and Romans 7.25, where Paul turns to thanksgiving. He then introduces the topic of the Holy Spirit in Romans 8.1.

On this interpretation, the point of Romans 7.14-23 is to explain that the law never produces good fruit, not even in Christian believers. Instead, the power to have victory over sin comes from the Holy Spirit (Rom. 8.1-11). Paul therefore triumphantly proclaims: "through Christ Jesus the law of the Spirit who gives life has set you free from the law of sin and death" (Rom. 8.2).

Romans 7.7-25 describes the function of the law, and Romans 8.1-17 describes the function of the Spirit. The law provokes sin and transgression, but the Spirit gives victory over sin. To be led by the Spirit is therefore to be free from the law. Those who "are led by the Spirit . . . are not under the law" (Gal. 5.18). They are free from slavery under the law and free to bear the fruit of the Spirit (Gal. 5.22-23). This fruit consists of virtues that build community and can be summed up as a fulfillment of the love commandment, also known as "the law of Christ" (Gal. 6.2).

The Law and the Christian

Paul's different statements regarding the law may therefore seem to contradict each other. In some passages, he says that the law brings death and condemnation and that Christians are free from the law (Rom. 7.3-4; Gal. 3.24-25). He also clearly says that there are several requirements in the law that are no longer binding for Christians (Rom. 14.5; Gal. 5.2; Col. 2.16).

But in other passages, he makes it clear that Christians "uphold the law" (Rom. 3.31), that "the righteous requirement of the law might be fully met in us" (Rom. 8.4), and that "love is the fulfillment of the law" (Rom. 13.10). In Ephesians 6.2-3, he quotes from the Ten Commandments when he gives exhortations to the church. We therefore need to examine what the New Testament has to say about how Christians should relate to the law.

Table 12.1 Different statements about the law

Statements affirming the law	Statements about liberation from the law
The law will not be abolished: "Do not think that I have come to abolish the Law or the Prophets; I have not come to abolish them but to fulfill them. Truly I tell you, until heaven and earth disappear, not the smallest letter, not the least stroke of a pen, will by any means disappear from the Law until everything is accomplished. Anyone who sets aside one of the least of these commands and teaches others accordingly will be called least in the kingdom of heaven, but whoever practices and teaches these commands will be called great in the kingdom of heaven" (Mt. 5.17-19).	Christ set aside the law: "For he himself is our peace, who has made the two one and has destroyed the barrier, the dividing wall of hostility, by setting aside in his flesh the law with its commands and regulations" (Eph. 2.14-15a).
Christians uphold the law: "Do we, then, nullify the law by this faith? Not at all! Rather, we uphold the law" (Rom. 3.31).	Christians are not under the law: "But if you are led by the Spirit, you are not under the law" (Gal. 5.18).
Christians fulfill the law: "And so he condemned sin in human flesh, in order that the righteous requirement of the law might be fully met in us, who do not live according to the sinful nature but according to the Spirit" (Rom. 8.3b-4).	Christians must not do the commandments of the law: "I, Paul, tell you that if you let yourselves be circumcised, Christ will be of no value to you at all" (Gal. 5.2).

Jesus and the Law

Jesus, as we meet him in the Gospel of Matthew, affirms that he has not come to abolish the law and the prophets, "but to fulfill them" (Mt. 5.17). But he also placed himself above the law (ch. 8), and there is a lot of scholarly discussion about his attitude to the law. From what we read in the Gospels, Jesus always obeyed the law of Moses. He paid the temple tax (Exod. 30.13), even though he may not have thought this law was binding for him (Mt. 17.24-27). Jesus touched people that were unclean (Mk 1.41), but that does not mean that he broke the law. Normally, those who touched the unclean also became unclean, and they had to be purified afterwards. But with Jesus, it would have been different. The unclean did not transfer their uncleanness to Jesus, but Jesus transferred his cleanness to the unclean and made them clean.

The conflicts between Jesus and the Pharisees did not usually concern the written law of Moses, but the oral tradition that the Pharisees observed. Jesus did not acknowledge these traditions and felt free to break them. He associated with people that were held to be unclean (Mk 2.15-17), healed on the

Sabbath (Mk 3.1-6), and spoke out against the oral traditions directly (Mk 7.1-23). Many Jews thought that Jesus broke the law when he was healing on the Sabbath (Mt. 12.1-8). In this respect, Jesus certainly disagreed with common interpretations of the law in his day, but whether he actually disobeyed the law is a matter of dispute.

What Jesus taught others about the law is a slightly different question. When it came to the issue of divorce, Jesus certainly differs from the Mosaic law. His teaching is much stricter than that of Moses (Mt. 19.3-12; see also Deut. 24.1-4). But regarding food laws, Jesus made it clear that no food can make a person unclean (Mk 7.18-19). The evangelist Mark clarifies that Jesus therefore "declared all foods clean" (Mk 7.19). When he did that, he also announced that the food laws in Leviticus 11 and Deuteronomy 14.3-21 were no longer valid.

We find Jesus' most detailed teaching about the law in the Sermon on the Mount. As we have seen, Jesus here places himself above the law (ch. 8). But that does not mean that he annulled the law or taught others not to keep it. Regarding the law and the prophets, he insisted that he had "not come to abolish them but to fulfill them" (Mt. 5.17). Scholars discuss what Jesus meant by "fulfilling" the law. Did he understand the law as a prophecy about himself, a prophecy that he had come to fulfill? If so, he was the one who would fulfill the law, but that does not mean that his disciples should fulfill it. Or did he mean that he came to ensure that the law was fulfilled? If so, both he and his disciples would have to obey the law. The context shows us that we must accept both of these interpretations. In v. 18, Jesus announces that everything will be "accomplished." That must refer to the law as a prophecy of what Jesus will do. But in v. 19, Jesus talks about "whoever practices and teaches these commands." This must mean that Jesus comes to ensure that his followers obey the commandments of the law.

Fulfillment of the Law

How can we explain the fact that the New Testament both affirms and rejects the Old Testament law? To understand all these statements, we must consider the context in which they were written. Paul's statements regarding our freedom from the law belong in his discussions of justification and of how we can be members of the people of God. In this context, the law has no place. It is only by faith that we are declared righteous by God and are included in God's people.

But even if Christians are justified freely, they have an obligation to live lives that are pleasing to God. They have been made holy, and are therefore called to be holy. Does the holiness of Christians mean that they should obey the law of Moses? Are Christians therefore obligated to fulfill the Old Testament law?

As we have seen, the New Testament seems to answer both yes and no to this question. Traditionally, Christians have solved this seeming contradiction by appealing to the threefold division of the law: moral, ceremonial, and civil. The civil law is then understood as the laws that Moses gave to Israel about the government of the people. These laws include instructions about how offenses are to be punished, about slavery, and about the organization of society. The ceremonial law concerns cleanness and uncleanness, sacrifices, and festivals in Israel. The moral law includes all the ethical requirements, first and foremost what we find in the Ten Commandments. Christians have then concluded that the civil and ceremonial laws are abolished, but the moral law is still binding for Christians.

But there are several problems with this understanding. The Bible does not give us a clear distinction between the moral, the civil, and the ceremonial laws. (The first person to use this terminology was Thomas Aquinas, in the thirteenth century CE.) We also see that the New Testament authors quote from what we would consider the civil and ceremonial parts of the law (Mt. 18.16; Rom. 12.1; 1 Cor. 9.9; 1 Pet. 1.16). They consider these parts to be authoritative, even if they give them a new interpretation.

When we turn to Jesus' teaching in the Sermon on the Mount, we see that he tells us to fulfill the law in a different way than what we can read directly in the Old Testament. In Matthew 5.21-48, he quotes several commandments from the law, but then he goes on to give an explanation that makes these commandments much more difficult. For example, he refers to the commandment "you shall not murder" and adds: "But I tell you that anyone who is angry with a brother or sister will be subject to judgment. Again, anyone who says to a brother or sister, 'Raca,' is answerable to the Sanhedrin. And anyone who says, 'You fool!' will be in danger of the fire of hell" (Mt. 5.22). Jesus makes it clear that it is not enough to obey the law with our actions. We must obey the law with our heart. True obedience includes our thoughts and attitudes as well.

When Jesus teaches us to fulfill the law, it is more than a literal fulfillment. This emphasis on a spiritual fulfillment is something we can also find in Paul's letters. We no longer bring animals as sacrifice to God. Instead, Paul says: "I urge you, brothers and sisters, in view of God's mercy, to offer your bodies as a living sacrifice, holy and pleasing to God—this is true worship" (Rom. 12.1). Our whole life is now a sacrifice.

The coming of Jesus therefore brings the law to its ultimate, eschatological fulfillment. This means first of all that the law points forward to Jesus Christ and the perfect salvation that we have in him. But it also means that Jesus' disciples are transformed from the inside, so that they obey God from their hearts, not only in outward observance. The new covenant that Jeremiah and Ezekiel expected (Jer. 31.33; Ezek. 11.19; 36.26) has now become reality (2 Cor. 3.3). As especially Paul explains, the disciples' transformation takes place through the power of the Holy Spirit (ch. 11).

When they obey God's will in this more perfect way, Christians fulfill all parts of the law, in their true, spiritual sense. The New Testament authors therefore give a spiritual interpretation of many of the Old Testament commandments (1 Cor. 9.9; Phil. 3.3; Heb. 13.16; 1 Pet. 2.5). The Old Testament prophets also knew that the law aimed at such a spiritual fulfillment (Deut. 10.16, 30.6; Jer. 4.4). But in the New Testament, it becomes clear that many of the Old Testament commandments are now irrelevant in their literal form. Christians do not have to observe the laws regarding clean and unclean food, circumcision, and festivals (Mk 7.19; Rom. 14.5; Gal. 5.2; Col. 2.16).

In the end, we therefore find that it may be useful to distinguish between the moral, the civil, and the ceremonial aspects of Old Testament law. But we should not think that Christians only fulfill the moral law. The whole law teaches us about God and his will, and Christians have an obligation to fulfill the whole law. They fulfill the whole law in a spiritual way. With respect to the moral aspects of the law, this means that Christians not only obey it outwardly, but also inwardly, from their heart. With respect to the ceremonial and civil aspects of the law, it means that they do not have to fulfill it in a literal sense, but that they do fulfill it in a spiritual sense.

In everything, Christians are called to fulfill the law of Christ and "love your neighbor as yourself" (Gal. 5.14; 6.2). Even though Christians are free with respect to the individual commandments of the Old Testament, they are always bound by this law. Oftentimes, Christians will need to set their own freedom aside in order to show love for their neighbor. Paul was free from the law of Moses, but he observed the law as an expression of his love for his fellow Jews. He explains: "Though I am free and belong to no one, I have made myself a slave to everyone, to win as many as possible. To the Jews I became like a Jew, to win the Jews. To those under the law I became like one under the law (though I myself am not under the law), so as to win those under the law. To those not having the law I became like one not having the law (though I am not free from God's law but am under Christ's law), so as to win those not having the law" (1 Cor. 9.19-21). For similar reasons, the apostolic council in Jerusalem instructed the Gentile Christians to obey certain dietary restrictions (Acts 15.20). These laws were not binding for Christians, but it would be unreasonably difficult for Jewish Christians to have fellowship with Gentiles who did not observe these basic rules. Even though they were free from these regulations, the Gentile Christians would therefore obey them out of love for their Jewish brothers and sisters.

Christians should not "seek their own good, but the good of others" (1 Cor. 10.24). They have the Holy Spirit. This Spirit causes them no longer to desire what the world desires, but to desire what is pleasing to God (Rom. 8.5-6). What they do, they do out of love for God and for their neighbor. Love is therefore the sum of the law (Rom. 13.8-10). When Christians are driven by this love, they do the kind of works that serve to build one another up. They are characterized by "love, joy, peace, patience, kindness, goodness, faithfulness, gentleness and self-control" (Gal. 5.22-23). They therefore go beyond the literal demands of the law. When Paul is appealing to the Corinthians to participate in the collection for the poor in Jerusalem, he does not want them to fulfill the law of tithing (Lev. 27.30-33; Deut. 14.22-25). Instead, he wants them to follow the example of Jesus Christ. He did not give only one-tenth of what he owned, but he gave up all his heavenly riches for the sake of his people (2 Cor. 8.9).

Other New Testament Writings

The other New Testament writings do not contain the detailed discussion of the law that we find in Paul's letters and the Synoptic Gospels (especially Matthew). But they also reflect the idea that Jesus brings the eschatological fulfillment of the law.

The letter of James holds the most positive view of the law in the New Testament. James does not reflect on the tension between the old and the new covenant, but refers to the law of Moses as authoritative (Jas 2.8). For him, Jesus has brought "the perfect law that gives freedom" (Jas 1.25).

In the Gospel of John and the epistle to the Hebrews, we find much more of a contrast between the old and the new. But the perspective here is also quite different from that of Paul's letters. These writings do not so much describe the law as something that brings death and condemnation (but see Jn 5.45), but as something that is old and that has now been replaced. Jesus brings the new and perfect revelation of God. For the author of Hebrews, the Sinai covenant is therefore precisely the old covenant (Heb. 8.13). It has been replaced by something better. The worship of the old covenant is for him what shadow is compared to reality (Heb. 8.5; 10.1).

In John's Gospel, it is a running theme that the revelation in Jesus Christ brings the genuine revelation of God (Jn 1.18). Moses could not bring the full reality of God's revelation. That only comes through Jesus Christ (Jn 1.17; 6.31-33). John therefore emphasizes that Jesus' revelation is "true" (Jn 1.9; 6.55; 15.1), which means that it is genuine and real.

Summary

Christians have been given a new life. Therefore, they should live a different life than those who are ungodly. They have been made holy, and they should live holy lives. The Holy Spirit drives them to put away sin and to put on new virtues. The foremost of these virtues is love, which is also the fulfillment of God's law. Christians therefore fulfill the law with their heart, not only with their actions.

With love and the other Christian virtues, Christians build a new community. This community enjoys the blessings of God in a way that has never been possible before, as we shall see in the next chapter.

Further Reading

Hays, Richard B. *The Moral Vision of the New Testament: A Contemporary Introduction to New Testament Ethics*. San Francisco: HarperSanFrancisco, 1996.

Matera, Frank J. *New Testament Ethics: The Legacies of Jesus and Paul*. Louisville: Westminster John Knox, 1996.

Thielman, Frank. *The Law and the New Testament: The Question of Continuity*. New York: Crossroad, 1999.

Thompson, James W. *Moral Formation According to Paul: The Context and Coherence of Pauline Ethics*. Grand Rapids: Baker, 2011.

Review Questions

What does it mean to be holy?

How does Paul describe the different effects that the law and the Spirit have on the believer?

In what way do Christians fulfill the law?

13

God's New Community

The Church

Chapter Outline

Jesus and the Church	180
Jesus' Words to Peter	181
The Church as God's People	183
The Church and Israel	183
The Body of Christ	184
The Temple of God	185
Peter	187
Hebrews	187
John	187
Election	188
The New Community	192
Spiritual Gifts	194
Offices in the Early Church	195
Church Discipline	199
Summary	201

In Jesus Christ, Christians have been reconciled to God and been given the Holy Spirit. They take part in an entirely new reality, the eschatological new creation (2 Cor. 5.17). This new reality becomes visible through the new community, the eschatological people of God.

Jesus and the Church

Many biblical scholars doubt that Jesus intended to form a church. The French scholar Alfred Loisy is often quoted: "Jesus foretold the kingdom, and it was the Church that came." According to Loisy, Jesus expected his own ministry to bring the end of the world. Then the visible kingdom of God would come. When the disciples realized that the kingdom had not come, they formed the church instead.

But this account does not do justice to the evidence in the New Testament. As we have seen, Jesus understood the kingdom to be present (and not only coming soon) in his ministry. At the same time, he thought the kingdom would become fully manifest in the future, when this world would come to an end. Jesus did not know when this end would come (Mk 13.32).

During his earthly ministry, Jesus gave clear indications that he wanted to form a new community, a community that would constitute the restored Israel. The most striking of these indications is the group of the twelve disciples. Even though Jesus had many followers, he chose a special group of twelve (Mt. 10.1-5; 1 Cor. 15.5).

There was an important reason why the number was twelve. The number corresponded to the number of tribes in Israel, a connection that Jesus pointed out when he promised the twelve that "at the renewal of all things, when the Son of Man sits on his glorious throne, you who have followed me will also sit on twelve thrones, judging the twelve tribes of Israel" (Mt. 19.28). After Jesus' resurrection, when Judas apostatized, the apostles knew that Judas had to be replaced, so that the number twelve could be maintained. In the book of Acts, the story about the choice of Matthias (Acts 1.15-26) appears immediately before the outpouring of the Holy Spirit (Acts 2.1-13). Matthias is never mentioned again in the book of Acts, so the reason why Luke includes him here has nothing to do with the person Matthias himself. But it was important for Luke to show that the number of apostles was twelve, and that this number had to be restored before the promise of the Holy Spirit was fulfilled.

When Jesus formed a community around himself, this community had strong symbolic ties to Israel. We can see this connection also in the Lord's Supper. The most important community meal in Israel was the Passover meal. This meal reminded the people of one of the most fundamental events in their history, their liberation from Egypt. Jesus' last meal with his disciples was a Passover meal (Mk 14.12), but Jesus gave this meal an entirely new meaning. He identified it with his own sacrifice (Mk 14.22; 1 Cor. 11.24) and his institution of the new covenant (Lk. 22.20; 1 Cor. 11.25). When Jesus changed one of the fundamental elements of Israel's community in this way, he showed that a new community was about to emerge.

It is also clear from Jesus' teaching that he envisions his followers as a community. He talks about his disciples as a "little flock" (Lk. 12.32), a "city" (Mt. 5.14), a planted field (Mt. 13.24), a group of wedding guests (Mk 2.19), and members of his family (Mk 3.34-35).

Jesus' Words to Peter

When we see how important the new community was in Jesus' teaching, it is not surprising that he also has something to say about the church directly. In Matthew's Gospel, after Peter's confession, Jesus tells him: "Blessed are you, Simon son of Jonah, for this was not revealed to you by flesh and blood, but by my Father in heaven. And I tell you that you are Peter, and on this rock I will build my church, and the gates of death will not overcome it. I will give you the keys of the kingdom of heaven; whatever you bind on earth will be bound in heaven, and whatever you loose on earth will be loosed in heaven" (Mt. 16.17-19).

The word for church (Greek: *ekklesia*) goes back to the Hebrew word *qahal*. This is the word that is used in the Old Testament for the assembly of Israel as God's people. Jesus now reestablishes this assembly with his words to Peter. Throughout the history of the church, there has been a lot of discussion about what Jesus referred to when he said that he would build his church "on this rock." Most interpreters think that this rock refers to Peter, and that there is a play on words here. The Greek word for "rock" is *petra*, which sounds very much like the word Peter (Greek: *Petros*). In the Roman Catholic church, this verse forms the basis for the special role they give to the pope as Peter's successor. Protestants have not accepted this idea, and have often provided a different interpretation of Matthew 16.18. They have argued that the rock is Jesus, or perhaps Peter's confession of Jesus. There are two main arguments for this interpretation: (1) the text uses two different words for Peter and the rock; and (2) Jesus says in Matthew 21.42 that he is the cornerstone. (However, the Greek word in Mt. 21.42 is not *petra*, but *lithos*.)

But the idea that Peter should serve as a foundation for the church is not unbiblical. Paul teaches that the church is "built on the foundation of the apostles and prophets, with Christ Jesus himself as the chief cornerstone" (Eph. 2.20). The context in Matthew 16 also favors this interpretation. In the conversation between Jesus and Peter, Peter first says something about who Jesus is, and Jesus answers by saying something about who Peter is. When Jesus refers to "this rock," there is no reason to think that he is talking about himself. The twelve apostles serve as the beginning of a reestablished Israel (see above). Here, Jesus addresses Peter as the representative of the twelve, as Peter has just made the confession that characterizes Jesus' disciples.

We may compare Jesus' words to Simon Peter with the stories about Abram and Jacob. God also gave them new names when he promised them that they would be the fathers of a people (Gen. 17.1-8; see also 32.22-32). This parallel between Peter and Abraham is even clearer in light of Isaiah 51.1-2, where Abraham is called a rock. John the Baptist also alludes to Isaiah 51.1-2 when he says that God may raise up children for Abraham "out of these stones" (Mt. 3.9). And this is exactly what Jesus does, when he makes the confessing Peter the rock and builds his church on him.

But there are more difficulties for the interpreter of Matthew 16.18. Jesus also promises that "the gates of death will not overcome it." But what are the gates of death? This expression usually simply refers to death (Isa. 38.10). But in some Jewish writings as well as in the New Testament, it stands for the domain of the ungodly dead and the evil spirits (see also 2 Pet. 2.4; Jude 6). These spirits can be associated both with the persecutions that the church has to suffer and with the deceptions of false teaching. There are therefore at least three possible interpretations of Jesus' promise: (1) the church will not be destroyed by death, but live in the resurrection; (2) the church will be protected against false teaching; or (3) persecution will never be able to destroy the church. It is difficult to be certain which one of these interpretations is the best. Perhaps none of them should be excluded.

Finally, Jesus draws a parallel between the church on earth and the kingdom of heaven: "whatever you bind on earth will be bound in heaven, and whatever you loose on earth will be loosed in heaven" (Mt. 16.19). In other words, the church is the earthly manifestation of the kingdom of heaven. In Rabbinic writings, the authority to bind and loose has to do with the authority to establish correct teaching, and many scholars believe that is the meaning also in Matthew 16.19. But the New Testament parallels direct us to a different interpretation. We find the same expression in Matthew 18.18, now in the context of forgiving sins. The authority to bind and loose must therefore be the authority to forgive or not to forgive sins. In Matthew 18.18, Jesus gives this authority to the whole church, and in John 20.23 he gives it to all the apostles. This is another reminder that Peter's role in this passage must not be understood as fundamentally different from that of other believers. Peter may be the foundational rock, but all Christians are living stones that together are built up as the house of God (1 Pet. 2.5).

The Church as God's People

We have seen that Jesus established the church and that this church was a reestablishment of God's people, Israel. This is also how the rest of the New Testament understands the nature of the church. The church is the people of God. What the Old Testament had to say about Israel as the people of God now applies to the church, consisting of Jews and Gentiles. Many Old Testament passages that speak of Israel are used in the New Testament to speak about the church (e.g. Rom. 9.24-26; 1 Pet. 2.9-10). In all these cases, there is no explanation for why passages that spoke about Israel can now be used to talk about Gentiles. This fact shows us that this understanding of the church was shared by all Christians, so there was no reason to explain it.

In the Old Testament, God uses the covenant formula to declare Israel his people: "I will be their God and they shall be my people" (Exod. 6.7; Jer. 31.33 etc.). In the New Testament, this formula is applied to the church (2 Cor. 6.16; Heb. 8.10; Rev. 21.3, 7).

Therefore, in the New Testament, God's people consists of those who believe in Jesus Christ. Like Israel in the Old Testament are called God's holy people (Exod. 19.5-6; Deut. 14.2), so are the believers called "the holy ones" in the New Testament (Acts 9.13; 1 Cor. 1.2; Rev. 5.8 NAB etc.).

The book of Revelation uses symbolic numbers to express the connection between the church and Israel. The number of the saved is 144,000 (7.4-8; 14.1-5). This number must not be understood literally, but can be broken down as follows: $12 \times 12 \times 1,000$. In Revelation, the number twelve is the number of the tribes of Israel (Rev. 21.12) as well as of the twelve apostles (Rev. 21.14). The number 1,000 stands for perfection. The 144,000 therefore represents the people of God in its completeness, both from the time of the Old Testament and from the time of the New Testament.

The Church and Israel

For a more detailed explanation of the relationship between the church and Israel, we have to turn to the apostle Paul. In Romans 9–11, he explains that

Israel, in the sense "God's people," was never an ethnic entity. "For not all who are descended from Israel are Israel" (Rom. 9.6b). Membership in God's people was never based on natural descent, but on God's election. The very history of Israel demonstrates this. Israel's ancestor, Abraham, had two sons, Isaac and Ishmael. But only Isaac was included in God's promise. Likewise, Isaac had two sons, Jacob and Esau. But only Jacob was chosen (Rom. 9.7-13).

In the time of the New Testament, Gentiles that believe in Christ have been included in Israel, God's people, like branches that are grafted into an olive tree. The natural branches of this tree (unbelieving Israelites) were cut off, and wild branches (believing Gentiles) were grafted in (Rom. 11.17-24). But in the end (Rom. 11.15), God will graft the natural branches back in (Rom. 11.23). Then all of ethnic Israel will be saved (Rom. 11.26).

The "Israel" in Romans 11.26 must be the same "Israel" as the "Israel" in Romans 11.25. In Romans 11.25, Paul says that "Israel has experienced a hardening in part." It is not God's people that have experienced hardening, but ethnic Israel. The "all Israel" that is saved in Romans 11.26 must therefore be ethnic Israel. This does not mean that every individual Israelite throughout the history of the world will be saved, but that Israel as a whole, Israel as a nation, will be saved in the end.

The Body of Christ

But the church is not only the continuation of Israel. The new eschatological reality in Jesus Christ also means something new for God's people. The new people of God are so intimately related to Jesus Christ that Paul refers to the church as the body of Christ: "Now you are the body of Christ, and each one of you is a part of it" (1 Cor. 12.27). This metaphor tells us that there is an organic unity between Christ and believers, but also among believers themselves (Gal. 3.26-29). The basis for this unity is Christ's death on the cross. Through baptism and faith, believers are joined with Christ in his death and resurrection (Rom. 6.3-5) and made members of his body (1 Cor. 12.13).

In his later letters, Paul develops further the concept of the church as Christ's body. In Romans and 1 Corinthians, Christ is identified with the body. But in Colossians and Ephesians, Paul is more specific. Christ is now called "the head of the body, the church" (Col. 1.18; see also Eph. 5.23). In this way, Paul shows that Christ provides direction for his people and that they depend on him for life and power (Col. 2.19). The idea of Christ as the head has cosmic and spiritual significance (Col. 1.17-18; Eph. 1.10, 23). Paul now focuses on the heavenly aspect of the church. Even though the church exists on earth, it is also a heavenly community because of its union with Christ (Col. 3.1-4; Eph. 2.5-6; see also Phil. 3.20).

In these later letters, when Paul focuses on the church as a heavenly community, he uses the word "church" differently than he does in his earlier letters. The word "church" now refers to the universal church, all believers throughout the world. Together, these believers form Christ's body (Eph. 5.23, Col. 1.18, 24). As Christ's body, the church all over the world is one (Eph. 4.4). In his earlier letters, however, Paul uses the word "church" with reference to the local community, the assembly of believers that come together in a particular place (e.g. Phil. 4.15; 1 Thess. 1.1).

The Temple of God

Because of their union with Christ, the people of God in the New Testament are much closer to God than what Israel was in the Old Testament. In the Old Testament, the temple represented the dwelling of God (1 Kgs 8.29). Now, the church is God's temple. This metaphor applies both to the church collectively (1 Cor. 3.16-17; Eph. 2.21) and to the believer individually (1 Cor. 6.19). Through the Holy Spirit, God dwells in believers.

In Ephesians 2.11-22, Paul explains what this means for Gentiles. Before, they "were separate from Christ, excluded from citizenship in Israel and foreigners to the covenants of the promise, without hope and without God in the world. But now in Christ Jesus you who once were far away have been brought near by the blood of Christ" (Eph. 2.12-13). In fact, they have come so near that they are far nearer to God than Israel ever was under the old covenant. Not only are they "fellow citizens with God's people," they are also "members of his household" (Eph. 2.19). What is more, as God's temple, they are now God's own dwelling, where he "lives by his Spirit" (Eph. 2.22).

The way that God has fulfilled his promises in Christ is so glorious that it goes beyond what anyone previously could have envisioned, even the Old Testament prophets. That is why Paul calls God's gift to the Gentiles a mystery or a secret (Eph. 3.3). In the Bible, a mystery is not something that is difficult to understand, but a secret that no one can know unless God reveals it to them (see also Dan. 2.19-23). The mystery that "the Gentiles are heirs together with

Table 13.1 Images of the church in the New Testament

The salt of the earth	You are the salt of the earth (Mt. 5.13a).
The light of the world	You are the light of the world (Mt. 5.14a).
Little flock	Do not be afraid, little flock, for your Father has been pleased to give you the kingdom (Lk. 12.32).
City	A city on a hill cannot be hidden (Mt. 5.14b).
A planted field	The kingdom of heaven is like a man who sowed good seed in his field (Mt. 13.24).
Wedding guests	How can the guests of the bridegroom fast while he is with them? (Mk 2.19).
Jesus' family	Here are my mother and my brothers! (Mk 3.34b).
God's chosen people	I will call them "my people" who are not my people (Rom. 9.25). But you are a chosen people, a royal priesthood, a holy nation, God's special possession, that you may declare the praises of him who called you out of darkness into his wonderful light (1 Pet. 2.9).
Members of God's household	You are no longer foreigners and strangers, but fellow citizens with God's people and also members of his household (Eph. 2.19).
The body of Christ	Now you are the body of Christ, and each one of you is a part of it (1 Cor. 12.27).
God's temple	Don't you know that you yourselves are God's temple and that God's Spirit dwells in your midst? (1 Cor. 3.16).
God's field	You are God's field, God's building (1 Cor. 3.9).
God's building	You are God's field, God's building (1 Cor. 3.9).
Jesus' sheep	I am the good shepherd; I know my sheep and my sheep know me (Jn 10.14).
Branches of the vine	I am the vine; you are the branches (Jn 15.5).
The bride of Christ	I promised you to one husband, to Christ, so that I might present you as a pure virgin to him (2 Cor. 11.2b).

Israel" (Eph. 3.6) was not clearly revealed in the Old Testament (Eph. 3.5). Now, Gentiles are so close to God that they are his temple (Eph. 2.22), and they enjoy this nearness only through faith, not through obedience of the law (Eph. 2.15).

As a result, Jews and Gentiles come together in unity; the law no longer separates them (Eph. 2.15-16). The unity of believers is so overwhelming that all status distinctions in this world become irrelevant (1 Cor. 12.13; Gal. 3.28; see also Phlm. 15–16). Through the church, in its unity, God proclaims his wisdom to the spiritual world (Eph. 3.10). In the letter to the Ephesians, God's wisdom is that he brings "unity to all things in heaven and on earth under Christ" (Eph. 1.10). God fulfills his purpose for the cosmos through the church and its demonstration of unity.

Peter

For the apostle Peter, the role of Israel was to point forward to the fulfillment of God's promises, just as the prophets in the Old Testament "were not serving themselves but you, when they spoke of the things that have now been told you by those who have preached the gospel to you by the Holy Spirit sent from heaven" (1 Pet. 1.12). In his first letter, Peter therefore addresses Gentile Christians as "God's elect, exiles scattered throughout the provinces" (1.1). They now have an entirely new identity. In Peter's eyes, they are no longer Gentiles (1 Pet. 2.12 NRSV). What God spoke to Israel at Sinai has now been fulfilled in them: "you are a chosen people, a royal priesthood, a holy nation, God's special possession, that you may declare the praises of him who called you out of darkness into his wonderful light" (1 Pet. 2.9). This idea controls everything that Peter has to say in his first letter. The Christians should understand themselves as the fulfillment of that to which Israel pointed. They should live their lives in fulfillment of what God spoke to Israel. They shall be holy because he is holy (1 Pet. 1.16; see also Lev. 19.2), and they shall present "spiritual sacrifices acceptable to God through Jesus Christ" (1 Pet. 2.5).

Hebrews

The author of the epistle to the Hebrews is also aware of the profound unity between the people of God in the Old and the New Testaments. Those who persevere in faith are surrounded by "a great cloud of witnesses" (Heb. 12.1) that consists of those who demonstrated their faith in the Old Testament (Heb. 11). At the same time, the letter to the Hebrews emphasizes that the new covenant is better than the old. For the people of God, this means that the New Testament believers are in a better position than Israel in the Old Testament. The New Testament believers are of the same family as Jesus, God's Son. Therefore, he calls them brothers and sisters (Heb. 2.11).

John

In the Gospel of John, the church is also defined by its relationship to Jesus, even though the word "church" does not occur. Instead, the church is the sheepfold with Jesus as the shepherd (10.1-18). These sheep are simply those who know Jesus' voice (10.4, 14). They are also described as the branches on the vine, where Jesus himself is the vine (15.1-17). This image emphasizes even more strongly that believers are dependent upon Jesus (15.4-6). The metaphor of the vine comes from the Old Testament (e.g. Isa. 5.1-7) and shows that God's people are now redefined through Jesus Christ, who also replaces the temple (Jn 2.21).

Jesus' high priestly prayer also demonstrates that there is an intimate relationship between Jesus himself and the church. Jesus prays for those whom the Father gave him (17.9) and those who will believe in him through their word (17.20). He prays that they may be one (17.21, 23) so that the world may believe that the Father has sent him (17.21, 23).

Election

The idea of divine election underlies much of what the New Testament has to say about the church. Jesus chose his twelve apostles, and the new community that emerged was the chosen, holy people of God. In the New Testament, the idea of God's election serves to explain the nature and identity of believers. They are God's people, not because there is anything about them that makes them especially attractive to God, but because God has chosen them in his mercy.

The most detailed description of God's election occurs in the letter that also provides the most detailed teaching regarding the church, Paul's letter to the Ephesians. For Paul, the thought of God's election is a source of comfort and assurance for believers. We can see the greatness of God's grace in that he chose us in Christ before the creation of the world (Eph. 1.4). The purpose of God's election was that we might be united with Christ and stand in the same relationship to the Father as he does, namely sonship: "he predestined us for adoption to sonship through Jesus Christ" (Eph. 1.5). In this way, all glory belongs to God (Eph. 1.6).

In Romans 8.18-39, Paul writes to assure the church of their future glory. His most compelling reason for this assurance is the purpose of God in election. The final glory of believers is assured because it depends on God's election: "For those God foreknew he also predestined to be conformed to the image of his Son, that he might be the firstborn among many brothers and sisters. And those he predestined, he also called; those he called, he also justified; those he justified, he also glorified" (Rom. 8.29-30). In Greek, all these verbs are in the aorist tense, which means that they are viewed as a complete action.

Even though the believers' glorification is not yet complete, Paul probably uses this tense because it is already complete in the counsel of God.

Because Paul refers to those God "foreknew" in v. 29, some interpreters conclude that God's election is based on his foreknowledge. The idea would then be that God chose some to be saved because he already knew that they would believe in him. But the meaning of "to foreknow" (Greek: *proginosko*) is probably not so much "to have previous knowledge of something" (Acts 26.5; 2 Pet. 3.17) as "to enter into relationship before" or "to choose before" (Rom. 11.2; 1 Pet. 1.2). The meaning is then that God was the one who initiated the relationship to believers. He decided to do so from eternity.

To be chosen by God means to "be conformed to the image of his Son" (Rom. 8.29). For Paul, this is the fundamental idea of election. God's election takes place "in Christ" (Eph. 1.4), and to be elected means to be so completely united with Christ that one shares everything with him. The elect share Christ's status; they have been adopted to sonship (Rom. 8.15; Eph. 1.5). They also share in Christ's sufferings. In fact, election and suffering are so inseparable that Paul in 1 Thessalonians 1.4-6 can refer to the Thessalonians' suffering as evidence of their election.

There is no reason for God's election other than his grace. God's election actually shows a tendency to choose the ones that do not appear great or attractive according to human standards. When God chose Isaac rather than Ishmael, he chose the son who was born as a result of his own promise, not the one whose birth was the result of human effort (Rom. 9.7-9). When God chose Jacob, he also chose the youngest. He made his choice before Jacob was born, so that it would be clear that his choice was not based on anything that Jacob had done (Rom. 9.10-13).

Paul sees a pattern in God's election: he chooses that which is unattractive. It is this pattern that works itself out when God later chooses the Gentiles. Through Hosea (2.23), God says: "I will call them 'my people' who are not my people; and I will call her 'my loved one' who is not my loved one" (Rom. 9.25). In the context of the book of Hosea, these words refer to how God will take Israel back after he has rejected them. But Paul finds a deeper principle at work in these words. He sees that God always chooses the opposite, those who are rejected, those who are not his people. This is why God chose Israel in the first place, when they were small and pitiful (ch. 5). And that is why he now has chosen the Gentiles.

In his choice of individual Gentiles, God has once again turned to those who are unimpressive. Paul explains to the Corinthians: "think of what you were when you were called. Not many of you were wise by human standards; not many were influential; not many were of noble birth. But God chose the foolish things of the world to shame the wise; God chose the weak things of the world to shame the strong. God chose the lowly things of this world and the despised things—and the things that are not—to nullify the things that are, so that no one may boast before him" (1 Cor. 1.26-29). This does not mean that those who are rich and powerful cannot be saved; there were several wealthy people in the Corinthian church. But it means that no one should think that God's election has anything to do with human qualities. Paul therefore describes God's election as a new act of creation. In his election, God creates something out of nothing. He chose "the things that are not" (1 Cor. 1.28) and made them into his people. He calls them "my people" who are not his people (Rom. 9.25; see also 4.17).

Since election is for the glory of God and based on God's mercy in Christ, those who are chosen have no reason to be proud. Paul is very critical of the Jewish tendency to view one's own elect status as a cause for boasting (2 Cor. 11.21-22; Phil. 3.4-7). He is also aware that Christians are in danger of making the same mistake, and he warns the Romans not to be arrogant because of their new status as the chosen people of God (Rom. 11.20-22).

Rather than a cause for pride, to be chosen is a motivation to change one's life. Those who belong to God should strive to display the virtues that are fitting for his holy people: "compassion, kindness, humility, gentleness and patience" (Col. 3.12).

The other New Testament authors do not discuss election in detail in the way that Paul does. But the idea of God's election is presupposed throughout the New Testament. In the Synoptic Gospels, those who are saved can also be called the elect or the chosen ones (Mt. 22.14; Mk 13.20; Lk. 18.7). The book of Acts reveals that those who come to faith in Christ and believe in the gospel have been predestined to do so (Acts 13.48).

In the Gospel of John, the idea of God's predestination underlies a number of passages. It is the Son who has decided who will receive life (Jn 5.21), and those who come to Jesus are those who are given to him by the Father (Jn 6.37). Only those who belong to God can hear what he says (Jn 8.47). The disciples did not choose Jesus, but he chose them (Jn 15.16). John describes salvation as a new birth, which depends on the will of God, not on the will of human beings (Jn 1.12-13).

For John, the idea of divine election is a comforting message. It means that the disciples' salvation ultimately depends on Jesus, not on themselves

(Jn 6.39-40; 17.2). In the book of Revelation, God's election means that believers are protected against any real harm, even though they may suffer persecution. God has put a seal on his people, which in Revelation is a symbol of protection (Rev. 7.3). That there is a fixed number that are sealed (for the interpretation of the 144,000, see above) probably means that believers are predestined by God.

God's election is for the purpose of transformation. The elect are chosen to be a separate people, a people that bears fruit (Jn 15.16).

This is also the purpose of election as Peter describes it. In his first letter, he ensures believers of their new identity. He explains that their election means that they are called to live a new life, a life that corresponds to who they now are: God's holy people (1 Pet. 1.15-16; 2.9).

The logical counterpart to election for salvation is that God also predestined unbelievers to damnation. But the New Testament does not draw this consequence. Whereas the cause of salvation is the grace of God in election, calling, and regeneration, the cause of damnation is human beings' own sin. When the Gentiles in Pisidian Antioch accepted the gospel, Luke explains that "all who were appointed for eternal life believed" (Acts 13.48). One would expect that those who did not believe were those who were not appointed for eternal life, but that is not what the book of Acts says. Instead, Paul and Barnabas announces to the Jews who refused to believe: "Since you reject it and do not consider yourselves worthy of eternal life, we now turn to the Gentiles" (Acts 13.46).

In Romans 9.22-23, Paul draws a parallel between "the objects of wrath" and "the objects of mercy," a parallel that may appear to apply to God's predestination: "What if God, desiring to show his wrath and to make known his power, has endured with much patience the objects of wrath that are made for destruction; and what if he has done so in order to make known the riches of his glory for the objects of mercy, which he has prepared beforehand for glory" (Rom. 9.22-23 NRSV). However, on closer inspection, we see that he makes an important distinction between the two. Only the objects of mercy are prepared *beforehand* (Greek: *proetoimasen*). Regarding the objects of wrath, Paul uses a different word (*katartizo*). This Greek word means "to cause to be in a condition to function well" or "to prepare for a purpose." In secular Greek, it often means to make soldiers ready for battle. The idea is that something or someone that already has a specific function or a specific purpose is prepared for that purpose (2 Cor. 13.11; 1 Thess. 3.10). When Paul says that God prepared the unbelievers for wrath, he does not say that God made them into people that deserved wrath. Rather, it may be implied that they were already such people. God brought to completion what they had already begun (by their own unbelief).

The doctrine of God's election does not eliminate human responsibility. The fact that no one can come to Jesus unless they are drawn by the Father (Jn 6.44) never stops Jesus from calling people to come to him (Jn 7.37). The seed is sown everywhere, even though it can only bear fruit when it falls on good soil (Mk 4.1-20). Paul knows that "those who are unspiritual do not receive the gifts of God's Spirit" (1 Cor. 2.14 NRSV), yet he makes an open statement of the truth, commending himself to everyone (2 Cor. 4.2). He has "become all things to all people, so that by all possible means [he] might save some" (1 Cor. 9.22).

The New Community

When Jesus came he brought the kingdom of God. This means that the devil had to flee and that the new creation was a reality (ch. 8). Prophecies like Isaiah 35.5-6 and 26.19 were fulfilled when Jesus performed his miracles (Mt. 11.5). Jesus also sent his disciples out to do the same miracles that he had done. He gave them power over demons (Mk 3.15; 6.7), power to cure diseases (Mt. 10.1; Lk. 9.1-2), and authority to forgive sins (Mt. 16.19).

Jesus' disciples continue Jesus' ministry. The kingdom of God continues to be a reality through the community of believers. This kingdom will not become fully manifest until Jesus comes again, but the church has a share in this new eschatological reality through the gift of the Holy Spirit. In the Old Testament, the Holy Spirit was only given to kings, prophets, and priests, but on the day of Pentecost the Holy Spirit was poured out on all the people of God, with no distinction between men and women, or young and old (Acts 2.17-18; see also Joel 2.28-29). The Holy Spirit is "a deposit, guaranteeing what is to come" (2 Cor. 1.22; 5.5). He is the first fruits of the final redemption (Rom. 8.23).

In the church, believers therefore enjoy the blessings of God's kingdom. Human sin had destroyed the relationships between human beings, but these relationships are now being healed. As a result of Christ's love, believers are united in spirit and mind (Phil. 2.1-4; see also 1 Cor. 1.10). They are all one in Jesus Christ (Gal. 3.27-28).

Since the church is such a unity, no believer should think of himself or herself as superior to others (Rom. 12.16). They should "be devoted to one another in love" and "honor one another above themselves" (Rom. 12.10). With such an attitude, they can "be patient with everyone" (1 Thess. 5.14) and "carry each other's burdens" (Gal. 6.2). Above all, they should "forgive one another if any of [them] has a grievance against someone" (Col. 3.13).

The believers' spiritual fellowship also comes to expression in material fellowship (Acts 2.44-45; 4.32-37; 1 Jn 3.17-18). The equality that they share in Christ manifests itself through equality in sharing material possessions (2 Cor. 8.13-15). This fellowship is not regulated by any law, but is completely voluntary (Acts 5.4; see also 4.32). The motivation to participate does not come from the law, but from the fellowship with Jesus Christ (2 Cor. 8.5, 9; Phlm. 8–9).

In this way, God's kingly rule extends throughout the earth, just as God intended when he created human beings (Gen. 1.28; see also ch. 3). The driving force is the Holy Spirit, who motivates believers from within. God's kingdom is never advanced through the use of force; the church can only be a fully voluntary fellowship. Jesus therefore admonishes his disciples to abstain from all forms of violence (Mt. 5.38-42; 26.52). His "kingdom is not of this world" (Jn 18.36).

The church is the anticipation of the eschatological people of God (Rev. 7.1-17). It is not complete until it consists of people from all nations (Rev. 5.9; 7.9). It is therefore the nature of the church to grow (Acts 2.41; 6.7; Col. 1.6) by being open to all people, regardless of their social status (Rom. 12.16; Jas 2.1-13), ethnic origin (Acts 8.4-25, 26-40; 10.1–11.18), and gender (Gal. 3.28). For the same reason, local churches have a vision that extends beyond their own territory and into areas where Christ is not known. The church in Antioch sponsored Paul and Barnabas as missionaries (Acts 13.1-3), and Paul received support from the church in Philippi when he proclaimed the gospel in Thessalonica (Phil. 4.16). He even counted on the support of a church that did not know him personally, the church in Rome, as he planned to take the gospel to Spain (Rom. 15.23-24).

The effectiveness of the church's witness is closely tied to the unity of the believers (Acts 1.14; 2.44 etc.). Paul therefore frequently admonishes his churches to demonstrate this unity (1 Cor. 1.10; Phil. 1.27). In John's Gospel, Jesus prays that "they may be brought to complete unity. Then the world will know that you sent me and have loved them even as you have loved me" (Jn 17.23).

Spiritual Gifts

The Holy Spirit gives his gifts to the church, so that they can continue Jesus' ministry and do the works that he did. Miraculous gifts therefore played a significant role in the New Testament church and caused the church to grow quickly (Acts 9.32-43; Rom. 15.18-19).

In Romans 12 and 1 Corinthians 12 and 14, the apostle Paul teaches us how to understand spiritual gifts. From these passages, we can divide these gifts into three groups: gifts of inspired speech (wisdom, knowledge, prophecy, discernment of spirits, tongues, interpretation of tongues, revelation, teaching, exhortation), powerful works (faith, healing, miracles), and services (assistance, ministry, giving, leadership, compassion).

For Paul, it is important to explain that none of the gifts should be seen as a sign that a person is specially favored by God. All believers, all those who share the basic Christian confession "Jesus is Lord" (Rom. 10.9), have the Holy Spirit (1 Cor. 12.3). One should therefore not look at the different gifts and think that one Christian is better than another because of the gifts they have been given. What is important is that all Christians have the same Spirit (1 Cor. 12.4). The different gifts are not given so that individuals should gain a higher status than others among the believers. In fact, the gifts should not be understood as individual gifts at all. Instead, we should see them as gifts that have been given to the church. The gifts that have been given to each individual have been given so that these individuals may use their gifts to serve the church, not themselves (1 Cor. 12.7; see also Rom. 12.3-8).

To emphasize this point even further, Paul then goes through the different gifts and explains that the highest honor should be given to those gifts that are less impressive according to human standards. He therefore mentions "different kinds of service" (1 Cor. 12.5) before he mentions the miraculous gifts that receive more attention: "different kinds of working" (1 Cor. 12.6).

He also takes the different gifts and compares them to the different parts of a body. In the Greek world, many speakers used this analogy. They would usually compare the stomach to the higher classes and the lower classes to the other members. The point was that it was necessary for the lower classes to work, like the members of the body. All the resources had to go to the upper classes, just like all the food went to the stomach.

In light of this background, Paul's use of the same analogy is quite remarkable. He does not advocate for class distinctions. Instead, he observes that "those parts of the body that seem to be weaker are indispensable, and the parts that we think are less honorable we treat with special honor. And the parts that are unpresentable are treated with special modesty, while our presentable parts need no special treatment" (1 Cor. 12.22-24). In the new eschatological community, the church, the believers lift up those who are weak and lack honor. In this community, the values of the world are turned upside-down.

The church is fundamentally a community of equals (Gal. 3.27-28). There can be no status distinctions in the community where all are in Christ and made holy in him.

The most important metaphor for the structure of the church is that of a family. As God's children, Christians are brothers and sisters. These are the most common "titles" for Christians in the New Testament. Since he views the church as a family, Paul compares himself both to a father (1 Cor. 4.14-15; 1 Thess. 2.11) and to a mother (Gal. 4.19; 1 Thess. 2.7) when he describes his own role as a minister.

All Christians have been given the Holy Spirit. Even though some have been given a special gift of prophecy (1 Cor. 12.10, 28-29; Eph. 4.11), all Christians have this gift in a fundamental way (Acts 2.17-18; see also Joel 2.28-29). All Christians have the mind of Christ and know spiritual things through their anointing with the Holy Spirit (1 Cor. 2.13-16; 1 Jn 2.27).

All Christians are therefore priests before God (1 Pet. 2.5, 9; Rev. 5.10). The Old Testament priesthood is not continued as a specialized ministry in the New Testament. When the New Testament uses the terminology of priestly service, it is not only applied to special ministers (Rom. 15.16; Phil. 2.17, 25, 30), but also to all Christians (Rom. 15.27; 2 Cor. 9.12; 1 Pet. 2.9).

Offices in the Early Church

In the early church, the different members used their gifts to build each other up. Many biblical scholars have seen a tension between this emphasis on spiritual gifts and the more fixed structure with various offices, such as elders and deacons. They argue that this structure is the result of later development, and that there were no such offices in the earliest Pauline letters.

But the evidence from the New Testament points in a different direction. There was no tension between gifts and offices. Those who had an office were given this office because of the gifts they had. In Acts 6.1-6, we get an insight into the process of electing them. Seven men who were "known to be full of the Spirit and wisdom" (Acts 6.3) were chosen to be the first deacons in the Jerusalem church.

In Paul's letters, we also see that spiritual gifts and offices function together. He makes no distinction between apostles, prophets, and teachers on the one hand, and the "gifts of healing, of helping, of guidance, and of different kinds of tongues" on the other (1 Cor. 12.28-30; see also Rom. 12.6-8; Eph. 4.11). But there is no clear structure of offices in the New Testament. There is considerable overlap between many of them, such as elders, overseers, and teachers. There is also no clear indication of a structure that goes beyond the local church. Those who hold these offices are understood as servants, not rulers (1 Cor. 3.5), and the function they have to serve is more important than their position or office. Paul therefore more frequently refers to his coworkers by their function (e.g. Rom. 16.23; 1 Cor. 16.15-16; 1 Thess. 5.12; Phlm. 1–2) than by their office (e.g. Rom. 16.1; Phil. 1.1).

Apostles

The first office in the early church was that of the apostles. This is the only office that Jesus himself instituted (Lk. 6.13; see also Mt. 10.2). The background for the New Testament understanding of apostleship is found in the Old Testament and Judaism. The Greek word *apostolos* corresponds to the Hebrew *shaliach*, which means "envoy" or a "commissary." The Jews eventually recognized the use of a *shaliach* as a legal institution. A *shaliach* could act on someone else's behalf, for example to contract an engagement or marriage, manage a divorce proceeding, or slaughter the Passover lamb. According to the Mishnah (a book completed ca 220 CE that contains Jewish oral traditions from the period 70–200 CE), "a man's *shaliach* is like the man himself" (*Berakot* 5.5; see also Jn 13.16). Regarding the age of the *shaliach* institution, scholars disagree, but most will at least agree that the Mishnaic and the New Testament concept both grew out of the idea of sending in the Old Testament.

Jesus himself was sent by God to the world. This sending corresponds to the sending of the prophets in the Old Testament and is the fulfillment of the promised Servant of the Lord, whom God would send to his people

(Isa. 61.1-2; see also Lk. 4.18). Jesus' sending of the disciples was modeled after God's sending of himself (Jn 20.21).

To be an apostle of Christ is therefore to serve as his authorized representative and to exercise his authority. As Christ's apostle, Paul understood that he was continuing Jesus' ministry. He could therefore describe his call as a prophetic call and his ministry as a fulfillment of the prophecies regarding Isaiah's Servant of the Lord (Gal. 1.15; see also Jer. 1.5; Isa. 49.1).

The criteria for an apostle of Christ was to have seen the resurrected Lord and to have received a special commission from him (1 Cor. 9.1; Acts 1.22). The fundamental distinction between apostles and other ministers is therefore that apostles have been called directly by Christ, whereas other ministers receive their call through the church. When Paul in Galatians 1.11-12 defends his apostleship, he emphasizes that he was called directly by Christ and that he received his gospel directly from him.

Jesus initially chose twelve apostles (see above), but after the resurrection this circle was significantly expanded (1 Cor. 15.5-9). It included James the brother of Jesus (Gal. 1.19), Paul, Barnabas (1 Cor. 9.5-6), and many others. As Paul refers in 1 Corinthians 15.7 to "all the apostles" and mentions himself as the last of them (15.8), we may conclude that there are no longer any apostles in this qualified sense.

But the New Testament also uses the term "apostle" in a looser sense, for someone who has been sent by the church (2 Cor. 8.23; Phil. 2.25; most English Bibles translate *apostolos* as "messenger" in these verses). Such apostles are not sent with the authority of Christ, but are authorized by a church. Their function may be to carry a message from one church to another (2 Cor. 8.23; Phil. 2.25) or to serve as what we today would call a missionary. When Apollos is called an apostle (1 Cor. 4.6, 9), it is most likely in this sense. We know that Apollos was converted at a later stage (Acts 18.24-26) and could not have been called by the risen Christ. The same probably goes for Junia and Andronicus (Rom. 16.7), who may have been among those visiting from Rome at Pentecost (Acts 2.10). Silvanus and Timothy are probably not referred to as apostles in 1 Thessalonians 2.7, even though they are included as the senders of the letter (1.1). Paul's discussion there concerns his personal ministry. As a late convert (1 Cor. 4.17; 1 Tim. 1.2; 2 Tim. 2.1), Timothy would in any case not qualify as an apostle of Jesus Christ.

The New Testament uses the Greek word *apostolos* both in a narrow and in a broad sense, therefore. In the narrow sense, an apostle is called directly by the risen Christ. We no longer have any apostles in this narrow sense. In the broad sense, an apostle refers to someone who is sent, for example by the church. In modern English, however, the word "apostle" is normally only used in the narrow sense (see also most English translations' rendering of *apostolos* in 2 Cor. 8.23 and Phil. 2.25). It is therefore misleading to use the word "apostle" for any Christian ministers today.

Elders and Deacons

From the Pauline letters, we know that there must have been a number of different offices in the early church, and it is not easy to know how they differ from each other. Regarding the offices of elders/overseers and deacons, Paul gives us more detailed instructions.

The institution of elders goes back to the church in Jerusalem (Acts 11.30; 15.2 etc.). Together with the apostles, they formed the ruling body of the church. The system was similar to that of the Jewish Council, the Sanhedrin. Elders were also appointed for the new churches that were established (Acts 14.23; 20.17-35). First Peter describes the elders as shepherds of the congregation (1 Pet. 5.2). The model is Christ himself (1 Pet. 2.25; 5.4). Detailed qualifications for elders (Greek: *presbuteros*) are listed in Titus 1.6-9 and for overseers (Greek: *episkopos*) in 1 Timothy 3.1-7. These criteria are so similar that we understand that they refer to the same office. Based on these descriptions, the functions of elders must have been to provide direction and leadership for the church, to provide pastoral and shepherding care for believers, and to teach the word of God.

Timothy and Titus themselves are not described as elders; they were rather special delegates appointed by the apostle Paul. There is no indication that the elders and overseers (sometimes *episkopos* is translated "bishop") had any function beyond the local church. The idea of a bishop as a superior of elders is a later development in the church (Ignatius of Antioch, around 110 CE).

Deacons are first mentioned in Acts 6.1-6. Their ministry was to take care of the distribution of food in the church. The list of qualifications for deacons in 1 Timothy 3.8-13 is very similar to that of overseers, but shorter, as the deacons do not seem to have been involved in preaching, teaching, and providing direction for the church.

Ordination

The lists of qualifications show us that equipment with spiritual gifts and being called by God and the church were constitutive of ministry in the New Testament, not ordination. But there are several references to the practice of laying on of hands to commit someone to ministry. Timothy was appointed to his ministry in this way (1 Tim. 4.14; 2 Tim. 1.6). Such laying on of hands is also described in Acts (6.6; 13.3). Ordination may also be mentioned in 1 Timothy 5.22.

Church Discipline

Through the gift of the Holy Spirit, the church is a manifestation of the kingdom of heaven. But the complete manifestation of this kingdom still lies in the future. Until then, the church is a mixed community, consisting of both genuine believers and people who have joined this community without having genuine faith in Jesus Christ. Several of Jesus' parables in the Gospel of Matthew makes this clear. Jesus mentions a man who entered the wedding banquet, but lacked wedding clothes and was cast outside (22.11-13). He also tells the parable of ten virgins that went out to meet the bridegroom. Five of them were foolish and five of them were wise. The foolish virgins did not bring oil for their lamps, and they were not ready when the bridegroom arrived (25.1-13). These characters represent those who belong to the church in this world, but who lack genuine faith and who will be condemned in the final judgment. For this reason, but also because genuine believers continue to be sinners (ch. 12), the church needs to know how to respond to sinful behavior among its members. The New Testament therefore provides relatively detailed instructions for church discipline.

When we compare New Testament disciplinary practices with those of other Jewish groups, one thing stands out: the focus in the New Testament is on restoration of the offender (Mt. 18.10-14). The goal of discipline in the New Testament is the salvation of the sinner, even in the grave instance of incest in Corinth (1 Cor. 5.5; see also 1 Tim. 1.20). At the same time, discipline is necessary for the sake of the holiness of the eschatological community (1 Cor. 5.6).

The New Testament procedure of discipline may be described as correction, repentance, and reconciliation (Lk. 17.3-4). The first step in discipline is always loving and humble correction in private (Mt. 18.15; Gal. 6.1-2). The one who corrects a brother or sister should not act in an attitude of superiority, but as someone who also is totally dependent on the grace of God. They should look at themselves as those who need God to take the plank out of their own eye, before they try to help others with the sawdust in their eye (Mt. 7.3-5). There are many more admonishments to forgive (e.g. Mt. 18.21-35; Lk. 17.3-4; 2 Cor. 2.5-11) than there are to punish. In the case of a sinner who refuses to repent, Jesus commands that the second step should also take place in private, with another witness (Mt. 18.16). Only as a last resort should the matter be brought before the whole church (Mt. 18.17). If the sinner still does not repent, excommunication becomes necessary. This means full exclusion from the Christian community. Paul emphatically says: "Do not even eat with such a one" (1 Cor. 5.11 NRSV). The wording shows that this instruction cannot be restricted to mean exclusion from the Lord's Supper, but must concern Christian fellowship in general.

The responsibility for excommunication rests on the church as a whole, as Paul shows us in his letters (1 Cor. 5.3-5; 2 Thess. 3.14-15). Some serious cases were also dealt with by an apostolic delegate (1 Tim. 5.20; Tit. 3.10-11) or by the apostles themselves (2 Cor. 13.1-2; 1 Tim. 1.19-20). Since the goal is always the salvation of the sinner, excommunication should also be used as an act of love. Even though the excommunicated are excluded from fellowship, they should be treated lovingly by the believers, as brothers and sisters (2 Thess. 3.15 CEB).

Offenses that result in discipline include incest (1 Cor. 5.1-5), unwillingness to work (2 Thess. 3.6-15), and divisiveness (Tit. 3.10-11). Paul also gives directions for discipline in cases of sexual immorality, greed, idolatry, verbal abusiveness, drunkenness, and stealing (1 Cor. 5.11; see also 6.9-10).

Doctrinal error is also cause for discipline in the New Testament. Paul pronounces a curse on those who proclaim a different gospel (Gal. 1.8-9), a reference to his opponents in Gàlatia who maintain that faith is not sufficient for justification. He also gives instructions to Timothy and Titus to correct the errors of heretics, and to excommunicate them, if necessary (1 Tim. 1.3-4; Tit. 3.10-11). Their heresy is difficult to define. Jewish teachers

(Tit. 1.10) claimed to be teachers of the law of Moses (1 Tim. 1.7; Tit. 3.9), were concerned with details in the law and futile speculations (1 Tim. 1.4; Tit. 1.14; 3.9), and advocated an elitist, ascetic form of religion (1 Tim. 4.3). In 2 Peter (2.1-3) and Jude (3-4), the chief problem appears to be antinomianism (2 Pet. 2.12-20; Jude 4).

From the letters of John, we learn that his churches were threatened by a heresy that denied the incarnation of Christ (1 Jn 2.22; 4.2) and was characterized by antinomianism (1 Jn 1.8, 10; 3.6, 9; 5.18). In his second letter, John therefore gives us the clearest commandment regarding heretics: "If anyone comes to you and does not bring this teaching, do not take them into your house or welcome them" (2 Jn 10). They should not be accepted in the churches.

Summary

Jesus established a new eschatological community. This community is a continuation of God's people in the Old Testament, but it enjoys a closer relationship to God than Israel did under the old covenant. Since the Holy Spirit lives in them, they are God's dwelling and share in the heavenly reality.

The gift of the Holy Spirit has been given to all believers, and they are all chosen to be holy and blameless in God's sight. They all share the status of God's Son, and there can therefore be no status distinctions within the church. Spiritual gifts do not lift individual believers up above others, but serve the whole church as a community.

The church is a visible demonstration of God's eschatological act of reconciliation and of his kingly rule. The church enjoys the blessings of God's kingdom. In the new community's covenant rituals, these blessings find their visible expression.

Further Reading

Minear, Paul S. *Images of the Church in the New Testament*. 1960. Repr. New Testament Library. Louisville: Westminster John Knox, 2004.

Schnackenburg, Rudolf. *The Church in the New Testament*. Translated by W. J. O'Hara. London: Burns & Oates, 1974.

Turner, Max. *The Holy Spirit and Spiritual Gifts Then and Now*. Carlisle: Paternoster, 1996.

Review Questions

In what ways does the New Testament show that the church is the continuation of the Old Testament people of God?

In what ways does the New Testament show that the church is something more than the Old Testament people of God?

What is the purpose of the New Testament language of election?

Spiritual gifts are given to build up the church. In what ways does this purpose inform what Paul has to say about these gifts?

14

The Covenant Rituals of the New Community

Baptism and the Lord's Supper

Chapter Outline

The Baptism of John	203
Christian Baptism	204
The Great Commission	205
Baptism in Paul's Letters	206
Faith and Baptism	207
Infant Baptism	209
The Lord's Supper	210
Abuse of the Lord's Supper	211
John and the Lord's Supper	212
Summary	213

Jesus instituted two communal rituals for the new people of God: baptism and the Lord's Supper. The church later used the word "sacrament" for these rituals, but we do not find that terminology in the New Testament.

The Baptism of John

The immediate background for Christian baptism is the baptism of John. He baptized "with water for repentance" (Mt. 3.11). Those who were baptized by him confessed their sins and repented (Mt. 3.6). Since God forgives the sinner who repents, John's baptism would therefore lead to forgiveness (Mk 1.4).

Because John's baptism was a sinner's baptism, John would at first not allow Jesus to be baptized (Mt. 3.14). However, Jesus explained to him that it had to be done in order "to fulfill all righteousness" (Mt. 3.15). In other words, Jesus' baptism was a necessary part of Jesus' mission to restore righteousness on earth. His baptism showed that he took the place of sinners (Jn 1.29).

Three significant events took place as Jesus was baptized (Mt. 3.16-17). First, heaven was opened. This meant that it was the time for the eschatological judgment (Isa. 64.1). Second, the Holy Spirit came down as a dove. This is an echo of Genesis 1.2 and tells us that the new creation is here. Third, God's voice from heaven said: "you are my Son, whom I love; with you I am well pleased" (Mk 1.11). The voice alludes to three different Old Testament passages: God's words to Israel's king and the Messiah (Ps. 2.7); God's words about Isaac (Gen. 22.2, 12, 16), and God's words to the Suffering Servant (Isa. 42.1). Jesus combines all the promises of the Old Testament. He is the Messiah, the fulfillment of the promise to Abraham, and the Suffering Servant. Because Jesus' baptism was a part of his vicarious ministry, his baptism is unique. We should therefore be careful not to draw conclusions regarding Christian baptism from Jesus' baptism.

John's baptism was not Christian baptism. John stands between the Old and the New Testament as the last of the prophets, and he points forward to the coming of Jesus (Mt. 11.7-15). John's baptism also points forward to the baptism with the Holy Spirit and fire (Mt. 3.11; see also Acts 19.1-5). We may therefore explain the relationship between John's baptism and Christian baptism as the relationship between promise and fulfillment. A comparison with Old Testament sacrifices may be helpful. The sacrifices did not in themselves have any power to atone for sin (Heb. 10.4). Nevertheless, those who offered them with a sincere heart were forgiven (Lev. 4.20 etc.). In light of the full revelation in the New Testament, we understand that forgiveness could take place on the basis of Jesus' sacrifice (Rom. 3.25). In the same way, John's baptism did not actually give the gifts that we receive in Christian baptism (Acts 19.1-5). Nevertheless, those who were sincere were forgiven (Mk 1.4).

Christian Baptism

We can therefore understand that Christian baptism would be much more powerful than John's baptism. John himself promised that Jesus "will baptize you with the Holy Spirit and fire" (Mt. 3.11). Christian baptism brings the new eschatological reality of the Holy Spirit, and fire can be a symbol both of judgment (Isa. 66.15-16) and of purification (Isa. 6.6-7; Zech. 13.9). The promised eschatological renewal (Ezek. 36.25-27) would now be reality.

In his speech on the Day of Pentecost, Peter explains that baptism is now the way in which the eschatological promises will become reality: "Repent and be baptized, every one of you, in the name of Jesus Christ for the forgiveness of your sins. And you will receive the gift of the Holy Spirit. The promise is for you and your children and for all who are far off—for all whom the Lord our God will call" (Acts 2.38-39). Baptism with the Spirit is now here. Baptism is now directly connected with forgiveness and the Holy Spirit.

The Great Commission

The Gospels do not tell us that Jesus ever baptized anyone (Jn 4.2). Instead, he sent his disciples to baptize. His Great Commission is recorded in Matthew 28.18-20: "All authority in heaven and on earth has been given to me. Therefore go and make disciples of all nations, baptizing them in the name of the Father and of the Son and of the Holy Spirit, and teaching them to obey everything I have commanded you. And surely I am with you always, to the very end of the age."

This commission begins with Jesus' assurance to his disciples that all authority belongs to him. He has come to establish the kingdom of God on earth. Now he makes himself known as the one who exercises the authority of the kingdom. Earlier he had claimed to have this power on earth (Mt. 9.6); now he claims to have this authority in heaven as well.

At the conclusion of the commission stands Jesus' promise to be with his disciples always. The divine presence is now the presence of Jesus (Mt. 1.23; 18.20).

The one who is omnipotent (all-powerful) and omnipresent (present everywhere) gives the disciples two commandments: (1) to go and (2) to make disciples. Compared to the Old Testament, the situation is now reversed. In the Old Testament, the Gentiles had to come to the people of God. But now the people of God are called to go to the nations. Missiologists refer to this idea as the centrifugal (away from the center) movement, as opposed to the centripetal (towards the center) movement in the Old Testament (ch. 5).

The second commandment is to make disciples, which is a comprehensive commandment. Mission aims to make followers of Jesus. To be a follower of

Jesus, or to be a disciple of him, means to imitate him. It cannot be defined as a particular task, but only by the person of Jesus. When Jesus called his disciples, he did not give them any specific commands. He simply told them to follow him (Mk 1.17; 2.14 etc.). Discipleship meant to be with Jesus, walk with him, eat and drink with him, listen to him, and watch him. Disciples are not called to do great things on their own, but to witness and participate in what Jesus does. To be a disciple is to be identified with Jesus (Mt. 10.24-25).

Jesus explains what it means to make disciples with the verbs "baptizing" and "teaching." Grammatically, these verbs are subordinate participles. This means that they serve as a further explanation of the main verb: make disciples.

The disciples will make disciples by "baptizing them in the name of the Father and of the Son and of the Holy Spirit" (Mt. 28.19). The Greek preposition that is translated "in" (*eis*) literally means "into." To be baptized is to be baptized "into" this name. That means that those who are baptized are now fundamentally determined by this name. They are radically changed human beings. They belong to a new name.

This new name is the name of the Father and of the Son and of the Holy Spirit. Christian baptism takes place in the name of the Triune God (ch. 1).

In the book of Acts, baptism is always said to be baptism in Jesus' name (Acts 2.38; 8.16; 10.48; 19.5). This appears to be different from what we read in Matthew 28.19. But we must remember that the account in Acts is a very brief summary. It is not a comprehensive account of everything that was said in connection with baptism. Rather than repeat the lengthy formula that the apostles used when they baptized, Luke summarized it and mentioned the name that was most characteristic of Christian baptism: the name of Jesus.

Jesus' Great Commission adds the verb "teaching," which also explains what it means to make disciples. Baptism cannot take place in isolation, but must be accompanied by "teaching them to obey everything I have commanded you." The teaching that must be obeyed includes everything that Jesus has commanded and is first and foremost found in the Sermon on the Mount (ch. 10).

Baptism in Paul's Letters

The apostle Paul also gives us detailed teaching regarding baptism. The most central text is Romans 6.1-14, where he explains that "we were therefore buried with him through baptism into death in order that, just as Christ was raised from the dead through the glory of the Father, we too may live a new life" (Rom. 6.4; see also Gal. 3.27; Col. 2.12). Baptism means that the old life in sin has been put to death and the new life in Christ has come into existence.

The background for Paul's teaching is the institution of slavery. Before they were baptized, believers were slaves to sin. A slave belongs to someone else, is ruled by someone else, and does the will of someone else. In the same way, the Romans belonged to sin and were ruled by sin (Rom. 6.6). But when slaves are dead, the owner cannot rule them anymore. When they were baptized, the believers died to sin. They no longer belonged to sin as their slave-master (Rom. 6.7). Instead they had a new life, with Christ (Rom. 6.4, 8).

Baptism therefore serves as a powerful motivation for Christians to live their lives in a new way. Paul urges them to consider what happened in baptism and put it into practice in their life. They died to sin; now they must understand themselves and think of themselves in this way: "count yourselves dead to sin but alive to God in Christ Jesus" (Rom. 6.11). Sin is no longer their master, so they must no longer obey their sinful impulses (Rom. 6.12-13a). Instead, they must use their lives in the service of God and righteousness (Rom. 6.13b).

Baptism is therefore the fundamental, life-transforming event. It represents the death of the old life under sin and the birth of the new life with Christ. Paul can also describe baptism as "the washing of rebirth and renewal" (Tit. 3.5; see also Heb. 10.22). Because of this connection between washing, new birth, and baptism, many biblical scholars also find a reference to baptism when the New Testament mentions washing or new birth (Gal. 4.5-7; Eph. 4.22-24). But we should be cautious about making this link in texts that make no explicit reference to baptism.

This makes it difficult to know if Jesus says anything at all about baptism in John's Gospel. Many scholars see a reference to baptism in Jesus' words about "being born of water and the Spirit" in John 3.5. But the phrase may simply be an allusion to Ezekiel 36.25-27, which describes the Holy Spirit's role in new birth. If so, this passage may not refer to baptism directly.

Faith and Baptism

Since baptism is so closely tied to becoming a Christian, some questions may arise: does a person become a Christian by being baptized or by believing in Jesus Christ? Does God give the Holy Spirit through baptism or through faith?

The New Testament does not address these questions directly. To the New Testament church, faith and baptism belonged together. Baptism was the way to express publicly that a person had come to faith in Jesus Christ. Peter explains that the flood in Noah's days "was a symbol pointing to baptism, which now saves you. It is not the washing away of bodily dirt, but the promise made to God from a good conscience" (1 Pet. 3.21 GNB). Baptism is accompanied by a genuine promise to belong to God.

To ask if the Holy Spirit is given through faith or baptism is therefore to separate what the New Testament holds together. The book of Acts shows us one instance where the Holy Spirit is given before baptism. In that case, baptism serves as a public confirmation (Acts 10.44-48). But the most common picture is that the Holy Spirit is given when someone is baptized (Acts 2.38; 9.17; 19.5-6; 22.16).

On one occasion, the New Testament reports the giving of the Holy Spirit as a separate event that takes place after baptism. Many Samaritans believed and were baptized when Philip proclaimed Christ in Samaria (Acts 8.4-13). But they did not receive the Holy Spirit until the apostles Peter and John came to Samaria, prayed for the new believers, and laid their hands on them (Acts 8.14-17).

Scholars have explained this unusual event in several different ways. Some suggest that the Samaritans actually did receive the Spirit when they were baptized. According to these scholars, what happened when Peter and John laid their hands on the believers was an extraordinary manifestation or a second giving of the Spirit. These explanations are unlikely to be correct, because Acts 8.16 says: "the Holy Spirit had not yet come on any of them." Other scholars have suggested that the Holy Spirit could not be given through Philip's ministry because he was not an apostle. It was necessary for some of the apostles to lay their hands on the believers in order for them to receive the Holy Spirit. This explanation is also difficult because the book of Acts does not usually mention that the apostles laid their hands on those who were baptized (e.g. 2.38, 41; 8.38).

There are two explanations that are better than the ones mentioned above. One possibility is that the Samaritans did not truly become believers when they were baptized. Elsewhere in the book of Acts, the gift of the Spirit serves as the proof that someone is genuinely a Christian (Acts 10.45, 47; see also 19.2). When Acts 8.16 tells us that "the Holy Spirit had not yet come on any of them," the point may simply be that they had not become genuine believers. We read that they "believed Philip" (v. 12), but never that they believed in Jesus. Their faith also seems to be focused more on the display of magical power than on an understanding of the gospel (vv. 9-12). Perhaps they understood the message about the kingdom of God (v. 12) in a political sense. In the case of Simon, we clearly see that his faith was not genuine (vv. 18-23). The problem with this interpretation is that it passes the same judgment on all the Samaritans as it does on Simon, whereas the text makes a distinction between them.

The most common explanation is that Acts 8.4-25 describes a unique event in salvation history. Up until this point, the gospel had only been proclaimed among the Jews. That God also gave the Holy Spirit to the Samaritans was a decisive new step in salvation history (Acts 1.8). The event in Acts 8.14-17 is therefore a "Pentecost of the Samaritans." If this is the correct interpretation, it is a little surprising that there was no similar validation in the case of the Ethiopian (8.26-40) or Paul (9.1-19). But this may still be the best explanation.

Infant Baptism

The New Testament does not address directly the question of whether infants were or should be baptized. To answer this question, it is necessary to consider dogmatic and historical issues as well.

Many Christians quote Jesus' words "Let the little children come to me" (Mk 10.14) and use them as an argument for infant baptism. But Jesus did not speak about baptism when he said these words. The only possible mention of infant baptism in the New Testament is when we hear that someone's household was baptized (Acts 16.15, 31-34). It is likely that there were small children in at least one of these households, but we cannot know for certain.

The basis for infant baptism is the covenant nature of our relationship with God. This covenant is modeled after God's covenant with the people of Israel. In this covenant, infants received the sign of the covenant, circumcision, on the eighth day. Paul also makes a comparison between baptism and circumcision in Colossians 2.11-12: "In him you were also circumcised with a circumcision not performed by human hands. Your sinful nature was put off when you were circumcised by Christ, having been buried with him in baptism, in which you were also raised with him through your faith in the working of God, who raised him from the dead." Baptism is the ritual that marks one's entrance into the new people of God (see above), and Jesus makes it clear that his kingdom is for small children. In Luke's Gospel, Jesus' words about children apply specifically to "babies" (Lk. 18.15). Many Christian churches therefore baptize infants.

The Lord's Supper

The other ritual that Jesus instituted with his disciples was the Lord's Supper. Sharing a meal plays an important role in biblical theology. The Old Testament describes the end time salvation as a banquet (Isa. 25.6-8). Jesus builds on these images when he uses meal fellowship in his ministry. He drew attention when he included sinners and outcasts in his meal fellowship (Mk 2.15-17; Lk. 15.1-2; 19.1-10). Jesus also used food miracles to reveal his own identity (Mk 6.30-44; 8.1-10; Jn 6.1-14). In the Gospels, we even see that Jesus' meals help his disciples understand the truth about him. After the resurrection, they recognized Jesus when he shared a meal with them (Lk. 24.30-31, 42; Jn 21.9-13). All of these meals serve as the general background for the Lord's Supper. In the early church, the Lord's Supper was therefore also known as the love feast (Jude 12). The distinction between the Lord's Supper and the love feast is the result of later developments in the church.

We find the account of Jesus' institution of the Lord's Supper in Matthew 26.26-29; Mark 14.22-25; Luke 22.15-20; and 1 Corinthians 11.23-26. The meal has a profound meaning related to salvation. When Jesus breaks the bread he says: "Take it; this is my body" (Mk 14.22 par.). He also says that the cup is his "blood of the covenant, which is poured out for many for the forgiveness of sins" (Mt. 26.28). This refers to Jesus' death as an atonement for sin.

The meal is the new covenant meal. In Luke's and Paul's accounts, we learn that the cup is "the new covenant in my blood" (Lk. 22.20; 1 Cor. 11.25; see also Jer. 31.31). Matthew and Mark refer to the "blood of the covenant" (Mt. 26.28; Mk 14.24) and allude to the blood of the covenant in Exodus 24.8. Half of this blood was sprinkled on the altar (Exod. 24.6). This symbolized that God accepted the people and forgave them. The other half was sprinkled on the people (Exod. 24.8). This symbolized their union with God in covenant. The Lord's Supper therefore represents the new covenant between God and human beings, based on the atoning sacrifice of Jesus Christ, the forgiveness of sins, and God's acceptance.

Jesus also explains that the Lord's Supper is a genuinely heavenly meal and that it has a uniquely eschatological significance. He tells his disciples: "I will not drink again of the fruit of the vine until that day when I drink it new in the kingdom of God" (Mk 14.25 par.). The Lord's Supper is a meal that will continue when the kingdom has reached its fulfillment. It shows that the church is the eschatological people of God.

According to the Synoptic Gospels, the meal that Jesus and the disciples shared together was a Jewish Passover meal (Mk 14.12 par.). Paul also associates Jesus' death with the Passover lamb (1 Cor. 5.7) and calls the cup of the Last Supper the cup of blessing, which is the name Jewish liturgy gave to the third cup during the Passover meal (*Mishnah Pesahim* 10.7).

The Passover meal was the most important community meal for the Jewish people. When they ate this meal, all Jews thought of themselves as if they belonged to the generation that was delivered from Egypt (*Mishnah Pesahim* 10.5). They identified the unleavened bread with the bread of affliction that they ate in Egypt.

When Jesus used this meal to institute the Lord's Supper, he redefined it. It no longer unites the participants with the generation that was saved from Egypt. Now it unites the participants with the saving effects of Jesus' sacrifice. He identifies the bread with his own body (Mk 14.22 par.; see also Jn 6.53). Luke's and Paul's versions also specify that Jesus' body is "given for you" (Lk. 22.19; 1 Cor. 11.24). This expression may be related to Isaiah 53.12, where we learn that the Suffering Servant "bore the sins of many." Rather than participate in the bread of affliction from Egypt (Deut. 16.3), the believers now take part in Christ's sacrifice (1 Cor. 10.16). Like the blood sprinkled on the Israelites at Sinai meant that they belonged to God's covenant people (Exod. 24.8), so does the sharing of the cup at the Lord's Supper mean that the believers belong to God's new covenant people. When Jesus tells his disciples to "do this in remembrance of me" (1 Cor. 11.24, 25), it means more than simply to remember it. It means to renew it in our experience (Deut. 8.18; Judg. 8.34).

Abuse of the Lord's Supper

In 1 Corinthians 11.17-34, Paul discusses a case of abuse of the Lord's Supper. This particular abuse was so serious that he had to conclude: "when you come together, it is not the Lord's Supper you eat" (1 Cor. 11.20). He even warned the Corinthians with these stern words: "those who eat and drink without discerning the body of Christ eat and drink judgment on themselves" (1 Cor. 11.29).

To understand what it is that Paul condemns so harshly, we must know what happened in the church in Corinth. The church came together in private homes to worship. The host of these gatherings was likely a wealthy member of the church. Close friends of the host would typically be allowed into the dining room, but others might have to stay in the atrium, which was not as nice. When the church came together for the Lord's Supper, everyone brought their own food.

In 1 Corinthians 11.21, Paul says that "some of you go ahead with your own private suppers." He uses the Greek word *prolambanei*, which is difficult to translate. It may mean "take beforehand" (TNIV). On this interpretation, the point is that the church members of higher status go ahead and eat their meal, but those of lower status could not take part in it. The word may also be translated as "devour." If so, what happened was that the rich ate all their good food while those who had nothing were watching. In either case, the New Living Translation captures the idea well: "some of you hurry to eat your own meal without sharing with others."

When Paul rebukes the Corinthians for eating or drinking "in an unworthy manner" (1 Cor. 11.27), it is important to note that "unworthy manner" (Greek: *anaxios*) is an adverb. It describes the way in which the Corinthians ate, not the Corinthians themselves. This verse does not concern people who are unworthy, but eating done in an unworthy way. This refers to the way in which the rich were eating without sharing with the poor. When the Lord's Supper is used to demonstrate status distinctions and disunity within the church, it is an unworthy way of taking the Lord's Supper. The Lord's Supper is a meal that should demonstrate the unity of the church. When Paul mentions "those who eat and drink without discerning the body of Christ" (1 Cor. 11.29), the "body of Christ" refers to the church, which is the body of Christ (1 Cor. 12.27; Eph. 4.12).

John and the Lord's Supper

The Gospel of John has not included an account of the Last Supper. But many scholars think that Jesus refers to the Lord's Supper when he talks about himself as the bread of life (Jn 6.35-50). In this passage, Jesus says: "I am the bread of life" (6.48). In other words, he identifies himself with the bread, just as he did in the Synoptic accounts of the Last Supper. But it is doubtful that this expression is directly related to the Lord's Supper. The background is the Old Testament's use of bread as a metaphor for the word of God (Amos 8.11-13; Prov. 9.5). In John 6.48, the point is that Jesus is the perfect revelation of God; he is the true bread of life.

A few verses later, it is possible that the perspective has changed. In John 6.51-59, Jesus uses different terminology. Up until this point, Jesus has only spoken about eating, not drinking (even though he mentioned thirst in v. 35). But now he specifically mentions eating his flesh and drinking his blood (vv. 51, 53, 54, 56). He promises that "whoever eats my flesh and drinks my blood has eternal life, and I will raise them up at the last day" (v. 54). In this passage the text uses a different word for eating. This word (Greek: *trogo*) emphasizes the realistic nature of eating and may almost be translated "chew."

Some scholars do not think these arguments are strong enough that we can find a reference to the Lord's Supper in these verses. They point out that Jesus had not yet instituted the Lord's Supper when he gave the speech in John 6.35-50. But there are good reasons to believe that the disciples after the resurrection would have thought of the Lord's Supper when they remembered Jesus' speech. The way John has recorded it leads us towards this conclusion.

Summary

Baptism and the Lord's Supper unite us with Christ and the saving effects of his death. Baptism gives a person a new identity. He or she now belongs to the Triune God, is united with Christ's death and resurrection, and receives forgiveness of sins and the gift of the Holy Spirit.

The Lord's Supper is a heavenly meal and shows that the church is the eschatological people of God. This community meal unites them with Christ's atoning sacrifice for their sins. The Lord's Supper is a meal that will continue in the future kingdom of God. By partaking in this meal, the church anticipates the blessings of the new heaven and the new earth.

Further Reading

Ferguson, Everett. *Baptism in the Early Church: History, Theology, and Liturgy in the First Five Centuries.* Grand Rapids: Eerdmans, 2008.

Hartman, Lars. *"Into the Name of the Lord Jesus": Baptism in the Early Church.* Studies of the New Testament and Its World. Edinburgh: T & T Clark, 1997.

Moloney, Francis J. *A Body Broken for a Broken People: Eucharist in the New Testament.* Peabody: Hendrickson, 1997.

Witherington, Ben, III. *Making a Meal of It: Rethinking the Theology of the Lord's Supper.* Waco: Baylor University Press, 2007.

Witherington, Ben, III. *Troubled Waters: The Real New Testament Theology of Baptism*. Waco: Baylor University Press, 2007.

Review Questions

What are the benefits of Christian baptism?

How does the Lord's Supper transform the Passover meal?

What does it mean to eat and drink the Lord's Supper "in an unworthy manner" (1 Cor. 11.27)?

15
Perfect Union
The Last Things

Chapter Outline

The Old Testament	215
The New Testament	216
The Gospels	218
Paul	218
The Rest of the New Testament	221
The Book of Revelation	221
The Victorious Lamb	222
The Beast	223
The Tribulation	223
The Millennium	224
Judgment	225
The New Creation	226
Summary	226

In the church, the gifts of God's kingdom are already present in this world. Nevertheless, the church looks forward to a time when she will enjoy these gifts in a more visibly glorious way.

The Old Testament

Many Old Testament prophecies look towards a new future for Israel. The people will be freed from captivity, return to the promised land, and enjoy its abundant fruit. They will be ruled by a good king and see peace and justice. God will give them a new covenant. Through this covenant, he will give them a new heart, so that they will obey God wholeheartedly. He will be their God, and they will be his people. He will pour out his Spirit on all flesh (ch. 5).

To fulfill all these promises means to restore the order of God's creation. Human beings will have an open relationship with God and enjoy the blessings of life in abundance, much like Adam and Eve did in the garden of Eden. In some Old Testament passages, it becomes clear that the fulfillment of God's promises will involve a radical transformation of the world as we know it. God will intervene in the world in a most decisive way and bring about a new creation. Through the prophet Isaiah, he announces: "See, I will create new heavens and a new earth. The former things will not be remembered, nor will they come to mind" (Isa. 65.17).

In the book of Daniel, this expectation is combined with a vision of the resurrection of the dead. This resurrection will be followed by God's judgment. "Multitudes who sleep in the dust of the earth will awake: some to everlasting life, others to shame and everlasting contempt" (Dan. 12.2). This is the clearest reference to a resurrection in the Old Testament. Some interpreters point to Isaiah 26.19 and Ezekiel 37.1-14 as well, but these passages may also be understood metaphorically. Elsewhere, the Old Testament is not very specific about hope for the afterlife.

The New Testament

As we have already seen, Jesus fulfills the promises of the Old Testament. He is the Messiah who leads his people to a new future (ch. 8). The political promises of freedom, land, peace, and life are fulfilled in a more fundamental way. Jesus has triumphed over the devil and set his disciples free from sin and death. Jesus therefore also sets people free from sickness and disease (ch. 12). Through him, they have a relationship with God that is not bound to any specific place; they worship God in spirit and truth (Jn 4.23). Through faith in Jesus Christ and the gift of the Holy Spirit, they have come much closer to God than anyone could under the old covenant (Eph. 2.19-22). They enjoy the fulfillment of the Old Testament promises regarding the land (Mt. 5.5). Jesus has established the new covenant (Lk. 22.20; 1 Cor. 11.25; Heb. 12.24) and given his disciples a new heart (2 Cor. 3.3). In Jesus Christ and through the gift of the Holy Spirit, Christians already enjoy the first fruits of the new creation (Rom. 8.23; 2 Cor. 1.22). That is why the apostle Paul can say that "if anyone is in Christ, the new creation has come" (2 Cor. 5.17; see also Gal. 6.15).

At the same time, Christians are still waiting for the full manifestation of the new creation (2 Pet. 3.13; Rev. 21.1, 5). Jesus announced the presence of the kingdom (Lk. 11.20; 17.21), but he also awaited this kingdom in the future (Mt. 6.10; Lk. 22.16-18). As the Son of Man, he would then return in glory (Mk 8.38; 14.62).

There is therefore a tension in New Testament eschatology between these two aspects. On the one hand, the end times are already here (Acts 2.17; 1 Cor. 10.11; 1 Pet. 1.20). The church enjoys the eschatological gift of the Holy Spirit (Acts 2.17), and the community of the church therefore represents the beginning of God's eschatological salvation.

On the other hand, Christians are still waiting for the fulfillment of the promises (1 Pet. 1.3-5). Theologians typically use the phrase "already and not yet" to account for this double nature of New Testament eschatology. The German biblical scholar Joachim Jeremias spoke of "eschatology that is in the process of realization."

Since the end time events are already underway, the New Testament authors are convinced that the final end is near (Rev. 22.10). They expect the present world order to come to an end when God intervenes in history. At that time, they look forward to a resurrection of the dead (Mk 12.18-27). God's judgment will bring rewards for the righteous and punishment for the wicked (Mt. 25.31-46; 2 Thess. 1.5-10; 1 Pet. 4.5 etc.). In Matthew 25.31-46, Jesus describes how he will come as the Son of Man in glory. "All the nations will be gathered before him, and he will separate the people one from another as a shepherd separates the sheep from the goats" (v. 32). Those on his right will receive their inheritance, "the kingdom prepared for [them] since the creation of the world" (v. 34), but those on his left will be sent "into the eternal fire prepared for the devil and his angels" (v. 41). Before this happens, there will be a time of tribulation for the righteous (Mk 13.5-23; 2 Tim. 3.1-5).

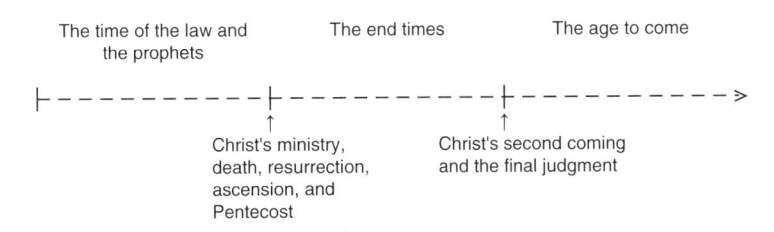

Figure 15.1 History and eschatology

The Gospels

The Gospels describe Jesus as the fulfillment of the promises regarding what God would do in the last days. Even God's judgment has already taken place in the person of Jesus Christ (Lk. 12.8-10; see also Rom. 3.25-26). In a fundamental way, Jesus' death anticipates the end of the world. The Gospel of Mark therefore describes Jesus' death in such a way that it recalls Jesus' own words about the end of the world in the Olivet discourse (Mk 13). In Mark 13.24, Jesus predicted the darkening of the sun. When he died, there was darkness at noon (Mk 15.33). He said that the temple would be thrown down (Mk 13.2), and when he died the temple curtain was torn (Mk 15.38). He warned about sleep (Mk 13.36), and his disciples all fell asleep before his death (Mk 14.34, 37). He also predicted that his disciples would be "handed over to the local councils," be flogged, and appear "before governors and kings" (Mk 13.9). All of this then happened to Jesus himself on his way to the cross (Mk 14.41, 53-65; 15.1-15).

As for the time when the final end would come, Jesus urged his disciples to be ready and look forward with expectation (Mk 13.32-37; Mt. 25.1-13). At the same time, he dismissed chronological speculation (Lk. 17.20) and admitted that even he did not know the time of his coming (Mk 13.32). God will decide the time based on his gracious concern for his people (Lk. 13.6-9). One of the things that has to happen first is that "this gospel of the kingdom will be preached in the whole world as a testimony to all nations, and then the end will come" (Mt. 24.14).

There are few differences between the four Gospels in their picture of the end. Luke gives more attention to the possibility that there will be a delay before Jesus comes again (Lk. 12.45; 19.11). John puts the strongest emphasis on realized eschatology, that the end time events are already a reality (Jn 5.25; 6.47; 12.31). But he is also aware that the full realization lies in the future (Jn 5.28-29; 6.39-40). Matthew highlights Jesus' role as the Son of Man in the final judgment (Mt. 13.41; 25.31).

Paul

Like the other New Testament authors, the apostle Paul knows that the end is already here (1 Cor. 10.11). In Jesus Christ, the new age has broken in (2 Cor. 5.17; Gal. 6.15). Jesus' resurrection is the fundamental eschatological event that marks the onset of the new age. He is the first fruits of the dead (1 Cor. 15.20, 23; see also Col. 1.18), and the guarantee of the believers' resurrection (1 Cor. 15.12). With Christ's death and resurrection, all evil forces have been completely defeated (Col. 1.20). This even includes physical death (2 Tim. 1.10). However, the full manifestation of this victory still lies in the future (1 Cor. 15.24-28).

This victory also involves the redemption of creation. Human sin caused damage that also affected the created world (Gen. 3.17-19; see also ch. 4). "The creation was subjected to frustration," but it "will be liberated from its bondage to decay and brought into the freedom and glory of the children of God" (Rom. 8.20-21).

Because he sees that the end is at hand, Paul has a very vivid expectation of the consummation. When he writes his first letter to the Thessalonians, he refers to "we who are still alive, who are left till the coming of the Lord" (4.15), so he seems to think that he would be alive when Jesus comes. But he also finds it necessary to correct the Thessalonians when they become too focused on the idea that Christ will come soon. There are some events that have to take place first, including the appearance of the lawless one (2 Thess. 2.3), who is elsewhere called the antichrist. One of the most cryptic statements in Paul's letters concerns the something and someone that are restraining the lawless one: "And now you know what is holding him back, so that he may be revealed at the proper time. For the secret power of lawlessness is already at work; but the one who now holds it back will continue to do so till he is taken out of the way" (2 Thess. 2.6-7). Traditionally, this restrainer has been taken to be law and order, represented by the Roman Empire and the Roman Emperor. Others have suggested that this restrainer is the preaching of the gospel, a divinely determined time period, or a spiritual being. But it is impossible to know for certain.

In 1 Thessalonians 4.16-17, Paul explains what will happen at the end: "For the Lord himself will come down from heaven, with a loud command, with the voice of the archangel and with the trumpet call of God, and the dead in Christ will rise first. After that, we who are still alive and are left will be caught up together with them in the clouds to meet the Lord in the air. And so we will be with the Lord forever." On the basis of these verses, some Christians believe that there will be a rapture of believers that will take place before Jesus' second coming. The supposition is usually that Christians therefore will not have to go through the end time tribulations. (This view is often called pre-tribulational premillennialism.) But there is no indication in Paul's letters that Christians will not have to go through these trials (Phil. 1.29-30; Col. 1.24; 1 Thess. 1.6). Paul's purpose in 1 Thessalonians 4.13-18 is very different. He is concerned to explain that those who are dead will not miss out when Jesus comes again. They will be resurrected when God's people are transformed. There is no reason to believe that this account describes two different stages: a rapture followed by the general resurrection. On the contrary, the resurrected and the transformed will be together (1 Thess. 4.17).

When the general resurrection takes place, it is also time for the final judgment. Paul's understanding of the final judgment is based on the Old Testament, but has also been transformed by the revelation in Jesus Christ. The Old Testament refers to the day of God's judgment as the day of the Lord (Isa. 13.6, 9; Joel 1.15; Mal. 4.5). For Paul, the day of the Lord is the day of Jesus Christ (1 Cor. 1.8; 2 Cor. 1.14). This is the time when those who belong to Christ will receive their inheritance (Rom. 8.17; Eph. 6.8; Col. 3.24), but the ungodly will be damned to an eternity of conscious suffering (2 Thess. 1.9).

Many scholars think that there is a development in eschatological thinking between the early and the late writings of the New Testament. They think that the first Christians waited for Jesus to come while they were still alive. When his coming was delayed, they had to adjust their expectations. Scholars who hold this view often use the Pauline letters as evidence. They believe that Paul in 1 Thessalonians 4 and 1 Corinthians 15 expected the resurrection to take place in his lifetime. But in 2 Corinthians 5.1-10 (Phil. 1.23; 2 Tim. 4.6), they argue, he thought he would experience death.

A better explanation for the differences is that Paul had different purposes when he made these different statements about the afterlife. The focus is on resurrection in 1 Corinthians 15, since there were some Christians in Corinth who denied it. In 2 Corinthians 5.1-10, on the other hand, Paul explains that the superior glory of his new covenant ministry is not visible now; it will only be revealed after death.

From the Old Testament, Paul had learned that the Gentiles would be included in the people of God in the end times. He also saw that this was being fulfilled in a very surprising way. The prophets describe the salvation of the Gentiles as something that follows the salvation of Israel (Isa. 2.2-4; 60.1-9). But Paul explains that the sequence actually is the reverse. The Gentiles are saved first, and then the salvation of Israel will follow (Rom. 11.25-32). Israel's salvation will lead to the general resurrection (Rom. 11.15). When this happens, the whole creation will be liberated from its bondage to decay (Rom. 8.19-23).

The Rest of the New Testament

We find the eschatological pattern "already, not yet" in all of the New Testament. The book of Acts teaches that Joel's end time prophecies (Joel 2.28-32) are fulfilled at Pentecost (Acts 2.16-21). But the full realization of the promises still lies in the future (3.20-21; 17.30-31).

When Jesus is about to be taken up to heaven, the disciples ask him: "Lord, are you at this time going to restore the kingdom to Israel?" (Acts 1.6). Jesus responds: "It is not for you to know the times or dates the Father has set by his own authority. But you will receive power when the Holy Spirit comes on you; and you will be my witnesses in Jerusalem, and in all Judea and Samaria, and to the ends of the earth" (Acts 1.7-8). This answer has been interpreted in different ways. Some think that Jesus affirms that the promises to Israel will be literally fulfilled, but others believe that his answer points to a fulfillment that includes the Gentiles through the gift of the Holy Spirit.

The epistle to the Hebrews also affirms that the last days have arrived (Heb. 1.2; 9.26) and that the promises of the eschatological new covenant (Jer. 31.31-34) have been fulfilled (10.15-17; 12.24). Nevertheless, the believers do not experience the goal of the promises yet. There is still a "rest" that remains for God's people (4.1, 6, 9).

For Peter, the time after the coming of Christ is the end of the ages (1 Pet. 1.20-21; 2 Pet. 3.3). But he is more focused on the time of his second coming, when believers will experience their salvation (1 Pet. 1.5, 9) and their glory will be revealed (1 Pet. 1.13; 4.13).

The Book of Revelation

The most detailed picture of the end times is found in the book of Revelation. In order to understand this book, it is important to remember that John wrote this book to Christians who suffered persecution from a totalitarian power. He wrote to help them look at what happened from the heavenly perspective, where God is on his throne and rules in sovereignty. The purpose is twofold: to comfort suffering Christians by assuring them of their final vindication, and to warn Christians that are tempted to enter into an alliance with the ungodly ruler: God's judgment is coming.

Revelation was not written to give us a timetable of end time events or a detailed description of them. It is wrong to try to use it in that way. The language of Revelation is steeped in symbolism. These symbols are taken from the Old Testament and from events in the first century, when the book was written. These events were familiar to the original audience of the book.

The book of Revelation presupposes the same eschatological understanding as the rest of the New Testament. Jesus' resurrection has inaugurated the new age (Rev. 1.5), and the believers belong to his kingdom (Rev. 1.6; 5.10). He will once again be revealed to judge the ungodly and to reward his people (Rev. 6.12-17; 19.17-21). At this time, he proclaims: "To the thirsty I will give water without cost from the spring of the water of life. Those who are victorious will inherit all this, and I will be their God and they will be my children. But the cowardly, the unbelieving, the vile, the murderers, the sexually immoral, those who practice magic arts, the idolaters and all liars—they will be consigned to the fiery lake of burning sulfur. This is the second death" (Rev. 21.6-8). Before that happens, there will be a time of deception and suffering (Rev. 11.7-10; 16.12-14).

The Victorious Lamb

The climax of the book of Revelation is the vision of Jesus Christ, who is both the victorious lamb (14.10; 17.14) and the slaughtered lamb (5.6, 9; 13.8). Because he is victorious, he is the only one who can open the scroll with the seven seals (5.1-5). The scroll probably represents God's plan to bring about the new creation through judgment and redemption. Christ is therefore the one who makes God's plan become reality.

Christ, the Lamb, is victorious (Rev. 5.5), precisely because he has been slain (Rev. 5.6). His eschatological victory is won through defeat. This view of Christ's victory must inform our view of the believer's victory as well. The faithful are frequently called "those who are victorious" (2.7; 21.7 etc.). This is a paradoxical title. They are victorious because they have refused to compromise with the evil power and have been willing to sacrifice their own lives (12.11).

The events that unfold in the book of Revelation do not occur in chronological order. After a detailed description of end time judgments (Rev. 6.1–11.19), John turns to the birth of Christ (12.1-5). We should therefore not believe that the various judgments follow each other sequentially. Instead, they provide different perspectives on how God judges the ungodly.

John portrays God's enemies in such a way that we see how they try to imitate God and take his place. In John's description, the ungodly powers form a "false trinity" (16.13-14): the dragon (Satan), the beast (the oppressive secular power, the antichrist), and the false prophet (false religious teachers).

The Beast

John's picture of the beast is based on the Roman Emperor. He demanded to be worshiped (Rev. 13.4, 12, 15), and there were temples dedicated to him in Pergamum (Rev. 2.13), Smyrna, and Ephesus. The number of the beast, 666 (13.18), is a threefold repetition of the number that is just short of being the perfect number for God, 7. It may be modeled after the Emperor Nero, whose name transliterated into Hebrew yields the number 666. (This result comes from taking a Greek form of "Emperor Nero" [*Neron Kaisar*], writing it out in Hebrew characters, and adding up the numerical value of each character. This is only one, and a rather ingenious, way of calculating the numerical value of Nero's name. This identification is therefore not completely certain.) The background for the description of the mark of the beast (13.16; 14.9) is the practice of branding or tattooing. In the first century, such branding was done to slaves. People who dedicated themselves to certain gods also let themselves be branded. This branding signifies ownership. In Revelation it stands for the total commitment that the Emperor demands of his subjects.

This does not mean that what Revelation says about the beast only concerns the Emperor of Rome. The first letter of John teaches us that there are many antichrists (1 Jn 2.18). Revelation gives us a typical description of these antichrists, based on a prime example of them: the Roman Emperor. It is therefore not as important to know who the beast represents as to know what characterizes him: he takes God's place and demands a level of obedience and commitment that only God can ask of us.

The Tribulation

Revelation repeatedly refers to a period of tribulation lasting three and a half years (11.3; 12.6, 14; 13.5). The background for this time period is found in the book of Daniel. God spoke to Daniel about seventy "sevens" or seventy weeks (Dan. 9.24-28). These weeks are usually interpreted as periods of seven years each. Towards the end of these weeks, a ruler would come and destroy Jerusalem and the sanctuary (Dan. 9.26). "He will confirm a covenant with many for one 'seven.' In the middle of the 'seven' he will put an end to sacrifice and offering. And at the temple he will set up an abomination that causes desolation, until the end that is decreed is poured out on him" (Dan. 9.27). This prophecy describes a time of terrible suffering for the people of God, a time that will last for the last half of the "seven" or week. Daniel's description refers to Antiochus IV Epiphanes, who ruled the Seleucid Empire (centered in what is now Syria) from 175 to 164 BCE. In 167 BCE, he conquered Jerusalem, made it illegal to practice the Jewish religion, dedicated the temple to the Greek god Zeus, erected a Zeus statue in the Most Holy Place, and sacrificed a pig there. The three and a half years of his rule stand in the Bible as a model or type of a period of terrible tribulation for God's people. It also corresponds to the period of about three and a half years from the Jewish revolt against the Romans in 66 CE to the fall of Jerusalem in 70 CE. When the book of Revelation refers to this time period, the point is not to say how long it will last, but to identify a period of persecution and suffering for believers. During this period, worldly rulers will attempt to crush the people of God.

The Millennium

Towards the end of the book of Revelation, John briefly mentions a period of 1,000 years, a millennium (Rev. 20.1-6). John sees an angel coming down from heaven, who "seized the dragon, that ancient serpent, who is the devil, or Satan, and bound him for a thousand years. He threw him into the Abyss, and locked and sealed it over him, to keep him from deceiving the nations anymore until the thousand years were ended. After that, he must be set free for a short time" (Rev. 20.2-3). Through the history of the church, there have been three major interpretations of this millennium. Amillennialists argue that these 1,000 years are symbolic of the time after Jesus came to earth, when Satan was bound (Mk 3.27). The word "amillennial" is formed by the word "millennial" with the prefix "a-," which means "not." Amillennialists do not believe in a literal millennium. Postmillennialists (the word "post" means "after") believe that Jesus will come again after the millennium. Before that, history will evolve into a period of wonderful progress for the gospel, a millennium where Satan is bound. This view is not very common today. Premillennialists ("pre" means "before") expect Christ to come before the millennium. When he comes, believers will be raised from the dead, Satan will be bound, and the believers will rule with Christ for 1,000 years. The number 1,000 may be interpreted symbolically. After this millennium, Christ will come for the third time, there will be a general resurrection, and the final judgment.

Those who hold to the premillennialist position argue that the millennium cannot be a part of regular history because it takes place after the resurrection of believers (Rev. 20.4b). Amillennialists see this resurrection as a spiritual resurrection. They take it as believers' spiritual rebirth. Premillennialists point to the parallel descriptions in Revelation 20.4b ("They came to life") and Revelation 20.5 ("The rest of the dead did not come to life"). They claim that these two occurrences of the same word, "came to life" (Greek: *ezesan*), must have the same meaning. In Revelation 20.5, the word can only refer to physical resurrection (unbelievers will never experience a spiritual rebirth). The words must therefore refer to physical resurrection in both verses. If so, the millennium must be a period after the physical resurrection of believers. Amillennialists respond that the word (*ezesan*) may very well be used with two different meanings. It may refer to spiritual resurrection in Revelation 20.4 and physical resurrection in Revelation 20.5. In a very similar way, John uses the words "life" and "live" in John 5.24-29, but the meaning switches between spiritual life and physical life.

Judgment

In any case, the book of Revelation teaches that history moves towards a final confrontation between Christ and the forces of evil (Rev. 19.11-21; 20.7-10). Christ will hand the evil forces their final defeat. This will take place without a real battle (note that Rev. 19.19 describes the armies of the beast and Rev. 19.20 describes their capture; there is no battle). The Lamb is already victorious (Rev. 14.10; 17.14).

After the final defeat of Satan, all human beings will appear before God's judgment (Rev. 20.11-15). Those who are written in the book of life, the people of God, escape judgment. The others are thrown in the lake of fire (Rev. 20.15). This and other images of judgment in the book of Revelation (14.11; 19.20) must not be taken literally, but they show that the ungodly are eternally conscious of their punishment.

The New Creation

In the end, John paints a picture of the new creation (21.1–22.5). Christians will not literally spend eternity in heaven because God's dwelling will come down to earth. This is what John saw:

> Then the angel showed me the river of the water of life, as clear as crystal, flowing from the throne of God and of the Lamb down the middle of the great street of the city. On each side of the river stood the tree of life, bearing twelve crops of fruit, yielding its fruit every month. And the leaves of the tree are for the healing of the nations. No longer will there be any curse. The throne of God and of the Lamb will be in the city, and his servants will serve him. They will see his face, and his name will be on their foreheads. There will be no more night. They will not need the light of a lamp or the light of the sun, for the Lord God will give them light. And they will reign for ever and ever. (Rev. 22.1-5)

In the new creation, God's relationship to human beings will be perfected. Revelation describes the people of God as the new Jerusalem, a city that is structured as a perfect cube; its height, length, and width are the same (Rev. 21.15-17). There is only one building in the Old Testament that has a similar structure: the Most Holy Place (1 Kgs 6.20). This means that in the new creation, God's people are his dwelling.

The new creation also restores the harmony that existed before the fall. The river of life (Gen. 2.10) flows through the city (Rev. 22.1). "On each side of the river stood the tree of life" (Rev. 22.2), the tree that also stood in the garden of Eden (Gen. 2.9). But now, this tree is far more glorious; it gives its fruit every month (Rev. 22.2; see also Ezek. 47.12). There is therefore both continuity and discontinuity between the old and the new creation. The new creation restores the old, but it brings a new level of glory.

In the new creation, God's people enjoy his gift of life, and they are completely free from death and all its consequences. God "will wipe every tear from their eyes. There will be no more death or mourning or crying or pain, for the old order of things has passed away" (Rev. 21.4).

Summary

The New Testament message can be summarized as the good news that the end is already here. God has already come to earth in Jesus Christ and defeated Satan. God's judgment has taken place on the cross where Jesus died. The new creation is a reality in Jesus Christ. God's victory, the salvation of his people, and the new creation will be fully visible when Jesus is revealed once again at the end of history. Then he will destroy all God's enemies and put an end to death. That will also be the time of the final judgment. Those who are already justified in Jesus Christ will enter into their inheritance, and the ungodly will receive the fruit of their own sins.

For God's people, the end will be the time when they will fully enjoy the gift they have been given in Jesus Christ. God will look upon them with favor, and there will be nothing to separate them from his love and care. He will be so close that it will be impossible to distinguish God's dwelling from God's people.

Further Reading

Gowan, Donald E. *Eschatology in the Old Testament*. 2d ed. Edinburgh: T&T Clark, 2000.

Hill, Craig C. *In God's Time: The Bible and the Future*. Grand Rapids: Eerdmans, 2002.

Witherington, Ben III. *Jesus, Paul and the End of the World: A Comparative Study in New Testament Eschatology*. Downers Grove: IVP, 1992.

Review Questions

Why do we describe New Testament eschatology with the expression "already and not yet"?

The book of Revelation describes a lot of suffering for Christian believers. At the same time, these believers are called "those who are victorious." How can both of these things be true at the same time?

How does the new creation compare to the original creation, according to the book of Revelation?

Scripture Index

The Old Testament
Genesis
1.1 4
1.2 12, 158
1.3 28, 116
1.26 11
1.26-28 28
1.27 27, 114, 169
1.28 27, 28, 29, 48, 49, 52, 64, 114, 193
1.28-30 28
1.29 27
1.31 19, 27
2.4 7
2.7 15, 31, 161
2.9 226
2.10 65, 226
2.15 27
2.16 27, 34
2.16-17 28
2.17 34, 68
2.18 27
2.19-20 27
2.24 27
2.25 28
3.1 33
3.1-7 19
3.2 34
3.2-3 34
3.3 34
3.4-5 34
3.5 20, 35
3.6 34
3.7 34
3.8 15, 58
3.10 34

3.12 34
3.15 84
3.16 34
3.17 34
3.22 11, 34
3.23 58
4.8 35
4.23-24 35
4.25-26 21
5.3-32 21
6.2 21
6.3 21
6.4 21
6.5 21, 35, 49
6.6 15, 48
6.7 48
6.14-16 49
6.18-20 48, 49
6.18-21 49
6.19-21 48
8.20 68
8.21 15, 49, 69
9.1 49, 52, 64
9.6 28
9.7 49
9.8-17 48, 49
9.11 49
11.4 35, 49
11.5-9 49
12.1-3 49
12.2 35, 64
12.7 57, 58
12.8 58
12.10-20 50
15.1-21 48

15.4 61
15.4-5 61
15.5 49
15.6 50, 151, 152
15.9-10 50
15.17 50
16.7 12
16.9 12
16.10 12
16.11 12
16.13 12
17.1-8 182
17.1-22 48
17.2 49, 52, 64
17.4-5 49
17.6 49, 52, 61
17.7 61
17.8 49, 50
17.9-14 50
17.23-27 50
19.13 13
20.1-18 50
21.1-5 50
21.4 50
22.1-18 50
22.2 103, 204
22.11 12
22.12 12, 103, 204
22.16 103, 204
24.43 78
25.23 50
26.3 60
26.3-4 50
26.25 58
27.1-4 50
27.5-29 50
28.12 58
28.13-15 50
28.14 64
28.15 58
28.19 58

31.36 37
32.22-32 182
32.28 50
35.7 58
35.11 64
35.11-12 50
35.12 64
42.22 37
49.8-12 84
49.9 84, 120
49.11 84

Exodus
3.2 12
3.4 12
3.5 12
3.6 12
3.7 12
3.8 57, 78
3.14 118
3.14-15 5, 6, 110
4.14 31
4.22-23 54, 57, 76
6.2-3 7
6.4 7
6.6 7
6.7 6, 7, 51, 183
6.8 7
12.7 71
12.12 71
12.21-23 130
12.24-28 71
12.26-27 126
12.46 130
13.8 126
13.21 117
13.21-22 58
14.31 56
15.17 58
16.3-9 55
16.10 58

Scripture Index

16.16 31
18.1 12
18.2 12
18.13 12
19.3-6 48
19.4-6 51
19.5 51
19.5-6 53, 183
19.6 55, 95
19.8 51
19.9 86
20.1 99
20.3 37, 38
20.12 98
20.13 99
20.24 9
23.7 143, 148
23.17 60
23.20 100
23.21 12
24.3 51
24.5-8 126
24.6 210
24.7 51
24.7-8 48
24.8 126, 210, 211
24.15-18 58
25.16 59
25.22 59
28.38 38
28.41 74
29.45-46 51
30.10 59
30.12 125
30.13 172
30.25-29 75
31.3 158
32.1-4 55
32.4 37
32.5 37

32.10 15
32.11-14 133
32.14 15
33.3 59
33.5 59
33.9 58, 59
33.11 59
33.11-23 103
33.20 8
33.20-23 116
33.23 8, 60
34.5-7 6, 7
34.14 10
34.23 60
35.31 158
39.1 168
40.20 59
40.34 58

Leviticus
1.3 68
1.4 68, 69
1.9 68
4.2 69
4.6 70
4.7 70
4.17 70
4.18 70
4.20 70, 204
4.25 70
4.30 70
5.1-6 39
5.16 71
5.18 71
6.1-7 71
6.7 71
6.12-13 68, 69
8.15 69
9.23 58
11 173
11.45 168

Scripture Index

16.2 8
16.2-34 59
16.5 70
16.6 70
16.9 70
16.6 38
16.11 38
16.14-15 70
16.21 68
16.21-22 70, 129
16.22 72
18.5 146
18.30 39
19.2 54, 168, 187
22.14 71
24.16 124
25.13 57
25.23 57
25.23-28 57
25.48-52 125
26.1-13 52
26.3-13 57, 59
26.9 52, 64
26.12 58
26.14-39 52, 57
26.18 80
26.27-39 41
26.40-46 52
27.30-33 176

Numbers
3.45-58 125
5.2-3 39
6.24-26 58
9.12 130
10.1-2 39
11.12 11
11.17 158
11.25-29 158, 158
12.1-8 103

13.31–14.10 55
14.20-35 55
16.30-33 13
20.2-3 40
21.8-9 155
22.3 39
22.31 18
23.21 95
24.14 84
24.17 84
24.17-18 84
24.17-19 84
26.53 57
27.18 158
35.33 39
36.2 57
36.6-8 57

Deuteronomy
1.20-21 57
1.26 37
1.33 58
4.12 37
4.15-19 37
4.38 57
5.7 38
6.4 10, 106
6.5 31, 99, 169
6.13 10
7.7-8 53
8.5 57
8.11-18 36
8.18 211
10.2 59
10.5 59
10.16 175
10.20 10
12.5 62
12.11 62
14.1 21

14.1-2 55, 168
14.2 55, 183
14.3-21 173
14.22-25 176
16.1-8 71
16.3 211
16.16 60
18.10-11 53
18.15 103
18.15-19 86
18.18 86, 114, 127
20.4 101
21.14 31
23.24 31
24.1-4 173
25.1 143
27.26 146
28.1-14 52, 59
28.15-68 52
28.25-57 41
29.1-29 48
30.6 175
31.23 60
32.5-6 21
32.8 22
32.9-14 54
32.17 22
32.18 11
32.39 13
33.2 18

Joshua
1.5 60
23.14 31
24.1-28 52
24.19-20 52

Judges
6.11-15 12
6.16 12
8.27 38

8.34 211
13.18 78
13.22 79

1 Samuel
2.6-7 13
4.3-11 9, 59
4.4 59
6.19 59
9.16 75
10.1 74
10.1-11 158
13.12 69
15.29 14
16.7 19
16.13 74, 158
16.14-15 24
18.10 24
24.17 144

2 Samuel
6.2 59
6.6-7 59
6.12-17 62
7.5-16 60–1
7.8-16 48
7.11 61, 75
7.11-16 75
7.12 61, 82
7.12-13 61
7.12-16 64, 78
7.13 61, 62, 75, 82
7.14 61, 62, 75, 78, 82
7.14-15 76
7.15 78, 82
7.16 61, 75
7.22 78
23.1-7 75
23.5 61
24.21 69

Scripture Index

1 Kings
6.1-38 62
6.20 226
8.10 62
8.17 31
8.27 9, 59
8.29 185
8.32 143
8.37-40 9
8.39 19
8.49 9
11.4-13 63, 77
11.36 62
12.28 38
12.30 38
17.17-23 99
18.12 158
19.16 74

2 Kings
2.3 21
2.16 158
4.18-37 99
6.17 18
17.14 63
25.8-12 41

1 Chronicles
15.25–16.1 62
16.22 74
17.1-15 75
22.19 168
28.2 59
28.5 94, 95
28.7 95
29.11-12 10, 94
29.22 74

2 Chronicles
3.1-17 62
6.18 9

7.1-3 62
18.18-22 19, 20, 24
24.20 158
28.19-21 57

Ezra
3.2 80
9.6 40

Nehemiah
2.1-10 80
9.16 63
9.20 158
9.29 37

Job
1.6 22, 76
1.8-12 14
1.8–2.10 19
19.9-11 131
1.12 14, 19
1.12-19 14
2.1 22
2.3-6 14
2.4-5 131
2.6 14, 19
2.7 14
4.17 145
6.4 14
9.8 118
9.17 14
12.10 13
16.11-14 14
28.20-28 105
33.4 12, 158
33.12 145
42.2-6 14

Psalms
2.1-3 95
2.4 15

Scripture Index

2.7 76, 82, 103, 204
2.8 82
2.8-9 76
2.8-12 76
2.9 76, 83
6.3 31
6.10 40
7.1-7 145
77.7-9 171
7.10-15 171
7.11 145
8.4 101
8.4-5 29
8.5-6 27
8.6-8 29
9.8 148
10.2-13 36
11.1-7 145
11.7 8, 116
14.1 43
14.3 43
16.10 86
18.2 54
18.50 76
22.1 85
22.7 85
22.18 85
22.22 85
27.4 60
31.2 54
33.6 158
33.9 10, 116
35.25 31
40 86
40.5 11
41.9 86
42.1-2 31
42.2 8, 116
44.23-24 14
45 76

45.4 82
45.6-7 112
51.2 39
51.4 38
51.7 69
51.11 157
51.17 31, 59
53.5 40
69.4 85
69.9 85
69.21 85
69.25 86
71.2 144
71.3 54
71.15 144
72 76
72.2 82
72.3 83
72.24 82
73.26 30
74.13-14 21
76.2 62
77.7-9 171
77.10-15 171
78.12 78
78.15-16 117
78.59 41
80.17 101
82.1 21
82.6-7 21
89.3-4 48, 76
89.4 82
89.19-37 76
89.23 83
89.26 82
89.27 106
89.28 61
91.11 18
98.2 148
99.1-5 94, 95

Scripture Index

100.3 54, 97
103.1 99
103.3 99
103.13 10, 48
103.19 10, 95
104.29-30 158
104.30 12
105.41 117
107.11 37
107.23-30 99
107.29 99
110.1 76, 83, 91, 101, 108, 111
110.4 77, 81, 83
118.22-23 86
118.25-26 86, 91
132 76
132.13-14 62
135.12 57
137.4 57
138.4 65
139.1-2 14
139.4 14
139.6 11
139.16 14, 109
139.23 14
139.7-12 9, 58
143.2 145
145.10-13 95
147.5 14
148.2 17
148.5 17

Proverbs
1.29 116
8.22 104, 107, 116
8.22-36 12, 104, 106
8.30 104, 116
8.35 116
9.4-5 116
9.5 212

10.30 54
12.21 54
13.14 116
14.10 31
14.31 39
16.24 30
17.15 143
18.4 116
20.9 38

Ecclesiastes
5.2 9, 30
7.20 38
12.4 99
12.14 97

Isaiah
1.2 37
1.3 104
1.4 7
1.11 71
2.1-4 65
2.2-4 220
2.4 79
2.6-22 36
2.9 36
2.11 39
2.12 36
5.1-7 188
5.5-7 54
6.1-3 8
6.1-4 8
6.5 8, 39
6.6-7 8, 205
7.2 31
7.9 56
7.14 78, 83
7.16 78
9.6 78, 83
9.6-7 78

Scripture Index

9.7 78, 82
10.20 56, 57
10.20-23 56
10.21 57, 79
10.22 145
11.1 79
11.2 83, 158, 159
11.2-3 79
11.3-4 82
11.4 83
11.4-5 79
11.6 79
11.6-8 82
13.1 19
13.6 220
13.9 220
14.3-21 36
14.12 20
14.12-15 19
14.14 36
24.5-6 52
24.21 99
24.21-23 95
25.6-8 210
25.6-9 96
26.19 94, 192, 216
27.9 68
27.12-13 57
30.2 39
31.1 39
32.15 158
35.5 94
35.5-6 100, 192
37.21-29 36
38.10 182
40.3 100
40.6-7 30
40.11 54
41.4 6
41.8-9 54

41.8-10 54, 56
41.14 125
41.22-23 14
41.23-24 10
42.1 84, 85, 103, 114, 158, 204
42.1-9 84
42.6 84
42.17 40
43.1-2 60
43.1-7 56
43.10 54, 56
43.12 56
43.14 125
44.3 158
44.8 56
44.9-17 22
44.28 10
45.5 6, 10
45.7 13
45.23 110
46.9-10 14
46.13 147, 148
48.18-19 52
49.1 197
49.1-7 84, 114
49.3 84, 85
49.5-6 84
49.15 11
50.1 41, 56
50.4-9 84, 114
50.8-9 84
51.1-2 182
51.1-8 145
51.8 144
51.9-10 21
52.13 84, 130
52.13–53.12 84, 114, 124, 136
53 85
53.4 136
53.4-6 84

Scripture Index

53.5 72, 84, 125, 136
53.6 136
53.7 72, 130
53.8 125
53.9 84, 136
53.10 72, 84, 125
53.10-11 85
53.10-12 125, 126
53.11 125, 127, 136
53.11-12 125, 127
53.12 101, 125, 127, 136, 211
54.5 10
54.10 64
55.3 64
55.7 97
57.15 9, 31, 79
60.1-9 220
61.1 75, 85, 94, 158
61.1-2 92, 197
61.1-7 85
61.2 92
61.8 64
62.1-2 147, 148
62.5 10
63.10-11 157
64.1 204
64.6 40
65.17 216
65.17-24 113
66.13 11
66.15-16 205

Jeremiah
1.5 109, 197
2.7 40, 48, 62
2.22 40
3.3 40
3.4 10, 48
3.10 39, 63
3.19 48
4.1-2 52
4.4 63, 175

5.7 56
6.10 63
6.15 40
6.20 71
7.3-6 55
7.4 9, 59
7.5-7 52
7.12-15 41
7.26 63
7.29 41
7.30 40, 62
8.12 40
9.26 63
10.3-11 22
10.10 95
10.16 63
11.2-13 52
11.3 146
11.6-8 146
11.11 41
14.11-12 41
14.12 59
15.20 60, 101
17.9 63
18.23 68
21.5 41
23.5 79, 81, 82
23.6 79, 82
23.24 9, 58
24.5-7 57
24.7 64
25.9-11 52
26.18 62
30.2 56
31.1 56
31.19 40
31.31 210
31.31-34 63, 221
31.33 63, 175, 183
31.34 64
33.14-26 79
34.18 50

Scripture Index

Lamentations
2.1 59

Ezekiel
1.4 58
1.5-24 87
1.26 8
1.27 8
1.28 8
2.1 101
5.11 40, 62
8.3 158
10.4 9, 40, 62
10.18-19 9, 40, 62
11.5 158
11.16 62
11.19 31, 175
11.24 158
12.11 52
16 56
16.3-5 56
16.6-14 56
16.8 48, 56
16.15-34 56
16.36 40–1
16.37 41
16.45-58 56
16.59-63 56
16.60-63 64
18.20 68
19.10-12 54
20.3 41
20.11 52
20.31 41
25.11 80
28.11-19 36
28.12 36
28.17 36
28.18 36
29.10 80
30.13 52
34.11-31 54
34.23 81
34.23-24 80
34.25 64
36.17-18 40, 62
36.25-27 205, 207
36.26 31, 175
36.27 158
36.35 58, 65
37.1-10 128
37.1-14 216
37.9 161
37.12-13 129
37.14 158
37.24 64
37.24-25 80
37.25 64
37.26 64
37.27 64
37.28 64
39.23 41
40.1–43.11 65
43.4 65
44.7 30
45.18-19 126
45.18-20 71
45.19 71
47.1 65
47.12 65, 117, 226

Daniel
2.19-23 185
3.25 76
4.22 36
4.25 36
5.23 13
6.13 10
6.26 95
7.1-8 87
7.7 21
7.13 86, 91
7.13-14 95, 101
7.14 87

7.15-28 87
7.27 87, 95
8.15-26 18
9.11 37
9.16 133
9.19 133
9.24 80, 83
9.24-27 80
9.24-28 223
9.25 80
9.25-26 75, 80
9.26 223
9.27 223–4
10.5 87
10.6 87
10.13 22
10.20 10
10.20-21 22
12.1 22
12.2 216
12.6-7 87

Hosea
1.2 10
1.9 41, 55
2.2 41, 56
2.2-8 38
2.23 56, 189
3.1 56
3.5 77
4.12 56
5.13 39
7.5 39
11.1 54, 76

Joel
1.15 111, 220
2.23-26 65
2.28 65
2.28-29 158, 192, 195

2.28-32 159, 221
3.17 65

Amos
3.2 35, 55
3.6 13
5.18-20 111
5.21-22 59
5.22 71
6.4-7 39
7.14 21
8.11-13 212
8.12 41
9.11 77
9.11-12 82
9.12 77
9.13 77
9.14-15 57

Obadiah
10 40

Mica
4.1-3 65
5.2 77, 83
5.4 78, 81, 82, 83
5.5 79
5.5-6 78
7.18 97

Habakkuk
2.4 146, 147
2.14 65

Zephaniah
2.3 57
3.1-2 40
3.5 40
3.12 57
3.15 95

Zechariah
1.8 81
1.12 12
3.1-2 131
3.8 81
3.8-9 83
3.9 81
4.2 159
4.6 159
4.6-10 80
4.7-10 81
4.10 159
6.2 81
6.9-14 80
9.9 81, 82
9.10 79, 81
13.7 81, 83
13.9 205
14.7 117
14.8 117
14.9 95
14.20-21 95

Malachi
1.2-3 50
3.1 100, 111
4.5 100, 111, 220

The New Testament
Matthew
1.1 90, 91
1.9-11 159
1.18 159
1.20 159
1.21 125
1.23 9, 78, 79, 100, 101, 205
2.1-4 91
2.2 84
2.6 78
3.6 204

3.9 182
3.11 203, 204, 205
3.14 204
3.15 204
3.16-17 204
3.17 127
3.17-19 219
4.1 19
4.6 128
4.1-11 20, 127
4.3 127
4.9 34
4.10 104, 121
4.14-16 79
4.24 24
5.3 31, 140, 141
5.5 216
5.6 140
5.7 20
5.13 186
5.13-14 169
5.14 181, 186
5.17 98, 172, 173
5.17-19 172
5.18 173
5.19 173
5.20 140
5.21-22 99
5.21-30 140
5.21-48 98, 140, 174
5.22 98, 174
5.38-42 193
5.38-48 170
5.44 140
5.48 140
6.1-4 141
6.9 10
6.10 97, 217
6.16-18 141
6.22-23 30

Scripture Index

6.24 42
6.26 13
7.3-5 200
7.11 44
7.14-21 25
7.21-27 97
7.28-29 98
8.5-10 141
8.8 99
8.12 139
8.13 99, 142
8.16-17 114, 124, 125
8.22 98
8.28-34 25
8.29 20
8.32 25
9.5-6 125
9.6 205
9.28 142
9.32 25
10.1 192
10.1-5 180
10.2 196
10.7-8 94, 95
10.24-25 206
10.28 30
10.38-39 169
11.5 192
11.7-10 100
11.7-15 204
11.19 105
11.25-26 102
11.27 102, 105
12.15-21 114
12.18 159
12.25-29 25
12.28 159
12.33-35 140
12.42 105
12.43-45 20
13.13-15 44

13.14-15 44
13.24 181, 186
13.27 110
13.41 218
13.54-58 92
14.33 104
15.18-19 140
15.21-28 141
15.26 141
15.27 141
15.28 141
16.16 92
16.17 90
16.17-19 181
16.18 181
16.19 182, 192
16.23 20
17.15 25
17.24-27 172
18.2-3 141
18.3 139
18.9-14 143
18.10 18
18.10-14 199
18.13 143
18.14 143
18.15 200
18.16 174, 200
18.17 200
18.18 182
18.20 9, 100, 159, 205
18.21-35 200
19.3-12 173
19.16-30 140
19.28 102, 180
20.16 139
20.28 128, 129
21.5 81
21.11 114
21.31 139
21.42 181

Scripture Index

21.42-43 81
22.11-13 199
22.14 190
22.41-45 92
23.1-33 140
23.10 90
24.14 218
24.31 18
25.1-13 199, 218
25.31 102, 218
25.31-32 99
25.31-33 102
25.31-46 97, 140, 141, 217
25.32 217
25.34 217
25.41 217
26.26-29 210
26.28 210
26.52 193
26.53 18
27.52-53 128
28.1-8 18
28.3 18
28.18-20 205
28.19 12, 206
28.20 9, 100, 101, 140, 159

Mark
1.1 90, 103
1.2-3 100
1.4 204
1.8 159
1.9-11 159
1.11 76, 103, 204
1.15 29, 94, 95, 138, 169
1.17 98, 169, 206
1.23-28 25
1.24 20, 96, 127
1.32 24
1.41 172
2.1-10 100

2.5 97, 139
2.7 97, 124
2.10 99, 102
2.14 206
2.15-16 139
2.15-17 172, 210
2.19 181, 186
2.20 124
2.28 102
3.1-6 173
3.6 124
3.11 103
3.15 192
3.22 19, 165
3.23-27 20
3.27 224
3.29 165
3.34 186
3.34-35 181
4.1-20 192
4.11-12 45, 102
4.35-41 99
4.39 99
5.1-5 25
5.1-20 25
5.7 20
5.21-22 44
5.27-28 44
5.28 44
6.1-6 92
6.7 192
6.9 102
6.30-44 210
7.1-23 173
7.18-19 173
7.19 173, 175
7.21-23 44
7.25 24
7.31-37 100
7.36 90
8.1-10 210

Scripture Index

8.17-18 45
8.22-26 100
8.31 102, 124
8.32 45
8.33 23, 45
8.34-35 169
8.36-37 31
8.38 18, 102, 217
9.1 76
9.7 86, 114
9.9 90
9.14-29 25
9.25 25
9.29 20
9.41 90
10.4 102
10.6-8 27
10.14 209
10.21 98, 169
10.45 101, 125, 126, 127, 129
10.46-52 100
10.47 91
11.9-10 86, 91
12.1-8 173
12.10-11 86
12.18-27 217
12.25 21
12.28-31 169, 169
12.30 31
12.35 75
12.35-36 91, 111
12.36 76
13 218
13.2 101, 218
13.5-23 217
13.9 218
13.20 190
13.24 218
13.26 87, 101, 102
13.26-27 102
13.31 98

13.32 18, 102, 180
13.32-37 218
13.36 218
13.37 218
14.12 180, 211
14.12-16 126
14.22 126, 180, 210, 211
14.22-25 210
14.23-24 126
14.24 210
14.25 97, 210
14.27 81
14.29 45
14.31 45
14.34 31, 218
14.36 10, 102, 103
14.37 218
14.41 218
14.53-65 218
14.58 101
14.61-62 90
14.62 87, 91, 101, 102, 111, 217
14.71 45
15.1-15 218
15.29 85
15.33 218
15.34 85
15.38 128, 218
15.39 103
16.5 18

Luke
1.6 111
1.11-12 18
1.11-20 18
1.13-20 18
1.17 111
1.19 18
1.26-38 18
1.32 75, 104
1.32-33 92

Scripture Index

1.33 75
1.34 78
1.34-35 44
1.35 159
1.43 111, 115
1.69 92
1.71 92
1.74 92
1.78 84
1.79 79
1.80 159
2.11 90, 92
3.9 93
3.15 75
4.1 159
4.14 159
4.16-27 92
4.18 81, 159, 197
4.18-19 92, 139, 159
4.18-21 85
4.19 92
4.23-37 124
4.24 114
4.33-37 25
5.32 92
6.13 196
6.20 141
6.20-21 92
7.11-17 114
7.16 114
7.21 24
7.22 92, 139
7.22-23 94
7.28 93
7.34 139
7.36-50 139, 142
7.48 139, 142
7.50 142
8.26-39 25
8.31 91
9.1-2 25, 192

9.23 142
9.37-43a 25
10.17-20 25
10.18 20, 127
10.21 159
10.29-37 170
11.20 29, 99, 165, 217
11.20-22 96
11.21-22 127
11.49 105
12.8-10 97, 218
12.32 181, 186
12.45 218
13.6-9 218
13.8 110
13.28-29 139
13.33 114
13.34 105, 115
14.26 98, 99, 169
15.1-2 210
15.8 162
16.16 93
17.3-4 200
17.11-19 142
17.19 142
17.20 218
17.20-21 96
17.21 29, 217
18.7 190
18.15 210
19.1-10 210
19.10 92, 102
19.11 218
19.44 44
22.3 20
22.10 127
22.15-20 210
22.16-18 217
22.19 211
22.20 181, 210, 216
22.27 129

22.37 85, 114
22.61 115
23.15 124
23.35 129
23.41-42 129
23.43 129
24.3 115
24.26 84, 94, 128
24.30-31 210
24.34 115
24.42 210
24.47 92

John
1.1 112, 116
1.1-2 107, 116
1.3 107
1.1-4 116
1.1-13 116
1.1-18 115
1.3 116
1.4 116, 154
1.9 177
1.10 45
1.10-11 44, 116
1.12 116
1.12-13 190
1.13 154
1.14 107, 116, 119
1.17 117, 118, 177
1.18 9, 11, 112–13, 116, 177
1.29 129, 204
1.41 90
2.1-11 84
2.4 130
2.11 116, 155
2.13-22 117
2.17 85
2.19 118
2.21 81, 101, 117, 118, 188
2.23 155

3.3-8 154
3.5 207
3.8 31, 155
3.9 155
3.13 130
3.14 130
3.14-15 131, 155
3.16 119, 155, 160
3.17 119, 130, 160
3.19 45, 130, 131
3.28 100
3.34 162
4.2 205
4.10 154
4.10-14 116
4.11 110
4.14 154
4.23 216
4.25 75, 90
4.25-26 90, 160
4.34 119
5.1-47 117
5.8-9 118
5.17-20 119
5.18 119
5.19 102
5.21 119, 190
5.22 119
5.24 119
5.24-29 225
5.25 218
5.26 154
5.28-29 218
5.36 160
5.43 119
5.45 177
6.1-14 210
6.1-47 117
6.14 86, 114, 127
6.15 91
6.20 112, 118

Scripture Index

6.27 154, 155
6.29 155
6.31-33 177
6.31-35 117
6.33 118, 130
6.35 116, 117, 118, 213
6.35-50 212, 213
6.37 155, 190
6.39-40 191, 218
6.44 155, 192
6.47 218
6.48 212
6.50-51 130
6.51 213
6.51-59 213
6.53 211, 213
6.53-58 130
6.54 213
6.55 177
6.56 213
6.59 160, 161
6.65 155
6.69 155
7.2 117
7.7 45, 160, 161
7.11-18 114
7.13 114
7.37 192
7.37-38 116, 117, 118
7.39 161
7.40 114
7.41-42 75
8.12 117
8.14 160
8.15 131
8.24 112, 118
8.28 118
8.28-29 119
8.31 155
8.42 160
8.44 19, 21, 45

8.47 190
8.51 155
8.58 112, 118
9.2-3 124
9.39 25
10.1-18 187
10.4 187
10.10 130
10.11 80
10.14 186, 187
10.22 117
10.24-25 90
10.27 155
10.30 119, 155
10.36 117, 118
11.50 130
11.15 155
12.15 81
12.23 130
12.27 130
12.28 130
12.31 218
12.31-32 131
12.34 101
12.38 114
12.46 45
12.47 131
12.48 131
13.1 130
13.1-3 119
13.3 160
13.16 196
13.18 86
13.19 118
13.20 119
13.27 20
13.34 169
14–16 162
14.6 160, 161
14.7 155, 160
14.9 160

14.11 155
14.12 130
15.5 186
16.13 161
14.16 158, 160
14.17 9, 160, 161
14.20 160
14.23 9, 155, 159, 160
14.26 160, 161
15.1 177
15.1-17 188
15.4-5 9
15.4-6 188
15.7-11 155
15.12 169
15.16 190, 191
15.23 119
15.25 85
15.26 160, 161, 164
16.3 160, 161
16.7 160, 161
16.8 161
16.8-11 160, 164
16.10 130
16.11 131
16.13 160
16.14 160
16.28 119, 160
17.1 102, 119, 130
17.2 191
17.3 155
17.5 119
17.6 155
17.9 188
17.11 119
17.18 119
17.20 188
17.21 188
17.23 188, 193
17.24 119

18.5 131
18.6 112, 119, 131
18.36 193
19.14 130
19.24 85
19.28 85
19.28-29 85
19.30 131
19.33-36 130
20.17 119
20.21 197
20.21-22 161
20.22 161, 162
20.23 182
20.28 112, 119, 121
20.31 155
21.9-13 210

Acts
1.6 221
1.7-8 221
1.8 164, 209
1.10 18
1.14 193
1.15-26 180
1.22 197
2 162
2.1-13 180
2.3-4 159
2.4 157
2.10 197
2.16-21 159, 221
2.17 217
2.17-18 157, 192, 195
2.25-31 86
2.34-35 77, 111
2.36 114, 115
2.38 162, 206, 208
2.38-39 205
2.41 193, 208

Scripture Index

2.44 193
2.44-45 193
3.13 114
3.20-21 221
3.22 86, 114
3.26 114
4.8 162
4.27 114
4.30 114
4.31 162
4.32 193
4.32-37 193
5.1-11 13
5.3 31
5.4 193
5.36-37 91
6.1-6 196, 198
6.3 196
6.6 199
6.7 29, 193
7.37 86, 114
7.53 18
7.55 162
7.56 101
8.4-13 208
8.4-25 193, 209
8.9-12 209
8.12 208, 209
8.14-17 208, 209
8.16 206, 208
8.18-23 209
8.26 18
8.26-40 193, 209
8.29 164
8.32-33 85
8.38 208
9.1-19 209
9.13 183
9.17 208
9.20 108

9.32-43 194
10.1–11.18 193
10.19 164
10.44-45 162
10.44-48 208
10.45 208
10.47 208
10.48 206
11.12 164
11.15 162
11.30 198
12.7 18
12.11 18
12.21-23 36
12.23 18
12.24 29
12.28-30 196
13.2 164
13.3 199
13.9 162
13.33 114
13.46 191
13.48 190, 191
14.23 198
15.2 198
15.8 162
15.14-18 77
15.20 176
16.7 158
16.15 209
16.31–34 209
17.25 13
17.28 13
17.30-31 221
18.24-26 197
19.1-5 204
19.2 208
19.5 206
19.5-6 208
20.17-35 198

20.28 113
22.16 208
26.5 189
27.37 31

Romans
1.3 30
1.3-4 108, 115
1.4 115
1.9 31
1.14 144
1.16 132, 144
1.16-17 144, 145
1.17 144, 147, 148
1.18 133, 144
1.18-3.20 41, 42, 133, 145
1.20-21 42
1.21 41
1.23 41, 42
1.24 34, 42
1.24-27 42
1.25 41
1.26 34
1.28 34
1.29 42
2.1-3.20 145
2.6-16 152
2.13 152
2.15 32
2.17-18 152
2.17-24 150
2.17-29 42
2.25 145
2.25-29 42, 150, 152
3.5 148
3.9 152
3.9-19 43
3.10-12 43
3.19 145
3.19-20 145, 152
3.19-21 147

3.20 151
3.21 133, 145
3.21-4.25 133, 144
3.22 80, 147, 148
3.23 42
3.24 147
3.24-25 132
3.24-26 148
3.25 132, 133, 148, 204
3.25-26 218
3.27-28 150
3.31 171, 172
4.3 147, 151
4.4-5 149
4.5 147, 148
4.6 147
4.9 147
4.9-12 150
4.10 151
4.11 147
4.17 190
4.18 151
4.18-21 153
5.10 133, 134
5.12 34, 41, 43, 44, 68, 124
5.12-13 43
5.12-21 44, 113
5.13 145
5.15 44
5.17 147, 148
5.18 44, 135
5.19 149
5.20 145
5.21 41
6.1-14 206
6.3-5 184
6.3-8 135, 168
6.4 169, 206–7
6.6 169, 207
6.7 207
6.8 207

Scripture Index

6.11 207
6.12 30, 41
6.12-13 31, 207
6.13 207
6.14 41
6.16 31
6.17-19 168
6.19 31
6.23 34, 41
7–8 171
7.7 43, 145, 150
7.7-8 43
7.7-14 42, 145
7.7-25 171
7.8 41
7.10-11 170
7.11-12 43
7.13 43
7.14 41, 43
7.14-23 170, 171
7.14-24 150
7.15 43
7.15-24 43
7.18 43
7.19 170
7.22 170
7.23-24 170
7.24 171
7.25 171
8.1 171
8.1-11 171
8.1-17 171
8.2 171
8.3 30, 43, 108
8.3-4 172
8.4 171
8.5 42, 163, 170
8.5-6 176
8.5-8 170
8.6 43, 170
8.7-8 171
8.9 158
8.9-10 162
8.11 164
8.13 163
8.14 102
8.14-17 108
8.15 10, 11, 102
8.16 31
8.17 220
8.18-39 188
8.20-21 219
8.23 164, 192, 216
8.26 163
8.27 14
8.28 14, 170
8.29 29, 114, 169, 189
8.29-30 188
8.34 111
9-11 183
9.2 31
9.5 30, 112, 113
9.6 184
9.7-9 189
9.7-13 184
9.10-13 50, 189
9.22-23 191
9.24-26 183
9.25 186, 189, 190
10.9 111, 194
10.13 111
11.2 189
11.15 184
11.17-24 184
11.20-22 190
11.25 184
11.26 184
12 194
12.1 30, 174, 175
12.3-8 194
12.6-8 196
12.10 193

Scripture Index

12.14 170
12.16 193, 193
13.8-10 150, 176
13.10 171
13.14 169
14.5 171, 175
14.10-12 152
15.16 195
15.18-19 164, 194
15.23-24 193
15.27 195
16.1 196
16.7 197
16.20 84
16.21 196

1 Corinthians
1.2 168, 183
1.8 111, 220
1.10 192, 193
1.18 132
1.19-25 42
1.26-29 189–90
1.28 190
1.30 79, 106, 108, 147, 149, 168
2.7-16 163
2.13-16 195
2.14 192
3.5 196
3.9 186
3.16 163, 186
3.16-17 185
4.4 32
4.6 197
4.9 197
4.14-15 195
4.17 197
5.1-5 200
5.3-5 200
5.5 19, 111, 199

5.6 199
5.7 211
5.10-11 42
5.11 200
6.9-10 200
6.11 168
6.19 185
6.19-20 132
6.20 132
7.3-4 171
7.5 20
7.22-23 132
7.34 30
8.4 22
8.4-6 10
8.6 106, 107, 112
8.7 32
8.7-8 22
8.10 32
8.19-23 220
9.1 197
9.5-6 197
9.9 174, 175
9.19-21 176
9.22 192
10.3 150
10.11 217, 218
10.16 211
10.19-21 22
10.24 176
10.28-30 32
11.1 169
11.15 220
11.17-34 211
11.20 211
11.21 212
11.23-26 210
11.24 180, 211
11.25 127, 181, 210, 211, 216
11.25-32 220

11.27 212
11.29 211, 212
12 194
12.2 186
12.3 111, 162, 194
12.4 194
12.4-6 13
12.5 194
12.6 194
12.7 163, 194
12.10 195
12.13 184, 186
12.22-24 195
12.27 184, 212
12.28-29 195
13.1-3 193
14 194
14.21 145
15 220
15.5 180
15.7 197
15.8 197
15.5-9 197
15.12 219
15.20 219
15.21-22 113
15.22 43
15.23 219
15.23-28 109
15.24 23
15.24-28 219
15.25 77
15.44-49 113
15.54-56 135
16.15-16 196

2 Corinthians
1.14 220
1.20 80
1.22 164, 192, 217

2.5-11 200
3.3 175, 216
3.6 146
3.7 146
3.7-9 151
3.8-11 146
3.9 146
3.9-11 146
3.10-12 146
3.18 29, 114, 169
4.2 192
4.4 29, 114, 169
4.5 110
5.1-10 220
5.5 192
5.10 152
5.14-17 113
5.17 114, 169, 179, 217, 218
5.18 133
5.18-19 134
5.19 133
5.19-21 149
5.21 80, 135, 148, 149
6.14-16 23
6.15 19
6.16 183
8.5 193
8.9 109, 176, 193
8.13-15 193
8.23 197, 198
9.12 195
10.3-6 23
10.17 42
11.2 10, 186
11.3-4 23
11.14 20
11.21-22 190
11.22 42
12.4-11 163
12.7 19

12.12-31 163
13.1-2 200
13.11 191
13.14 13

Galatians
1.8-9 200
1.11-12 197
1.15 197
1.19 197
2.3 150
2.16 151
2.20 135, 149, 162
3.6 147
3.10-12 146
3.11 147
3.13 132, 145, 149
3.15-18 147
3.17-19 145
3.19 18, 145
3.21 145
3.24-25 171
3.26 102
3.26-29 184
3.27 162, 169, 207
3.27-28 192, 195
3.28 186, 193
4.4-5 108
4.4-7 109
4.5-7 207
4.6 10, 102, 158, 162, 163
4.13 124
4.15 124
4.19 195
4.21 145
4.24 146
5.2 150, 171, 172, 175
5.14 175
5.16-17 43
5.17 42
5.18 167, 170, 171, 172

5.20-21 42
5.22-23 163, 171, 176
6.1-2 200
6.2 171, 175
6.8 152
6.11 124
6.14-16 113
6.15 169, 217, 218

Ephesians
1.4 149, 188, 189
1.5 149, 188, 189
1.6 188
1.7 132
1.10 185, 186
1.13 162
1.21 23
1.23 185
2.2 23
2.3 44
2.5-6 185
2.8-9 150, 151
2.11-22 168, 185
2.12-13 185
2.14-15 172
2.15 186
2.15-16 186
2.18 18, 163
2.19 185, 186
2.19-22 216
2.20 81, 181
2.21 185
2.22 185, 186
3.3 185
3.5 186
3.6 185–6
3.10 186
3.12 18
3.15 11
3.18 168
4.3-4 163

4.4 185
4.11 195, 196
4.12 212
4.11-13 163
4.22-24 163, 207
4.31 42
5.5 42
5.23 184, 185
5.25 11
6.2 193
6.2-3 171
6.8 220
6.10-20 23

Philippians
1.1 196
1.19 158
1.20 31
1.23 220
1.27 193
1.29-30 220
2.1-4 192
2.6 109
2.6-7 109
2.6-8 109
2.7-8 110
2.7 109
2.9 9, 110
2.11 110
2.17 195
2.25 195, 197, 198
2.30 195
3.3 43, 151, 175
3.4-6 150
3.4-7 190
3.5 42
3.5-6 42
3.6 146
3.7-9 150
3.9 80, 147, 150
3.10 135

3.13 135
3.19 42
3.20 185
4.5 111
4.15 185
4.16 193

Colossians
1.6 29, 64, 193
1.10 29
1.13-17 109
1.13-20 108
1.14 132
1.15 29, 106, 107, 108, 114
1.15-20 106
1.16 23, 106, 107, 169
1.16-17 24
1.17 107, 108
1.17-18 185
1.18 184, 185, 219
1.20 219
1.22 30
1.24 185, 220
2.6 110
2.8 20
2.9 9, 111
2.10 24
2.11-12 209
2.12 207
2.15 25, 128
2.16 171, 175
2.18 23
2.19 24, 185
3.1-3 168
3.1-4 185
3.4 149
3.5 42
3.9-10 169
3.12 168, 190
3.13 193
3.24 220

3.23-25 152

1 Thessalonians
1.1 185, 197
1.4-6 189
1.6 169, 220
1.9-10 108
2.7 195, 197
2.11 195
3.5 20
3.10 191
3.11 111
4 220
4.7 168
4.13-18 220
4.15 219
4.16 18
4.16-17 219
4.17 220
5.2 111
5.12 196
5.14 193
5.23 30

2 Thessalonians
1.5-10 217
1.7-8 18
1.9 220
2.3 219
2.3-4 36
2.6-7 219
2.16-17 111
3.5 111
3.6-15 200
3.14-15 200
3.15 200
3.16 111

1 Timothy
1.2 197
1.3-4 200

1.4 201
1.7 201
1.15 150
1.19-20 200
1.20 199
2.6 125
3.1-7 198
3.8-13 198
4.1 20
4.3 201
4.4 19
4.14 199
5.20 200
5.22 199

2 Timothy
1.6 199
1.10 219
2.1 197
3.1-5 217
4.6 220

Titus
1.6-9 198
1.10 201
1.14 201
2.13 112
2.14 132
3.5 151, 207
3.9 201
3.10-11 200

Philemon
1–2 196
8–9 193
15–16 186

Hebrews
1.1 47, 112
1.2 107, 108, 221
1.3 77, 107, 108
1.5-14 108

Scripture Index

1.5–2.9 24
1.6 18
1.7 17
1.8 112
1.8-9 112
1.14 17, 18
2.6-9 29
2.11 187
2.11-12 85
3.2-6 108
4.1 221
4.6 221
4.9 221
4.12 31
4.14-15 109
4.16 18
5.6 108
5.11–6.3 136
6.4-6 165
7.13 108
7.15-17 108
7.27 80, 81
8.5 135, 177
8.10 183
8.13 177
9.4 135
9.9 72, 135
9.11 72, 81
9.12 80
9.13 135
9.14 135
9.24 135
9.26 135, 221
10.1 71, 72, 177
10.3 72, 135
10.4 71, 204
10.5 30
10.5-10 86
10.10 136, 168
10.11 71

10.14 80, 81, 136
10.15-17 221
10.22 207
10.26-31 165
11 187
12.1 187
12.24 216, 221
13.16 175

James
1.5 153
1.7-8 153
1.12 170
1.15 34
1.18 153
1.19 153
1.25 176
1.26 153
2.1-13 153, 193
2.8 176
2.17 153
2.18 153
2.19 20, 153
2.24 152
2.26 30, 153
3.1-12 153
3.17 163
4.8 153

1 Peter
1.1 187
1.2 154, 189
1.3 136, 154
1.3-5 217
1.5 154, 221
1.8-9 154
1.9 31, 221
1.9-10 154
1.10-12 108
1.11 93, 158
1.12 18, 187

1.13 154, 221
1.14 154
1.15-16 168, 191
1.16 174, 187
1.18 136
1.20 108, 217
1.20-21 221
1.22 154
1.23 154
2.2 154
2.3 111
2.4 86
2.5 136, 175, 183, 187, 195
2.6-8 81
2.7 86
2.9 186, 187, 191, 195
2.9-10 183
2.10 154
2.12 187
2.22 85, 136
2.24 136, 154
2.24-25 85
2.25 198
3.8-9 170
3.12 15
3.18 136, 154
3.19-20 25
3.20 21, 49
3.21 208
4.5 217
4.7 154
4.13 221
5.2 198
5.4 198
5.8 19, 20

2 Peter
1.1 112, 154
1.4 154
2.1-3 201
2.4 20, 182
2.12-20 201
3.3 221
3.11-14 154
3.13 217
3.17 189

1 John
1.1 116
1.8 201
1.10 201
2.1 160
2.3 155
2.4-5 155
2.18 223
2.22 201
2.27 195
3.2 9, 116
3.6 201
3.8 21, 45
3.9 201
3.10 21
3.17-18 193
3.20 14
3.24 155
4.2 201
4.6 158
4.7-10 170
4.15 119, 155
4.20 170
5.12 119
5.12-13 155
5.18 201
5.20 112, 119

2 John
9 155
10 201

Jude
3-4 201
4 201

6   20, 182
9   18
12   210

Revelation
1.4   159
1.4-5   13
1.5   222
1.5-6   121
1.6   222
1.8   6
1.13   87
1.20   22
2.1   22
2.7   222
2.13   223
2.13-14   23
2.14   45
4.8-11   120
5.1-5   222
5.5   84, 120, 131, 222
5.6   120, 131, 222
5.8   183
5.8-14   18
5.9   193, 222
5.9-10   29
5.10   222
5.9-12   120
5.10   195
5.11   18
5.11-12   24
5.13   120
6.1-6   35
6.1-11.19   222
6.12-17   222
6.16   120
7.1-17   193
7.3   191
7.4-8   183
7.9   193
8.2   18

8.3   168
8.10   20
9.1   20
11.7-10   222
11.3   223
11.15   120
12.1-5   222
12.1-6   22
12.3   20, 21
12.5   76, 131
12.6   223
12.7-9   22
12.9   19, 20, 84, 131
12.10   19
12.11   23, 131, 222
12.14   223
13.1   20
13.2   23
13.4   223
13.5   223
13.8   222
13.11   20
13.12   223
13.4-17   45
13.15   223
13.16   223
13.18   223
14.1-5   183
14.9   223
14.10   120, 222, 225
14.11   225
14.19   120
15.1   120
15.2   131
16.12-14   222
16.13-14   223
17-18   46
17.3-4   46
17.5   23
17.14   120, 131, 222, 225
18.2   23

Scripture Index

18.7 46
18.14 31
19.10 18, 121
19.11-21 225
19.12 20
19.15 76
19.17-21 222
19.19 225
19.19-20 131
19.20 45, 225
20.1-6 224
20.2-3 224
20.4 45, 225
20.5 225
20.7-10 225
20.11-15 225
20.15 225
21.1 217

21.1–22.5 226
21.3 183
21.4 226
21.5 217
21.6-8 222
21.7 183, 222
21.12 183
21.14 183
21.15-17 226
22.1 226
22.1-5 226
22.2 226
22.3 112
22.3-4 120
22.8-9 18, 121
22.9 17
22.10 217
22.16 84

Index of Ancient Writings

Apocrypha

Tobit
8.1-3 25

Wisdom of Solomon
7.22 107
7.23 104, 107
7.25 105, 107
7.26 105
7.26 104–5, 107

The Wisdom of Jesus
 Son of Sirach
24.8 105, 107, 116
24.9 107
24.21 116

1 Maccabees
2.52 152

2 Maccabees
1.5 134
7.33 134

Pseudepigrapha

4 Ezra
7.118 43

2 Baruch
54.19 43

Psalms of Solomon
17.22 90
17.30 90

1 Enoch
6–16 21
62–63 101

Testament of Moses
10.1 95

Other Jewish Writings

Josephus
Antiquities of the Jews
8.45-49 25

Philo
Life of Moses
1.66 109

Mishnah
Berakot 5.5 196
Pesahim 10.5 211
Pesahim 10.7 211

Subject Index

144,000 183, 191
666 223
70 weeks 80, 223

Adam and Eve 28–9, 33–4, 43–4, 58, 64, 83–4
Adam, new 29, 113–14
altar 58
Angel of the Lord 12, 78–9
angels 17–18
　fallen 21
　of the nations 21–2
　as representatives 18, 21–2
anointing 74–5, 92
antichrist 219, 223
　see also beast, the
Antiochus IV Epiphanes 117, 224
apostles 196–8
atonement 68, 70, 72, 129–30, 132–3, 148–9, 210

Babel, tower of 35
Balaam's prophecy 84
baptism 162, 204–10
　faith and 207–9
　infant 209–10
　see also Christ, baptism of; John the Baptist
beast, the 20, 21, 31, 131, 223
　mark of 45, 223
blessing 13, 28, 49, 50, 52, 58, 64, 65, 192, 216
body 30
burnt offering 68–9

canonical interpretation 2
children 139
Christ 89–122
　baptism of 103, 159, 204
　body of 184, 194
　commandments of 97–8
　crucifixion of 85–6, 103–4, 118, 129, 130, 131, 155, 218
　death of 123–37
　divinity of 106, 108, 109–10, 111
　　see also Christ, as God's equal
　glorification of 130, 131
　as God 111–13
　as God's equal 94–101
　as head of the body 184–5
　miracles of 98–9
　preexistence of 87, 105, 107, 108–9, 116, 119
　as priest 135
　resurrection of 86, 108, 111, 115
　second coming of 97, 219–20
　as shepherd 187
　Transfiguration of 103
　see also Adam, new; "I AM"; image of God; Immanuel; incarnation; Lord; Messiah; Moses, prophet like; Servant of the Lord, Suffering; Son of God; Son of Man
Christological development 114–15
Christology 89–122
church 64, 179–202
　as family 195
　as mixed community 199

offices of 195–9
unity of 192–4, 212
church discipline 199–201
circumcision 63, 209
Commission, Great 140, 205–6
communion *see* Lord's Supper
conscience 32
covenant 6, 7, 47–52, 144, 183, 209
  with Abraham 49–50
  ark of the 59
  conditional 51
  with David 60–2, 75–6
  new 62–5, 187, 210
  with Noah 48–9
  old 177
  from Sinai 51–2, 145–6
  unconditional 49, 50, 62, 63
creation 4, 10, 13, 27–8, 49, 104, 106–8, 116, 117, 144–5, 158, 161, 169, 190
  mandate from 64
    see also Gen 1.28 in the Scripture index
  new 57, 58, 65, 79, 84, 96, 113–14, 139, 158, 161, 162, 169, 179, 204, 216–17, 219, 222, 226
criminals at the cross 129
cross, take up 142
curse 52, 146

David 54
  see also covenant, with David
Day of Atonement 70, 72, 129–30
deacons 196, 198
death 68
demons 20–1, 22–5, 96, 109, 127, 153, 165, 182
  occupation by 24–5
  possession by *see* occupation by
devil *see* Satan
disciples 45, 140–3, 169, 205–6
  twelve 180

Eden *see* creation, new
elders 198
election 50, 53, 54, 56, 187, 188–92
Elijah 100
empire, Roman 23, 219
enemies of God and his people 20, 21, 95, 96, 222–3
  see also Satan; demons
eschatology 215–27
  see also covenant, new; creation, new; Christ, death of; Christ, as God's equal; Christ, second coming of; judgment; Messiah; Son of Man
eternal life *see* life
exile 41, 52, 54, 55, 57, 62
exorcism 25
expiation 69, 133

faith 142, 147–8, 150–1, 153, 155, 207–9
fall away 165
fall in sin 19, 33–4
family 98
festivals 117
flesh 30, 43
forgiveness 70, 71, 72, 97, 99, 142, 182, 204
fulfillment 1, 91

Gentiles 77, 84, 104, 162, 176, 183–7, 189, 205, 220
God 4–15
  being with us 60
  as bridegroom 38, 41, 56
  dwelling of 58, 64, 226
    see also temple
  and evil 13–14
  face of 60
  as Father 10–11
  foreknowledge of 189
    see also knowledge of
  and gender 11

Subject Index

glory of 58 *see also* image of God
knowledge of 14–15
   see also foreknowledge of
name of 5–7, 92, 118–19, 120, 206
presence of 9, 58–60
regret of 14–15
rejection by 41, 55, 189
rule of 28, 29, 49, 55, 76, 94–6, 114, 138–9, 193
to see 8–9, 116
to take the place of 20, 34, 35, 36, 223
uniqueness of 9–10
wisdom of 12, 104–8, 115–16, 163, 186
wrath of 133
greed 42
guilt offering 70–1

hardening 44
heart 31
   new 63
heresy 200–1
holiness 7–8, 54–5, 136, 167–8, 183, 190
Holy Spirit 79, 157–66, 170–1, 192, 194, 205, 208–9
   as Advocate 159–62
   filled with the 162
   as first fruits 164
   fruit of 163
   gifts of *see* spiritual gifts
   sin against 165

"I AM" 6, 118–19, 131
   see also Yahweh
idolatry 9–10, 22, 37, 38, 42, 45
image of God 27–9, 42, 55, 106, 107, 114, 169, 188–9
Immanuel 9, 78, 83, 100–1
"in Christ" *see* union with Christ
incarnation 116
indicative and imperative 168
Isaiah 7–8

Israel 51–7, 180, 182, 183–4, 186, 187, 215–16, 220–1

Jesus *see* Christ
Job 13–14
John the Baptist 93, 100, 203–4
judgment 34–5, 39, 41, 55, 62, 77, 93–4, 97, 131, 140, 145, 149, 152, 217, 218, 220, 222, 225
justification 143–53

kingdom of God 94–7, 138–41, 169, 180, 182, 192
   see also God, rule of

Lamb of God 120–1, 129–30, 131, 222
land 57, 77
law of God 37, 42–3, 145–6, 170–7
   abolishment of 172–4
   fulfillment of 172–7
   threefold division of 174
life 154–5
linen, man dressed in 87
Lion of Judah 84, 120, 131
Lord 5, 92, 106, 110–11, 115
   see also Yahweh
Lord's Supper 210–13
   abuse of 211–12
love 169–70, 175–6
love feast 210

magic 53
Mary 78
meal fellowship 210
Messiah 74–83, 90–4, 127–8
   divinity of 76, 79, 83, 91
   as God's Son 75–6, 92
   Jesus as 90–4
   as Lord 91
   as political ruler 90–1, 92
   preexistence of 77
   as priest 77, 80–1

Subject Index

as shepherd 79, 80, 81
  suffering of 81, 83, 91–4, 123–4
messianic secret 90–1
method 2
millennium 224
miracles 106–7, 155, 192
mission 29, 164, 193, 205, 218
  see also Gentiles
Moses 5–7
  prophet like 86, 114
mystery 185

Nebuchadnezzar 36
new birth 153, 154–5
Nicodemus 155

obedience 103, 206
ordination 199

Passover 71, 117, 126, 130, 136, 180–1, 211
Pentecost 159, 161, 205, 209
persecution *see* suffering
Peter 45, 181–3
poor, the 39, 92, 141–2, 212
  in spirit 140–1
prayer 10, 99, 102, 103, 111, 134, 163, 188
predestination *see* election
pride 35–6, 190
priests 195
prophet *see* Moses, prophet like
prophetic perspective 93
propitiation 69, 132–3
purification offering *see* sin offering

ransom 125, 132
reconciliation 133–4
redemption 7, 125, 132–3
remnant 56–7
repentance 59, 63, 71, 177, 204
replacement 117

responsibility, human 192
resurrection 128, 216, 225
revelation 4, 5, 6, 7, 103, 117, 158, 177
righteousness 140, 143–5, 147–8

sacrifice 67–73, 125, 129–30, 133, 134, 135, 149, 175, 204, 211
salvation 56–7, 62, 93–4, 95–6, 138–56, 164, 220
Samaritans 208–9
sanctification 136, 167
Satan 19, 84
  victory over 84, 127–8, 131, 225
security, false *see* sin as misplaced trust
self-righteousness 150
Sermon on the Mount 97–8
Servant of the Lord, Suffering 72, 84–5, 101, 103, 114, 123–5, 130, 136, 197
shame 40
sickness 132
sin 33–46, 145, 199–201, 207
  as attitude 4, 44
  corporate 46
  as misplaced trust 34, 35, 36, 39, 41–2, 55, 56
  original 43–4
  as power 41, 43
  see also God, to take the place of; pride
sin offering 69–70, 84, 126–7
Solomon 62
son of God 75–6, 102–4, 119–20
Son of Man 86–7, 101–2
soul 31
spirit 31
spiritual gifts 163, 194–5
spiritual warfare 23
substitution 134
suffering 13, 45, 85–6, 134, 189, 219–20, 221–2, 223–4

Subject Index

tabernacle 9, 40, 58, 70, 116, 135
temple 9, 40, 101, 117, 185
   curtain of 128
   see also tabernacle
temptation 34, 127–8
tithing 176
transformation of believers 163, 175, 191, 207
Trinity 11–13, 105, 162, 206
trust 42, 142, 150–1

uncleanness 39, 69, 135
union with Christ 149, 188, 189, 207, 210–11

values, reversal of 139
vine 188

witness 56
works of the law 150–1
worship 37, 38, 45, 59, 104, 120–1
   of the emperor 45, 110, 223

Yahweh 5, 110
   see also "I AM"; Lord

Zion 62